ANGEL DE CORA, KAREN THRONSON, AND THE ART OF PLACE

IOWA AND THE MIDWEST EXPERIENCE

Series editor, William B. Friedricks,

Iowa History Center at Simpson College

ANGEL DE CORA, KAREN THRONSON, AND THE ART OF PLACE

HOW TWO MIDWESTERN WOMEN USED ART TO NEGOTIATE MIGRATION AND DISPOSSESSION

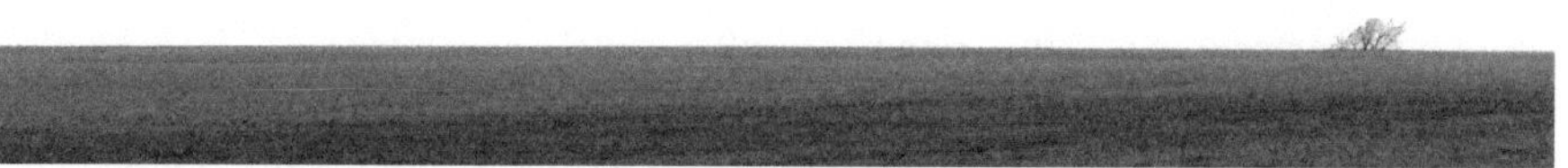

Elizabeth Sutton

UNIVERSITY OF IOWA PRESS, IOWA CITY

University of Iowa Press, Iowa City 52242

www.uipress.uiowa.edu

Printed in the United States of America
Design by April Leidig

Printed on acid-free paper

Library of Congress Cataloging-in-Publication Data
Names: Sutton, Elizabeth A., author.
Title: Angel De Cora, Karen Thronson, and the art of place: how two midwestern women used art to negotiate migration and dispossession / Elizabeth Sutton.
Description: Iowa City: University of Iowa Press, [2020] | Series: Iowa and the midwest experience | Includes bibliographical references and index. | Identifiers: LCCN 2019026586 (print) | LCCN 2019026587 (ebook) | ISBN 9781609386870 (paperback) | ISBN 9781609386887 (ebook)
Subjects: LCSH: Henook-Makhewe-Kelenaka. | Thronson, Karen, 1850–1929. | Winnebago women—Biography. | Norwegian American women—Biography. | Women artists—Social networks—Middle West. | Women artisans—Social networks—Middle West. | Art and society—Middle West.
Classification: LCC N6537.H3892 (ebook) | LCC N6537.H3892 S88 2020 (print) | DDC 704/.0420977—dc23
LC record available at https://lccn.loc.gov/2019026586

To my mother, Jean,
and all our mothers

CONTENTS

FOREWORD

TWO DECADES AGO I packed up my van and took a road trip from northern California to Green Bay, Wisconsin, and back. I wanted to learn about my father's Ho-Chunk (Winnebago) ancestors, whose origin story begins at Red Banks near Green Bay in the seventeenth century. President Andrew Jackson's dictate to remove all Native tribes "west of the Mississippi" instituted five government removals for the Ho-Chunk, beginning in the 1830s. I followed their "migration" through Wisconsin to Fort Atkinson, Iowa, to Long Prairie and Mankato, Minnesota, to Crow Creek, South Dakota, and finally to Winnebago, Nebraska, where the Ho-Chunk found a permanent reservation in 1865.

With Genevieve "Jane" Manégre Waggoner, my great-great-grandmother, as my spirit guide, I lived in the past in the present as I visited such places as the Winnebago Agency House in Portage, Wisconsin, where Jane's parents worked. Jane was a Ho-Chunk Métis and a descendant of civil chief Chougeka DeCarrie (or "Decora"), the first-born child of the first recorded marriage between a Ho-Chunk woman and a French-Canadian. Jane was born near Green Bay, grew up a French-speaking Catholic in Portage, and married a white man; they had ten children. She gave birth to the youngest, my great-grandfather, near Mankato, Minnesota, less than two months after thirty-eight Dakota were hanged in the town square, one the son of Jane's half-sister.

I drove to the site of the hanging and discovered that Jane had later lived only two blocks away. What did she think when she passed that place? Did she feel its despair? The site was not just a primal scene for the Dakota, who were executed, imprisoned, and banished from the state. In the decade that followed the largest mass execution in the United States, the fate of the Ho-Chunk as one people became irrevocably disjoined. Some, like Jane, became naturalized citizens in 1870 to retain their Minnesota allotments; some joined the Winnebago tribe of Nebraska; others, who eluded removal from their homeland, became the Wisconsin Ho-Chunk.

Although only one Ho-Chunk warrior was convicted for participating in battle, Minnesota citizens demanded the Ho-Chunk be banished along with the Dakota. After traveling by steamboat they disembarked in June 1863 at a barren wasteland guarded by the military at Crow Creek, South Dakota. I arrived there on the sandy Missouri River bank in the summer with the bag of tobacco my father had given me to offer. I had learned that one-third of the tribe succumbed to disease and starvation at this eerie place. The survivors escaped in dugout canoes down the river to northern Nebraska, where their cousins, the Omaha, offered them refuge.

I drove south along the Missouri River to the reservation in Winnebago, Nebraska. I met my distant Decora cousin, the late Dave Smith, who served as tribal historian. Dave took me to a pretty wooded area to show me the reservation cemetery. Without pretense, he lit cigarettes and quietly placed them on headstones of the people he honored.

I stayed at his former family home, which he had converted into the Ho-Chunk Historical Society. Several paintings of prominent Ho-Chunk people that he had commissioned from photographs hung on the walls. One portrait struck me in particular. It was a photo of Angel De Cora taken in 1907 when she was a nationally recognized artist. De Cora's great-grandfather and Jane Waggoner's grandmother were siblings, so she felt like kin. To me, De Cora's dignified demeanor represented the survival of the Ho-Chunk, despite thirty-five years of traumatic upheaval that did not end with her parents. De Cora was born on the reservation in 1869, but Smith told me she had been abducted as a teenager and taken to Indian boarding school in Hampton, Virginia. She died in Massachusetts in 1919, where she is buried. I wondered how she would view her portrait hung back home in its honored place. A few years later Dave and his mother granted me permission to write her biography.

In the following pages art historian Elizabeth Sutton contrasts the migration, life, and artwork of Angel De Cora with that of her great-grandmother, Norwegian immigrant Karen Thronson. Sutton encountered Angel as she crossed paths with Thronson in Iowa. She wondered, given De Cora and Thronson's similar family migrations across the Midwest, how were they different and how the same. The results of her query became the subject of this informative and fascinating story that carefully analyzes De Cora and Thronson's lives and work through "the art of place."

As Sutton finds, racist government policies toward Indigenous Americans and a settler colonialism that benefited immigrants distinguished the women's parallel journeys.

Although gender and artistic pursuits united Sutton's subjects, white privilege and historical trauma clearly divided them. While "De Cora had to distinguish herself as a Native American woman artist to find community," explains Sutton, "Thronson already fit into one as a Norwegian woman." Thronson's parents made the choice to emigrate from Norway to America to seek a better life for their children. Thronson "crafted connections" to her native Norway as she migrated west across America's river land and plains. Sutton succinctly demonstrates how this maintained a tight-knit Norwegian female immigrant community.

In contrast, De Cora was taken to the East, where educators attempted to "Americanize" her. They soon discovered she had talents beyond the very few occupations then open to Native women: domestic service, nursing, and teaching. After graduation, De Cora studied with some of America's most famed artists of the period, gaining national recognition as the "Greatest of Redskin Painters." By 1905, she turned her attention to "Native Indian" design to develop both her "latent aboriginal talents," as she perceived them, and to meet the consumer desires of the Indian craze. For this market she designed lettering, book covers, furniture, rugs, and other household items.

In 1906 De Cora took control of the innovative Native Indian art department at Carlisle Indian and Industrial School in Pennsylvania. Here she mentored the next generation of Indian boarding-school children, inspiring them to be "Indian craftsmen" and craftswomen. Soon after De Cora rose to become a prominent figure in America's Arts and Crafts movement and was often invited to broadcast her esoteric knowledge of the abstract elements of Native American design.

Finally, Sutton shows us that Thronson and De Cora shared a poignant nostalgia for *home* and used "visual culture to connect to homeland and to situate herself." Through her migration to the United States and the Midwest, Thronson transformed *place* into *home* by designing and crafting traditional objects and with them cementing community ties. On the other hand, Sutton discovered that cultural knowledge and community were severely disrupted for De Cora. My journey to De Cora also found this to be so. This left De Cora to promote "pan-Indian" designs to serve as symbols of home and community for her Native students and peers, as well as for herself. As Sutton astutely concludes, although the women's lives were radically different, Thronson and De Cora both found themselves and their communities through creating "an art of place."

Linda M. Waggoner
Author of *Fire Light: The Life of Angel De Cora, Winnebago Artist*

PREFACE

I SPENT LABOR DAY 2016 camping in Badlands National Park, South Dakota. I was on sabbatical from my position as an art historian at a regional public university, and in the centenary year of national parks, I wanted to visit Yellowstone, and Glacier, too, before climate change rendered these landscapes unrecognizable. There was a lot of road time driving through the Dakotas, Wyoming, and Montana. I spent many hours thinking about how I had come to where I was at that point in my life—tenured and relatively successful in northeast Iowa. I jotted many thoughts about my academic matrilineage and my blood matrilineage in the notebook I carried with me. I realized that I knew very little about my own roots beyond my mother's stories. I had few details; all I knew was that my great-great-grandmother had immigrated to the United States from Norway, from somewhere near Bergen. And as my husband and I drove through the windy plains and mountains, I thought about previous trips I had taken as a child with my family, led by my mother: to camp in the Badlands, to eat fry bread at Pine Ridge, to canoe in the Boundary Waters. I was fortunate to attend a public high school in Minneapolis that had a Native American "All Nations" magnet program; my mother was a lawyer for the Department of Interior; and my father worked for a time as a secretary at an Indian law firm that often represented Minnesota and Wisconsin tribes. Thus, Native people were ever-present—as individuals and members (or not) of tribes—and Native rights were conversation topics at the dinner table. As a teacher in Iowa, I often am appalled at the ignorance of my students about Native American history—and indeed, ignorance of Native presence—in Iowa, of all places!

Driving through western towns, the Black Hills, and national parks—sacred lands for many Native Americans—I took note of signs of continued cultural negotiation between Native communities and the U.S. colonial government. Billboards, advertisements for knickknacks and stores, restaurants and entertainment: all show a visual confluence of cultures that continues, for the most part, to be uncritically consumed by whites.

That fall of 2016, I was dismayed by the willful ignorance of elites (politicians, media, law, corporate bodies, and stakeholders) toward Native sovereignty and the ecological ramifications of shortsighted profit seeking. Water protectors defending sacred land and water at Standing Rock Indian Reservation in North Dakota put centuries old injustices into relief. Twice I drove to Oceti Sakowin, in October and December, to be a witness for the landscape, to observe the defense of sacred land and water, and to be in solidarity with water protectors. At the same time, I understood that I could use my privilege most effectively by writing and teaching. I could try to forge understanding about the roots of my privilege, and I could try to find similarities across cultures to explain why conservation is important and how women, particularly, have contributed and continue to contribute to causes that value and sustain life. We are protecting family. For many Indigenous people—whether Native American or farmers in pre-Christian Norway—land, water, and animals all are family. Women often cultivate family, not only as mothers but as caregivers, in many ways. We expand the concept of family to include natural phenomena and human communities of mutual aid. Indeed, I see *care* and care ethics as the foundation of feminist practice. It does not exclude men but, rather, suggests that men, too, benefit from a foundational care and concern for others.

This book is both historical and personal. It necessarily took some unanticipated directions. It is still an attempt to use my privilege in a positive way by addressing the convergence of cultures and asserting the continued significance of art and nature, together, in the ever-unfolding circle of life—a circle in which, for now, humans are lucky enough to participate.

ACKNOWLEDGMENTS

I AM GRATEFUL FOR the assistance and support of many individuals and institutions throughout my work on this project. The University of Northern Iowa College of Humanities, Arts and Sciences provided financial support for travel to archives and libraries and provided subvention for some costs associated with image publication. UNI's Graduate College granted me a summer fellowship to write. Institutions gave me valuable material resources, and individuals gave me energy and direction. I am indebted to the staff at various offices for their help in tracking down sources and records. Thank you to the staff in the Jewell County, Kansas, Recorder's office (here's to you, Amanda), in Mankato, Kansas; the Hamilton County, Iowa, Auditor and Recorder's offices, in Webster City, Iowa; the Dallas County Recorder's office, in Adel, Iowa; the Story City, Iowa, Historical Society; and the Swarthmore College Special Collections. Thanks, too, to Aimee Brown, St. Olaf College Special Collections; Milianna Carlson, Immanuel Lutheran Church, Story City, Iowa; Andreese Scott and Daniella Maupin, Hampton University Archives, Virginia; Cara Curtis and staff, Cumberland County Historical Society, Carlisle, Pennsylvania; and Jennifer Kovarik, Vesterheim Museum and Library, Decorah, Iowa.

I greatly appreciate the correspondence of former colleague Carol Colburn regarding immigration and fashion history, the Norwegian transcription and translation of some of Immanuel's records by Harald Dyrkorn, and the emotional and intellectual support of my dear friend, Leisl Carr Childers. Through Leisl I met Kent Blansett, and through Kent I was able to solicit Linda Waggoner to write a foreword, without her having met me. Their generosity and graciousness exemplify collaboration and mutual aid at work! Thank you all!

The manuscript is better because of reviewers' and editors' comments and feedback. Of course, any mistakes are mine alone.

CHRONOLOGY

Listings in this chronology relating to the Thronson, Severson, and De Cora families appear in roman type. Historical events appear in italic type.

1850	Karen Helgesdottir (Severson) born in Landås, Norway
1854	*Kansas-Nebraska Act*
1861	*Kansas statehood*
1862	*Homestead Act*
1862	*Railroad Act*
1865	*End of U.S. Civil War; Ho-Chunk acquire Winnebago Reservation, Winnebago, Nebraska, from the Omaha, after having fled there from Crow Creek, South Dakota*
1867	Severson family and Mons Thronson immigrate to the United States through Québec on the *Helvetia*
1868	Mons Thronson files for U.S. citizenship in Dane County, Wisconsin
1868 or 1869	Angel De Cora born in Winnebago, Nebraska
1870	Mons Thronson and Karen record their marriage in Dallas County, Iowa
1871	Rasmus Thronson born in Iowa
1872	*Kansas-Missouri Pacific Railroad finished through Mankato/Jewell Center, Kansas*
1872	Thronsons and Seversons move to Mankato/Jewell Center, Kansas
1872	*Wisconsin Ho-Chunk removed to Winnebago, Nebraska*
1872	Carl Thronson born in Kansas
1875	*Last Wisconsin Ho-Chunk removed to Winnebago, Nebraska*
1880	Thea Helen Thronson (1880) born in Kansas

1882 Helge S. Sletten and Mons Thronson each receive a patent for 160 acres via the Homestead Act; Rachel Kristina Thronson born December 28

1883 De Cora and six other Native children taken from Nebraska to Hampton Institute, Virginia

1884 Mons Thronson dies in September and is buried in West Lutheran Cemetery, Mankato, Kansas

1885 Karen's younger brother, Ole Severson, granted patent homestead in Jewell County, Kansas

1887 General Allotment Act (Dawes Act)

1887 De Cora returns to Winnebago for the summer; meets Alice Fletcher

1888 De Cora returns to Hampton Institute

1888 Kvinden og Hjemmet *(The woman and the home) founded in Cedar Rapids, Iowa*

1891 De Cora completes her course of study at Hampton; enrolls first in Burnham Classical School for Girls and then in Smith College, where she studies with William Tryon

1895 De Cora attends Lake Mohonk Conference as a Smith student

1896 De Cora graduates from Smith; enrolls at Drexel Academy, Philadelphia, where she studies with Howard Pyle

1897–98 De Cora visits Fort Berthold, North Dakota; takes photographs and paints *Firelight*

1898 De Cora's work exhibited in Indian Building at Trans-Mississippi International Exposition in Omaha, Nebraska

1899 De Cora studies with DeCamp, Tarbell, and Benson in Boston, Massachusetts; *Harper's New Monthly* publishes De Cora's illustrated stories "Sick Child" and "Gray Wolf's Daughter"

1899 Helge Severson dies in February and is buried in West Lutheran Cemetery, Mankato, Kansas

1900 Rachel and Carl Thronson recorded as living with their cousin Hiram Severson (Ole's son) in Ionia Township, Jewell County, Kansas

1900 De Cora's illustrations for Francis LaFlesche's *Middle Five* published

1901 De Cora's work exhibited by Office of Indian Affairs at the Pan-American International Exposition in Buffalo, New York; illustrations for *Old Indian Legends,* by Zitkála-Šá, published

1901 Karen and Carrie sell Kansas farms and move to Story City, Iowa; on January 6, Karen and Rachel become members at Immanuel Lutheran Church

1902 De Cora moves to New York City to work as an illustrator; elected to National Academy of Design

1904 De Cora installation is part of Office of Indian Affairs exhibit at the Louisiana Purchase Exposition in St. Louis, Missouri

1905 *Francis Leupp appointed Indian Commissioner by Theodore Roosevelt*

1906 De Cora accepts position at Carlisle Indian Industrial School; illustrations for Mary Catherine Judd's *Wigwam Stories* published

1907 De Cora marries William "Lone Star" Dietz; Leupp Art Building opens at Carlisle, funded entirely by football revenue; De Cora and Franz Boas meet; De Cora's designs for Natalie Curtis's *Indians' Book* published

1909 *Journal "Indian Craftsman" debuts*

1911 Rachel Thronson and E. Roy Parrett marry; move to Batavia, Jefferson County, Iowa

1914 De Cora's illustrations for *Little Buffalo Robe* and *Wakondah* published

1915 Karen recorded as age 64, farm manager, in Story City, Ellsworth Township; Esther Parrett born November 26, Jefferson County, Iowa, to Rachel and E. Roy Parrett

1915 De Cora resigns from Carlisle; works at Charles Eastman's Camp Oahe, Granite Lake, New Hampshire

1916 Carrie Severson dies and is buried in West Lutheran Cemetery, Mankato, Kansas

1917 *Carlisle closes in response to World War I needs*

1917 Karen sells farm in Ellsworth, Iowa

1919 Angel De Cora dies from influenza and is buried in Northampton, Massachusetts

1929 Karen dies and is buried in West Lutheran Cemetery, Mankato, Kansas

ANGEL DE CORA,
KAREN THRONSON,
AND THE ART OF PLACE

ONE | MAPPING MIGRATIONS

In the following pages, I write about the migrations of Europeans and Native Americans — specifically, Norwegians and the Ho-Chunk/Hoocąągra (Winnebago) and Kanza (Kaw) people they displaced from the Great Lakes to the Great Plains. Ho-Chunk artist Angel De Cora (Hinook-Mahiwi-Kalinaka, ca. 1870–1919) and Karen Severson Thronson (1850–1929) have related stories — they literally map onto one another in a spatial and temporal overlay, as many European immigrants' journeys to land ownership map onto the stories of Native American land dispossession. Both women left their childhood homes, although under vastly different circumstances. Karen Thronson grew up among the fjords in southwest Norway, while Angel De Cora spent the first fourteen years of her life on the Winnebago reservation in Nebraska, until she was taken to Hampton Institute, a boarding school in Virginia. Karen Severson Thronson and her parents and brothers migrated across the ocean, great lakes, and seas of grass. They settled on homesteads in Iowa and Kansas, on land that had been the hunting grounds of the Kanza and, in Iowa, in an area used by De Cora's people, the Ho-Chunks, before their removal farther west. De Cora was an active illustrator, designer, and teacher of Native Arts at Carlisle Indian Industrial School in Pennsylvania.

This book is about two nineteenth-century women from different backgrounds, each of whom made things in order to connect to place and validate self and group identity. Karen Thronson and her family benefited from their whiteness and Protestantism and from their ability to form a cohesive ethnic community within the United States. They and other European settlers were enfranchised through property ownership afforded by the 1862 Homestead Act and through naturalization policies friendly to Western European immigrants. In contrast, U.S. policies and Indian reform groups sought to forcibly eradicate De Cora's ethnic identity through industrial education and land dispossession. These policies were purposefully contrary to Indigenous cultural norms.

While the stories here focus on the experiences of Angel De Cora and Karen Thronson, this book is not meant to be a biography of either.[1] Rather, these women's stories help illuminate the realities of power and hierarchy that made each woman's experience—and concomitantly, each woman's art—different. Both women, however, used visual culture to connect to homeland and to situate herself. Neither was immune to the dominant culture of elite Yankee values (*Yankee* referring mostly to native-born white American citizens with Anglo-Saxon Protestant heritage) regarding art making and, more generally, Yankee expectations regarding immigrant and Native American women's roles within the U.S. economy. Generally speaking, "fine" art was a man's pursuit and women did "craft," producing useful items for the home, at home. Institutions (including schools, churches, and government bureaus) and their policies shaped and perpetuated these expectations. Sometimes these demands came directly from powerful individuals within the structure—for De Cora, teachers and government officials—and sometimes they came from more indirect sources of cultural reproduction, such as advertisements and magazine articles.

Whites born in the United States expected both immigrant and Native American women to assimilate, but while Norwegian immigrants largely settled in ethnic enclaves, Native American communities and cultural traditions were forcibly eradicated. Norwegian immigrant women like Thronson established schools and churches in their rural communities. These sites fit in with broader Protestant gender and labor ideals and provided women with economic, social, and ethnic independence within spaces geared toward maintaining traditions in visual culture, language, and religion. As a Norwegian American immigrant, Karen Thronson inherited beliefs that helped her and her daughters survive and thrive in the United States. Karen and her children immigrated to cultivate the so-called frontier, to elevate themselves, and, thereby, to contribute to what most white Americans considered progress by civilizing the American West.

Karen Thronson and her family domesticated the plains by plow and by decorating their homes with straw and lace following the traditions of Norway. Thronson used straw and lace to express her nostalgia for her homeland and its traditions. Traditional crafts connected her to her heritage, and she was able to retain this heritage within the institutions of school and church. Thronson and her daughters also made straw ornaments and needlework to connect to each other and to maintain their kinship and community. At the same time that these traditions connected Norwegian immigrant women to their homeland, their handcrafts also fit within the dominant white American labor expectations for consumerist, domesticated women.

In contrast, Angel De Cora's tribal values conflicted with the American myths of the frontier and white settler colonists' perceived Manifest Destiny to own, cultivate, and consume.[2] While elite white reformers thought that uplifting the "squaw drudge" through work—notably handwork—was the key to assimilating all Native Americans into white, patriarchal, capitalist society, De Cora rejected total assimilation in her design and production. She used her art, and later her teaching, to preserve her and her students' tribal memories. Although physically distanced from her home and community, De Cora affirmed her identity with natural and sacred designs, even while ostensibly working within the whites' expectations of her. She was able to resist the parameters of their gendered and racialized expectations and policies. Both Thronson's and De Cora's art reflects how each woman maintained her respective ethnic values, shaped by tradition and religion, even as she responded to the expectations of the dominant white culture.

These dynamics of cultural power—the legacy of settler colonialism and gendered knowledge and the assumptions regarding gender roles, race, and community reproduced in visual culture and social relations—are still present in the United States today. Both De Cora and Thronson worked in media—handcraft, illustration, and design—that conventional art history has undervalued. As an art historian and educator, I consider Angel De Cora a kind of grandmother, while Karen Thronson is my great-great-grandmother by blood. Their stories relate and engage cultural views toward place, handmade objects, and the ways two very different women formed their identities within their natural and social environments and how they, in turn, contributed to those environments.

Karen Severson Thronson's Immigration to North America

Karen Severson Thronson was not yet born in 1825, but that year set the stage for her future: it was the year the first Norwegian immigrants to the United States boarded a tiny boat bound for New York from Stavanger. Also in that year the Kanza ceded part of their territory near what would become Mankato, Kansas, to the U.S. government. Farther east, Ho-Chunk participated in a U.S.-sponsored council in Prairie du Chien, Wisconsin, to define boundaries between the Anishinaabe (Ojibwe), Meskwaki (Sac and Fox), and Ho-Chunk (Winnebago) tribes, precipitating future land cessions. This first group of fifty-two Norwegian settlers moved west, making homes in Wisconsin and Illinois and later in Iowa.

Like Karen Thronson and her family, subsequent boatloads of Norwegian immigrants came just after the U.S. Civil War, encouraged by promises of free land, easy train travel, and the support of established Norwegian communities.[3] Especially after the ratification of the Homestead Act in 1862 and the end of the Civil War in 1865, Norwegians pushed west, using steamboats and steam engines, across the Great Lakes, into Illinois, Wisconsin, Iowa, then on to Minnesota and the Dakotas, and eventually to Utah and Washington, as U.S. agents removed Native Americans to reservations.[4] Mons Thronson and the Seversons came to the United States through Québec in 1867; they were later among a few Norwegians who tried their luck in Kansas.

Karen was from Norway's Vestlandet, or West Country. She and her family members are listed on the manifest as from Landås, near Bergen. Bergen and Landås are in the Hordaland *fylke* (county) district. Hordaland is split from southwest to northeast by the deep Hardangerfjord, one of Norway's largest fjords. Vøringsfossen and Skykkjedalsfossen are two well-known waterfalls in the district. Because of Norway's population growth and meager quantity of arable land (less than 3 percent of Norway is suitable for agriculture), emigration to the United States seemed a good opportunity to many Norwegians in the latter half of the nineteenth century, especially after Congress passed the Homestead and Railroad Acts.

Families probably gained information about America from letters read aloud in their community and from guidebooks and advertisements by railroad companies and the new western states and territories seeking white settlers. The enticing visions of open farmland created by letters, pamphlets, and images prompted hundreds of thousands of Norwegians to make the journey from the fjords to the plains of Iowa and Kansas.[5]

Born in July 1850, Karen was about seventeen (although the passenger list records her age as thirteen) when she emigrated with her parents, brothers, and Mons Thronson. Arriving in Québec on the bark *Helvetia* on June 17, 1867,

Helge initially identified himself using the name Sletten, the area they came from in Landås, near Bergen.[6] He was Helge Sjursen Sletten: Helge, son of Sjur. His wife is listed as Karen Olesdottir Sletten; she is later listed in U.S. census accounts as "Carrie." Helge's five children were all recorded on the manifest as Slettens.[7] When the family arrived in the United States, however, they quickly dropped the use of Sletten. Sjursen, likewise, seems to have evolved to the more easily pronounced and spelled Severson, as the family's U.S. records indicate their physical and linguistic migration over time.

According to family history, Carrie Severson, Karen's mother, was persuasive in the decision to emigrate. Helge Severson (Sjursen) had been a deep-sea fisherman, obliged to be absent for six to eight weeks at a time. Carrie did not want her sons to be seafarers. As was the case for most emigrants from Norway, the Seversons were not wealthy.[8] Because of Norway's topography, farming or fishing alone were generally inadequate to support a household. Individuals in a peasant household typically performed a variety of jobs, including farm labor, lumbering, fishing, and rosemåling painting for men and dairying, haying, childcare, and weaving for women. These tasks varied seasonally and according to the resources available in the region.[9] Carrie persuaded Helge to emigrate in order to acquire land for their sons, Sever (Sjur), Ole, and Marthinus.

Although Helge was not inclined to give up his trade, he relented. He met a captain in Bergen, Erik Larsen, with whom he bargained for passage for his family in exchange for working as part of the crew. Thus the Seversons boarded the *Helvetia* in May for the difficult six-week journey. Although Helge was offered more work on the bark, the family had already arranged transport to Wisconsin, where Norwegian enclaves had become established.

Many Norwegian immigrants initially settled along rivers and among trees, feeling more familiar with the landscape of the Great Lakes region than with the flat, grass prairies. These river and forest landscapes were often rocky, however, and thus unsuitable for the scale of farming required to make a homestead viable. Frequently, too, desirable land was unavailable. As the wife of a Wisconsin preacher wrote in 1854,

> I believe the entire population of Wisconsin is on the way west now. . . . [T]here is no land to be had for them here now. Those who are thus traveling [in wagons] are either newcomers who have spent the winter in

> Wisconsin or else people who have sold their small farms to older Norwegians and are now going to regions where they can easily get much land at low prices.[10]

Norwegians seeking land pushed west. Native American removal and U.S. land policies facilitated the immigrants' westward migration to Iowa, Minnesota, and Kansas. Iowa became a state two years before Wisconsin, in 1846; Minnesota in 1858; and Kansas in 1861. The Indian Removal Act of 1830 set the stage for Native dispossession of land through subsequent land cession treaties in the western territories. Government Indian agents coerced tribes to cede huge areas, precipitating statehood; states and railroad companies actively sought white settlers.

Statehood, Indian policy, and land policy are inextricably bound to notions of citizenship, of who is included and who is excluded. Before the Civil War, only white men were enfranchised as citizens. In most states, women could not own property, enter contracts, testify in court, serve on a jury, or vote.[11] Women's legal status was defined by coverture, which restricted adult women's legal rights and assumed her husband acted in her (and his other dependents') interest. Beginning in 1839, some states passed Women's Property Laws allowing women to retain their own property at marriage; such laws further distinguished white women from Native Americans and slaves, who were also not considered citizens. Indeed, as Evelyn Nakano Glenn has shown, coerced labor (by women and slaves) and notions of cultural inferiority justified a systematic, structural struggle to enfranchise or disenfranchise various groups.[12]

Through the Homestead Act of 1862, settlers could receive from the U.S. government free patents to 160 acres if they developed and cultivated the land within five years of staking the claim. Radically, the Homestead Act allowed women to apply for patents. Also in 1862, President Lincoln opened huge swaths of public land to corporate and individual entrepreneurs willing to develop it. Railroads received grants to build across the nation via the Pacific Railroad Act. In 1868, African American men gained citizenship and then suffrage—but, very explicitly, Native Americans and women did *not*.

In less than one hundred years, the U.S. government moved various Indigenous people, and white settlers drastically altered the midwestern landscape. The northerly portion of Kansas, where Mankato is today, had been ceded by the Kanza in the Treaty of St. Louis in 1825, the same year the first Norwegians immigrated to the United States.[13] Like their Dakota-Lakota neighbors to the north, the Kanza had farmed, hunted, and gathered across territory extending from Missouri on the east to Oklahoma in the south to central Kansas and Nebraska. By 1872, the Kanza had been removed to Oklahoma. Following the admission of Missouri to statehood in 1821 and the subsequent opening of the Santa Fe Trail, the government sought to create reservations for the forced removal of the Shawnee, Delaware, and Kickapoo people. The Kanzas agreed to reduce their twenty-million-acre domain to a two-million-acre reservation. For this huge cession the Kanzas were to be awarded a $3,500 annuity for twenty years; a quantity of cattle, hogs, and domestic fowl; a government blacksmith and agricultural instructor; and schools. Just east of the new reservation, the U.S. government also granted in fee simple 640-acre plots along the Kansas River to twenty-three mixed race Kanza.

Dispossessed of the range that sustained their traditional ways of life, the continued eradication of buffalo by white hunters, the incursions of the railroad, and lack of support for agriculture, in 1846, when U.S. treaty annuities ended, the Kanza were in a desperate situation. Factionalism and poverty led to further cessions, codified in the 1846 treaty of Mission Creek. In 1854, Congress ratified the Kansas-Nebraska Act and removed Native Americans to reservations. Before the Civil War, Kansas bled as settlers battled over whether the state would be free or slave — it also bled Native blood as tribes resisted or were removed to make way for white settlement.

The 1854 Act not only precipitated violence, it revealed its crafters' attitudes toward corporations and Native Americans: in the words of historians Craig Miner and William Unrau, "[v]irgin soil, railroad rights of way, and lucrative town sites were more important than stuffy statistics [about population densities in other states and territories] and a permanent Indian policy."[14] In Kansas, the Delaware were forced to accommodate railroads through their reservation. But in Nebraska the railroads that applied for right-of-way through reservations were seen as a boon: back east, the Society of Friends overseeing Nebraska tribes reported on the railroad's progress through the reservations and sought to use them to "secure a better arrangement . . . for sending the contributions of Friends of the Indians under our care."[15]

Henry Dawes, however, author of the Dawes Act of 1887 that authorized U.S. government surveys of Native American tribal lands and their subsequent division into allotments for individual Native Americans, lamented the railroads' influence: "something stronger than the Mohonk Conference has dissolved the reservation system. . . . The greed of these people for the land has made it utterly impossible to preserve it for the Indian."[16] Miner and Unrau conclude:

> In retrospect it seems clear that the end of Indian Kansas and the obliteration of diverse Indian cultures were virtually assured the moment a group of fumbling, short-sighted politicians opened the door to white settlement in 1854, and that all that was left was to work out the details—in Washington cloakrooms, corporate boardrooms, in the so-called halls of justice, at potential town sites and railroad centers, and on the fertile, timbered Indian reserves that all assumed were the measure of progress.[17]

"Progress" seemed to make its way to the Norwegian town of Decorah, Iowa, the center of Norwegian heritage and learning in the United States. Ironically, Decorah is named after Waukonhaga (Waukon) Decorah, the nephew of Angel De Cora's great-grandfather Chougeka, the Ho-Chunk chief forced to capitulate his tribe's lands under the pressure of settlement via treaties with the U.S. government in the 1830s and 1840s.[18] Ho-Chunks were moved from Wisconsin into Iowa, Minnesota, South Dakota, and, finally, onto the reservation in Nebraska in 1865.

Between 1867 and 1871, the Seversons and Thronsons traveled together westward across Canada and into the United States. Like most Norwegian immigrants, they would have booked passage through from Québec to a more western destination. After physical examination and quarantine on Grosse Île, about thirty miles from Québec on the St. Lawrence River, a steamboat tugged the bark to Québec. From there, most passengers boarded a train to Montreal and took a steamer across Lake Ontario to Buffalo or Detroit, continuing on to Milwaukee or Chicago, central hubs where they could purchase tickets on any of the many railroad spurs that by then crisscrossed the country. The Seversons and Thronsons followed these well-worn paths, using a transport company to get to Wisconsin from Québec and later shipping the possessions that did not fit in a wagon by rail to Kansas.

Mons Thronson applied for citizenship in the Circuit Court of Dane County, Wisconsin, in October 1868, but not long after, he and the Seversons continued west to Iowa. Edward Roy Parrett (E. Roy, Karen's son-in-law), states in his 1976 memoir that they attempted to settle in Dallas County, Iowa. Similar to

Dane County, an established community of Norwegians lived in and around Story City, Iowa. Mons and Karen recorded their marriage in Dallas County on May 22, 1870, probably anticipating a future homestead. In Iowa in 1870, couples were not required to record their marriages with the state. That Mons and Karen did so suggests their desire to assert their presence in the new country and to be recognized by and within U.S. government structures.[19] Homesteading gave them a path to U.S. citizenship: Mons had been homesteading in Kansas eight years when he was naturalized as a U.S. citizen, on September 20, 1880; in the United States, immigrant wives had been derivatively naturalized via their husbands since 1855.[20] But a homestead in Dallas County was not to be. As the story goes, Irish claim jumpers scared the Seversons and Thronsons off land in Iowa, and the families packed their things in late spring of 1871 and made their way to Mankato (at that time, Jewell Center), Kansas.[21] Railroad maps and advertisements may have enticed them to Kansas, where only a handful of Norwegians had as yet settled. In 1872, the same year that Jewell Center was platted, Karen, Mons, their babies Rasmus and Kansas-born Carl, along with Helge, Carrie, and their six children, were recorded among its first residents.[22]

An account left by Helge Anderson Ruud describes the conditions the Seversons and Thronsons encountered. Ruud and Hans Olsen established the first Norwegian settlement on the border of Jewell and Cloud counties, near Jamestown, Kansas, in 1869.[23] Jamestown is thirty miles southeast of Mankato and eleven miles west of the General Land Office in Concordia. Ruud wrote that when he first arrived in Kansas the land was full of "buffaloes and wild Indians." In a letter to Martin Ulvestad, compiler of *Norwegians in America* (1907), he explained:

> Once the Indians drove us east, where we gathered together and prepared to defend ourselves. It was seventy miles [from there] to the land office, and we had to walk because there was no railroad and we owned no vehicles. Our first homes were sod huts. We began growing wheat and maize, but several years passed before we had anything to sell since the drought and grasshoppers destroyed our crops. Now it is better in every respect.[24]

Although this memory registers the threat of violence as Native Americans resisted removal and white encroachment, it also dismisses them, proclaiming the pioneers' triumph over the wild forces of nature, insects, and Indians. This brief and to-the-point description is very similar to E. Roy's account describing the Thronsons settling in Kansas. E. Roy did not relate any interactions between the homesteaders and Native Americans. As early as 1838, Ole Rynning suggested in his emigrant guide that "[t]he Indians have now been transported away from this part of the country far to the west."[25] In the widely popular *Pathfinder for Norwegian Emigrants to North America and Texas,* first published in 1844 under the title *Veviser for Norske emigranter til de forenede Nordamerikanske stater og Texas,* Johan Reinert Reiersen explains that no emigrant need fear being "molested by the completely harmless Indians," and that the U.S. government has "pursued a just and peaceful Indian policy from the beginning. . . . If driving the Indians from their hunting grounds and the graves of their forefathers can be defended it must be on the basis of principle: the red man was a monopolist. He took possession of more land than could be reconciled with the welfare of the human race. And he was a barbarian, hostile to the useful occupations and fair arts of a civilized life."[26] As Reiersen suggested, U.S. Indian policy sought to solve the "Indian problem" of Native possession and existence through removal.

The triumphant pioneer whose civilizing values cultivate both nature and Native is a typical trope in Scandinavian immigration stories and survives today in frontier and pioneer legends and narratives.[27] Maps precipitated and perpetuated the frontier myth by showing wild, open land available to be possessed and cultivated. When Karen, Mons, and their baby Rasmus arrived in Kansas in 1872, buffalo were still abundant and were even hunted from the new trains running west.

Kanza and many other tribes still hunted the buffalo through the prairies' blue grama, junegrass, and wheatgrass, although they, too, were being pushed west. It was not until May 1872 that the Kanza were forced from their territory onto a new reservation in Oklahoma.[28] But the open spaces depicted on a railroad map from 1869 belie the presence of any Indigenous inhabitants. (See figure 1.) These peoples' lives and territories are not marked on this colored map. The map clearly demarcates the "Buffalo Range" in its center, just north of the Solomon River fork and just west of the Republican River, in what is now north-central Kansas. The land granted to the railroad by the federal government is a color block of green. It extended twenty miles on either side of the track. The map advertises millions of acres of land for sale, land the railroad

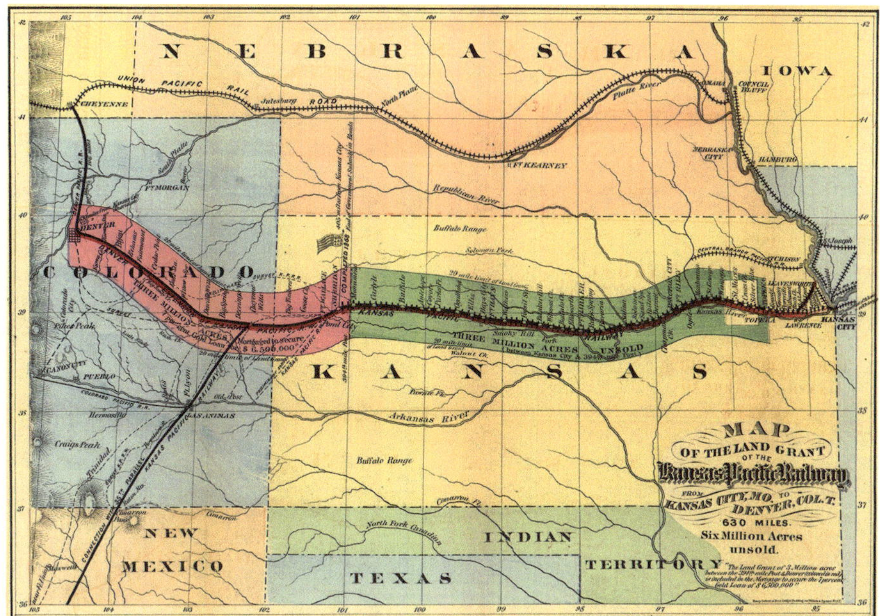

FIGURE 1. A map from 1869 showing Kansas Pacific Railway land for sale.

hoped to sell to settlers. By selling the land, the railroad not only made money, they also ensured continued profit from moving goods, livestock, new settlers, and visitors. The map shows the area surrounding the colored land grants as vast and vacant, seemingly unoccupied and undeveloped. Only the railroad and the towns popping up along its path indicate human presence—the cultivated civilization of industrial progress.

Today, the land that was the Thronson and Severson homesteads is virtually treeless and waterless. (See figure 2.) Mixed-grass prairies, such as those near Mankato, at the ninety-sixth meridian, typically receive less than twenty inches of rain a year, sometimes much less, while the semiarid West experiences great fluctuations in rainfall and temperature. Most Kansas agriculture relies on wells connected to deep aquifers to sustain cereal crops and the cattle and hog feedlots that have replaced the buffalo range. Both in the United States and abroad railroad companies aggressively advertised resource-rich lands and job opportunities. For example, the Kansas Pacific Railway (later

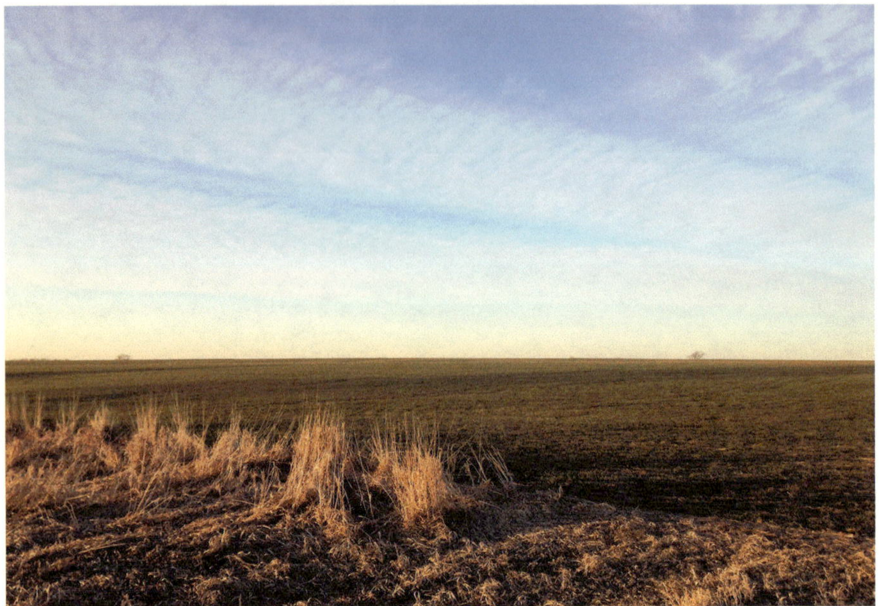

FIGURE 2. Mankato, Kansas, homesteads, December 30, 2016. Photo by author.

part of the Union Pacific network) published a pamphlet in Norwegian aimed at attracting immigrants. (See figure 3.) The pamphlet included information about Kansas's natural resources and its opportunities for education and work, illustrating it with an image of the Solomon River at Solomon City. The scene looks more like a fjord valley than a mixed-grass prairie. The image showcases abundant water and foliage and a river waterfall to provide power and irrigation for plant life, while the train in back signals industry and civilization, bridging both water and tall grass with steel. Pamphlets, maps, and pictures such as these were commonplace and were distributed in multiple languages from the 1860s on.[29]

As this brief history indicates, Karen Thronson's immigration directly overlapped the forced migration of various tribes, including those of Angel De Cora's Wisconsin ancestors and the Kanza. To facilitate white settlement, agents of the U.S. government removed Native Americans from their traditional homes, fracturing their communitarian ways of living and their collective sense of identity and place.

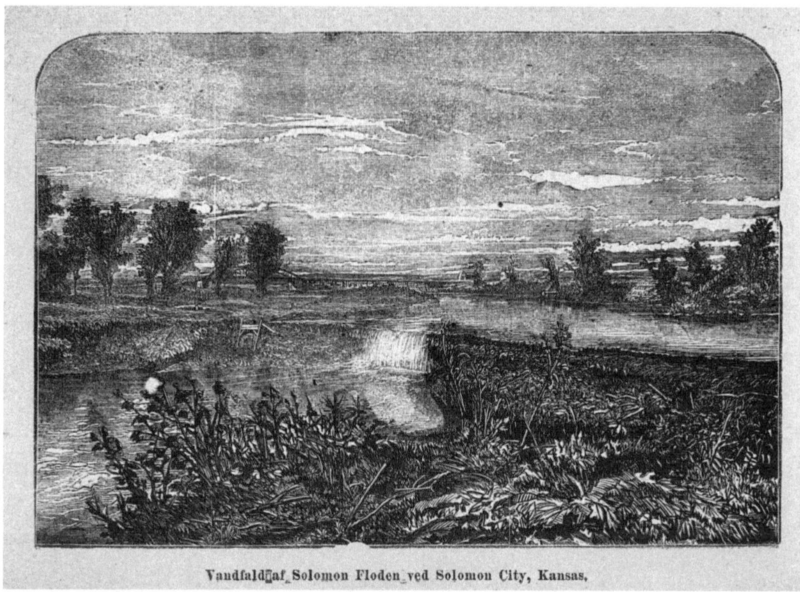

FIGURE 3. Engraving showing Solomon, Kansas, in 1877. See https://www.kshs.org/km/items/view/210135.

Angel De Cora's Migration across North America

Like other Native Americans, De Cora's story begins with her people's removal from their ancestral land as a result of pressures from white settlers. In *Fire Light,* her biography of Angel De Cora, Linda M. Waggoner details the horrors of Ho-Chunk removal and De Cora's family history, filling in the background of De Cora's exceptional creativity.

De Cora's great-grandfather, part of the Thunderbird clan, had been the chief of a large village near Portage, Wisconsin, and was party to the delegation of Ho-Chunk that signed treaties ceding land to the United States in 1832 and 1837.[30] Like their Kanza neighbors to the west, the Ho-Chunk, under the 1832 treaty, moved from their territories along the Mississippi River to Neutral Territory in north-central Iowa. Ho-Chunk were to receive $10,000 per year for twenty-seven years for ceding the eastern land. As with so many of the early treaties between tribes and the U.S. government, however, the land that was supposed to be reserved for them was not.

In 1837, the United States imposed a new treaty on the Ho-Chunk nation. This new treaty confirmed the Ho-Chunk land cessions in Wisconsin and at the same time reduced the size of the Neutral Territory. In response, Chiefs Heetshcawausharpskawkau and Kar-i-mo-nee led a delegation of younger men to Washington, D.C., to plead for restitution of their lands. They purposefully did not bring with them representatives of the Bear clan, because Ho-Chunk protocol required full representation to sign any treaty. By sending a delegation of young men with no Bear clan members, they sought to ensure that no land would be sold.[31] The delegates, however, were held in Washington until they signed the new treaty. Although they were led to believe that they would have eight years to move, the actual treaty required that the people move in eight months. The governor of Wisconsin was so desperate to remove the Ho-Chunk that he threatened that if the federal government did not remove them quickly, he would raise a state militia to remove them by force.

Immigrant settlers, including the Norwegians moving from Wisconsin to Iowa, and tensions between the Meskwaki (Sac and Fox) to the south and Dakota to the north rendered the so-called Neutral Territory not very neutral at all. In effect, the Ho-Chunk were buffers between their historical allies, the Meskwaki and the Dakota, but Ho-Chunk presence in Iowa enflamed the tensions between them. The Ho-Chunk people were suffering violence, disease and starvation. Their chief, Little De Cora wrote frequently to the agent in Iowa for the assistance the treaties had promised. As a lame response to the tribe's requests, in 1846—the year Iowa gained statehood—the U.S. government moved the Ho-Chunk farther north onto the Long Prairie Reservation in north-central Minnesota.

Conditions in Minnesota were not much better, as the Ho-Chunk at Long Prairie were again buffers: this time between Dakota and Anishinaabe (Ojibwe) territories and tensions. After not even ten years at Long Prairie, the Ho-Chunk left again, moving to a small reservation about eighteen miles square in southwestern Minnesota, in Blue Earth County. It seemed this would be their permanent home, and by 1859 more than fourteen Ho-Chunk families were raising oats and wheat on 1,600 acres of cultivated land. At that point about two thousand Ho-Chunk lived at Blue Earth.[32]

Their tenure there was limited, however. Factors including Minnesota statehood (1858) and the concomitant influx of industry and settlers, the outbreak of Civil War, and the violent resistance of Dakotas to white settlers near Mankato and New Ulm in 1862—a reaction to the suffering imposed on them by the government's broken treaties and constant pressure from white settlers—again precipitated Ho-Chunk removal. A small group of Ho-Chunk (only thirteen individuals, twelve of whom later were acquitted)[33] had taken up arms with the Dakota, although Little De Cora had tried to keep the peace. The government responded to the 1862 uprising with the largest mass hanging in U.S. history—the executed became known as the Dakota 38—and by removing the Ho-Chunk from the Blue Earth reservation.

The United States did not have a reservation set aside for them, so they moved the Ho-Chunk to Crow Creek, in South Dakota. This removal impacted the Ho-Chunk especially hard—of the two thousand individuals removed to the desolate Crow Creek Agency, more than five hundred died during the winter of 1863–64 alone. Finally, in 1865, the U.S. government purchased land from the Omaha in Nebraska and created the Winnebago reservation.

These assaults on the Ho-Chunk homeland and tribal identity by the colonizing government precipitated constant instability and led to factionalism. The Ho-Chunk became permanently divided, although they overlapped in their social relations.[34] Some abided by the treaties and moved to Neutral Territory, then to Minnesota, and finally to the present reservation in Nebraska in 1865; others remained fugitives on their own land in central Wisconsin, despite the U.S. government's continued attempts to remove them. Land from the Omaha added to the Nebraska reservation in 1873 was meant to accommodate these resisters, but by 1875, many, including Angel De Cora's father, had returned to Wisconsin. Today, they are recognized separately as Wisconsin Ho-Chunk.

The Winnebago Reservation lies just west of the Missouri River, the natural boundary that separates Iowa from Nebraska. Winnebago is a rolling canvas of mixed grasses and farms, with an area of more than 107,000 acres. Babbling creeks flow toward the Missouri, while small groves of trees provide shade for the tribe's herd of buffalo. Today, the earth seems to rise up around the flat two-lane highway that enters the reservation. The tribal college, including the Angel De Cora Museum, sits on a hill overlooking terraced fields.

Angel De Cora grew up on the reservation. Probably born in 1869, she related in a short autobiography, published while she was at Carlisle in 1912, that she was born in a wigwam, and that

> as a child, my life was ideal. . . . [A]s early as I can remember, I was lulled to sleep night after night by my father's or my grandparent's recital of laws and customs that had regulated the daily life of my grandsires for generations and generations, and in the morning I was awakened by the same counselling.[35]

She further relates how in 1883, as a young girl, she was taken from her Nebraska home to Hampton Institute in Virginia. De Cora writes that initially she hid herself from the white man, but later she joined six other Ho-Chunk children in a wagon ride to Sioux City, Iowa, with "Mr. H." From there, they rode three days on a train to Hampton. In this autobiography, as well as in letters extant in the Hampton University Archives, De Cora recounts her mother's worry (unimaginable!). De Cora was aware that her experience of coercion and the denial of her mother's right to know her child's whereabouts paralleled that of many Native children taken to boarding schools. This kidnapping was the beginning of De Cora's white education, first at Hampton Institute in Virginia and later at Smith College and at art schools in Philadelphia and Boston.

De Cora's experience of being taken from the Winnebago reservation during President Ulysses Grant's "Peace Policy," followed by her stays at eastern educational institutions, reflected Yankee reformers' ideas about assimilation. To assuage the violence of removals, to fulfill the needs of new white settlers after the Civil War, and, ostensibly, to address corruption among Indian agents, President Grant created a Board of Commissioners of Indian Affairs consisting of ten men "eminent for their intelligence and philanthropy, to serve without pecuniary compensation" in conjunction with the Secretary of the Interior. The control of Indian agencies was delegated to Protestant religious organizations, especially the Society of Friends (Quakers). These groups appointed agents and other personnel. The idea was that such "moral" groups would be unaffected by politicking and would have a pacifying effect on the Native Americans, particularly through Christian missionary activity. As Francis Prucha has noted, however, "Indian resistance to white encroachment and refusal to be quietly herded onto reservations resulted in wars that kept the plains and mountains aflame for more than a decade, making a mockery of the 'peace policy.'"[36]

The broad outlines of Native American cultural genocide are fairly well known. The ideals of "progress" and Manifest Destiny that brought both Yankee and Norwegian settlers west traumatized Native Americans. After removal, institutional prerogatives advanced by so-called "Friends of Indians" shaped and underscored government policies promoting assimilation via industrial education and allotment. Marinella Lentis summarizes:

> As the advancement of the self-conceived "great" American nation—foretold in ideas of manifest destiny that equated civilization with white, Protestant society—was slowed down by non-assimilated Indian presence, policy makers and self-appointed reformers, such as members of the Lake Mohonk Conference of the Friends of the Indians, envisioned a solution to the so-called Indian problem: it consisted of the total assimilation of the Indigenous population into American society through the adoption of mainstream behavior, values, language, and work habits. This was to be achieved through a breakup of the reservation system and the tribal customs of holding land in common, and eradication of tribal cultures and identities through education, and a transformation of men and women into self-sufficient and law-abiding citizens through manual labor. By the late 1870s, total assimilation became the goal of the federal government for its wards.[37]

Each of these reforms attempted to break up tribal political and social structures, attempting to replace tribal governments, kinship ties, and shared tradition with private land ownership (with the "remainders" devolving to the U.S. government) and the industrial (that is, vocational rather than classical) education of Native children to create a subordinate working class.

Various organizations with well-meaning supporters were galvanized to discuss mechanisms and policies to address the "Indian problem." Reform, for these individuals, meant addressing the "problem" by finding means of assimilation rather than extermination. These values, in turn, were conflated with "American"—elite, often eastern, U.S.-born, Protestant, capitalist—values. Protestant ideals of the morality of work and the importance of individual property ownership, and the assumed link between physical labor, material accumulation, and the right to thrive, underpinned these policies. In 1873, Commissioner of Indian Affairs Edward Smith said that "[a] fundamental difference between barbarians and a civilized people is the difference between a herd and an individual."[38]

In 1883, Albert K. Smiley, a Quaker member of the Board of Indian Commissioners, began inviting individuals interested in Indian issues to his resort at Lake Mohonk, near New Paltz, New York. These yearly conferences became significant forums for presenting ideas and drafting policy recommendations. Prominent Native Americans attended; De Cora went in 1895 while a student at Smith College. At the turn of the century, Merrill Gates, board commissioner and presiding officer at numerous Lake Mohonk conferences, held firmly to the principles that had guided Indian reformers for a quarter century. He wanted Native Americans to desire material things and money, to have plots of their own and give up communal living and sharing. Like many reformers, he believed that individual property ownership, along with a Christian education, would help Native Americans become "intelligently selfish" and, thereby, help the Indian to one day exercise "intelligent citizenship."[39] Reformers believed that ownership and education would change everything and everyone for the better.

To white reformers, making an "intelligent" Indian meant making him a Christian, property-owning producer and consumer. It meant breaking up tribes, breaking up kinship bonds, and castigating the mutual aid of community. Indeed, these modes of support—kinship bonds and shared resources of "tend and befriend" to survive and cope—are often utilized by women in patriarchal societies where their labor and selfhood are marginalized and devalued. The communal—what reformers often called "communistic"—ways of many Native Americans were an affront to the ideals inherent to settler colonialism. That Native Americans had been forcibly removed, put into foreign landscapes, and prevented from exercising traditional means of sustenance were not seen as causes behind conditions on the reservations. Prucha concludes: "The Protestantism of the Friends of the Indian merged almost imperceptibly into Americanism. In a period when traditional values seemed threatened by hordes of immigrants coming to American shores—immigrants from eastern and southern Europe who seemed to fit only with difficulty into the accepted culture—the reformers insisted on the Americanization of all unfamiliar elements."[40] The phrase "immigrants from eastern and southern Europe" meant Jews and Catholics. As Protestants, Norwegians were less threatening because they shared values with the dominant culture regarding education, land proprietorship, cultivation, and religion, even though they still kept to themselves in dense enclaves where they could speak Norwegian and carry on their traditions.

In Nebraska, the Society of Friends supervised the Indian agencies with jurisdiction over Ho-Chunk (at the Winnebago reservation) and the other tribes in Nebraska.[41] Between 1869 and 1884, the Society of Friends oversaw the Northern Indian agency and emphasized "civilizing" Native Americans by assimilating them to dominant white cultural norms. Records of the Society of Friends (extant at Swarthmore College) describe a white perspective on Ho-Chunk "progress" toward assimilation. In line with the board of commissioners and discussions at Mohonk, the Quakers' patronage emphasized "civilizing" the Native Americans on the Winnebago and other Nebraska reservations through education, religion, and agricultural work.

De Cora was intimately familiar with all aspects of these Indian policies: as a student of compulsory industrial education in the 1880s, a recipient of a land allotment in the 1890s (land that she, like so many, later sold), and finally, as a Native arts teacher at Carlisle in the first decade of the twentieth century. Indian Commissioner Francis Leupp called for a gentler assimilation of "improvement" rather than total "transformation." Leupp embraced Native arts as a uniquely significant mechanism for bringing Native Americans into the domestic economy. De Cora's evolution as an artist and human being reflects the confluence and conflict of the Native and white ideals she learned.

The reforms of the last quarter of the nineteenth century prescribed De Cora's roles making and teaching art. She seemingly acquiesced to white expectations of assimilation and "Indian" authenticity, but she also resisted by affirming her individual identity and adding complexity in her own way. While expected to conform and assimilate, De Cora transformed the system from within. As an adult, De Cora sold illustrations to magazines, exhibited her work at international expositions, and taught Native arts at Carlisle. She made things that whites liked, but using her own references and imagery; she submitted her work to government exhibitions to serve as a success story and taught at an Indian boarding school, but also wrote letters describing her distaste at being identified only by her ethnicity and gender; she sold her land allotment, but never purchased any property off the reservation. At Carlisle, De Cora nurtured her Native students' memories and ethnic identities through creative design, and in so doing she attempted to affirm a Pan-Indian community, all the while retaining her autonomy through her own complex, layered designs and her flexible, Indigenized art curriculum and pedagogy.

Art of Place

Both Karen Thronson and Angel De Cora left their birthplaces, but each woman's journey reveals how art formed a link to tradition and community and became a means of coping with the displacing physical and psychological effects of (im)migration. Communities can be real or imagined and can contain infinite complexity, but at its most basic definition, community is "a network of social relations marked by mutuality and emotional bonds," where individuals share "a common interest in a particular locality."[42] Cultural or social bonds can transcend physical boundaries, such that Norwegian immigrant women might feel part of a virtual ethnic community just by reading the same Norwegian-language magazine and De Cora might feel community with any individual, white or Native, sharing knowledge of and interest in her tribe and homeland. Objects mediate these relations between humans, phenomena, and place. This is a phenomenological knowing of the world through "seeing" and "grasping" things — an epistemology of touch and sight in which objects are fundamental to locating the self physically, emotionally, and psychologically.

For Norwegian immigrant women, connection to place shifted over the generations from the fjords of Norway to the plains of the Midwest, as they built communities on the prairies. Karen Thronson sought to connect her community in Kansas to her homeland in Norway by establishing a church and school and by making traditional decorations. For Karen "home" became her family, her work, and the objects she made with women who shared her memories and images of Norway. After Mons died, Karen's social connections with fellow Norwegians were especially important to her livelihood and identity. She left her homestead in Kansas with her mother, Carrie, and with her daughter, Rachel, to rejoin the Norwegian community near Story City, Iowa.

Although De Cora's and her family's movements initially were forced, through her art she retained a connection to her homeland and to the sacred beliefs or her people, thereby resisting total assimilation and affirming her individual and cultural identity. In "Gray Wolf's Daughter," De Cora dressed her fictional counterpart in traditional buckskin to dance the night before leaving for a white school. As a teacher, De Cora Indigenized the curriculum by promoting students' awareness of their distinct tribal heritages in order to create Pan-Indian designs. She helped them remember their individual and collective identities, and in so doing, she helped herself remember and find meaning in her heritage and community within a larger Pan-Indian idea.

Handmade objects and images, some brought from home, others referencing home, connected Karen and her family and De Cora to their respective heritages and homelands. It may seem obvious that objects hold memories: we can see it is true simply by observing how people cherish and hold onto particular things—a blanket, a photograph, a ticket stub. These objects are not mere receptacles of memory, however; in every interaction with the object, the person re-creates and re-narrates origin stories.[43] Mihaly Csikszentmihalyi and Eugene Rochberg-Halton have noted that people "make order in their selves, (i.e.: 'retrieve their identity') by first *creating* and then *interacting* with the material world. . . . Thus the things that surround us are inseparable from who we are."[44] [Emphases added.] These phenomena help people transmit meaningful information about who we are, via various material modes of expression, to ourselves as well as to others.[45] Objects are part of an intersubjective act of remembrance; they are traces of being, phenomena that both shape and are shaped by place and people. From Karen Thronson's wheat stars to De Cora's abstracted thunderbirds, culturally specific imagery conveys both physical and symbolic associations with place, community, and identity. They hold meaning and memories and preserve the makers' sense of self and being.

The objects I discuss operate on the borders of areas delineated as "art," "craft," "folk," and "fine" art, themselves gendered and racialized categories.[46] The reification of these hierarchies in the late nineteenth century included further distinguishing from "fine" art not only "folk" and ethnic art, but also Indigenous and female arts: all were seen as "primitive" and in contrast to industrial progress.[47] Neither straw weaving nor crochet are usually seen as art—at least, not within the compass of nineteenth-century dictates[48]—but through the process of making, women creatively resisted certain prescriptions for assimilation and defined themselves.

The structures within which Karen Thronson and Angel De Cora worked at the turn of the twentieth century were those of settler colonialism and industrial capitalism, themselves intertwined and presuming white male supremacy and property ownership as the requirements to self-determination: the right to exist freely and exercise choice. Understanding that settler colonialism is itself a structure that employed the rhetoric of industrial "progress," where things that were handmade (by women and non-whites) became quaint folk art to be relegated to history and the museum, was part of a nationalistic evolutionary narrative about the United States' destined greatness through industry.[49]

The movement of labor from farms to factory was one strand of the various processes that decentered women's labor contributions, relegating their work for home or farm to "craft" and simultaneously reifying class boundaries.[50] For the white female elite, such crafts became mere hobbies or items for consumption and social distinction within the Arts and Crafts movement. The Arts and Crafts movement in England and the United States sought to imbue unique, handmade objects with an improving moral ethic: aesthetics as counter to the ills of industrialization. This impulse, too, implicitly reified class and gender distinctions, since such objects necessarily became luxury goods to be commissioned and collected by the well-heeled. De Cora, although following many of the general tenets of the Arts and Crafts movement, has often been left out of its dominant historical narrative, even though her work is similarly informed.[51] She integrated design and decoration, inspired by midwestern natural surroundings.

Similarly, the middle and upper classes (particularly white bourgeois women with time on their hands) saw elevating handcrafts as a method to address the plight of the working class and to reform (Eastern European) immigrants and Native Americans, particularly the so-called "squaw drudge."[52] Many of the leading figures of England's Arts and Crafts movement were socialists, but their politics did not necessarily lead them to support women's rights, feminism, or racial equality generally; these liberal strains were submerged into workforce manual training.[53] "Craft" was seen as separate from the male-dominated institutions of intellect and power and as dividing industry from nature: as a result of these simple binaries, it became devalued.

Handwork was feminine and domestic and seen as such. Although millwork absorbed the labor of great numbers of poor women and girls, in more financially secure families, industrial society largely confined women to the home, where handwork kept them from idleness. Such work underscored their presumed moral superiority and their attendant duty to assume the roles of virtuous housewife, caretaker, and moral arbiter, traits marking a realm explicitly contrasting to the perceived immorality pervading the male world of business and public affairs. At the same time, gendering such handwork preserved "fine" arts and business for white men. De Cora's promotion of Native arts can be seen both as acquiescing to dominant expectations and as resisting them by asserting her identity as a female Native artist.

De Cora was a professional artist, in that she was academically trained, sold some of her work, and taught in her field, but she barely eked a living through sales of her art. (Her teacher and friend Cora Folsom noted in De Cora's obituary that she often gave her work away—the action of giving and sharing providing another reflection of her cultural values.)[54] In the multiple expositions displaying her work, De Cora's art was not shown in the fine arts buildings. Rather, reformers and government school officials exhibited it as demonstrations of a Native success story. Through her teaching position at Carlisle, however, De Cora was able to give cultural knowledge and the means of individual expression back to her Native American students, empowering them with visual tools to hold their own in a social order that sought to minimize their freedom and homogenize their heritages.

Norwegian immigrant women also sold some of the objects they made, but through collectives, such as ladies' aid societies. Sale of handmade decorative and functional items supplemented other farm production, and the women's volunteer (unpaid) work brought them together to make things that could be sold to support the church, its mission, and, at times, struggling families in the community. These kinds of contributions by women at the microeconomic level are often overlooked and devalued, even though they were highly significant to literally building midwestern communities.[55]

As Barbara Handy-Marchello concludes in her discussion of women's work on the Dakota plains: "Farm women were not only workers but producers. They made products to hold in their hands, to trade, to sell, to display, to admire. They felt the pride of accomplishment and the satisfaction of supporting themselves and their families even when the field crops failed."[56] Indeed, building community and sharing handwork at social gatherings, together, was especially important when so many women's daily lives were full of chores and relative isolation.

Strikingly, the products changed over time, as the crafters hybridized their Norwegian patterns with the forms of products necessary for the American home. To fit in, immigrant women both made and consumed objects with patterns that retained traditional geometries. As shown in the articles and advertisements in *Kvinden og Hjemmet* (The woman and the home), it was acceptable to conform to some of the dominant culture's social expectations when Norwegian traditions could be maintained too.

Both white and Native women could exert moral and economic power in the domestic realm through their skilled work, undermining conventional ideas and binaries through creative expression and what might be considered visual coding.[57] Women passed on knowledge or ideas that otherwise would have been suppressed; appropriation, ironic mimicry, and symbolic inversion especially draw attention to what might have been excluded or lost. Handcrafts such as needlework (quilting or lace making) as well as decorative design could convey meanings that evaded detection by those otherwise acculturated.[58] We will see how De Cora appropriated English text and type by resetting it using Native designs and how she mimicked a standard lesson using butterflies to open rich creative and interpretive possibilities for her Native students. Similarly, needlework done in the home or with other women in ladies' aid societies provided women like Karen Thronson with creative and social outlets as well as some economic power, veiled behind the domestic function of a simple doily or pillow. Finally, the dissemination of women's and other magazines provided Norwegian American women and, to an extent, Angel De Cora and her students a means of networking virtually through the appropriation of a medium traditionally used by men to legitimize their knowledge.[59]

Chapter Organization

Chapter 2 explores how straw weaving and embroidery connected Karen Thronson and her daughters to traditional Norwegian beliefs that honored the land. These beliefs attained longevity as communal knowledge by being passed down through women's handwork, despite being undervalued because of associations with nature, animism, and the feminine. At the same time, Karen Thronson, and her daughters, enfranchised through land and naturalization policies, was able to grow her family and maintain ethnic traditions.

In chapter 3, Angel De Cora's illustrations for *Harper's New Monthly*, specifically those she created for her semiautobiographical story "Gray Wolf's Daughter," show how the style, subject, and medium each indicate aspects of the shift from her childhood home on the Winnebago reservation in Nebraska — both its cultural values and the physical landscape — to the values and expectations taught to her at Hampton Institute, Smith College, and Drexel Academy of Art and Design. De Cora's landscape paintings and designs were also exhibited at three international expositions, exhibited as examples of a success story for the Indian boarding schools' process of transformative assimilation. Despite this training, I argue, De Cora retained meanings that continued her connections to her home and family, thereby subtly resisting the whitewashing of her heritage.

Chapter 4 focuses on how women formed virtual and physical communities through magazines and ladies' aid societies. Creative making brought Norwegian immigrant women together as they were adjusting to life in the United States and transitioning from time-consuming needlework, such as Hardanger embroidery, to crochet. The Iowa-based Norwegian American publication *Kvinden og Hjemmet* promoted both traditional handcrafts and new products and applications, and immigrant women used *Kvinden og Hjemmet* as a virtual community, sharing information and connecting to each other and their heritage. They also found community and some economic autonomy by forming *kvindeforening,* or ladies' aid societies, in their church congregations.

The graphic designs created by De Cora and her students at Carlisle Indian Industrial School are the focus of chapter 5. De Cora used design to Indigenize her curriculum within the rigid standards set by reformers. Design became a signifier of identity and a way to form a broad Pan-Indian community for De Cora and her students—Native Americans who had been taken from their ethnic communities and told their identities must change. Following Anne Ruggles Gere's assertion that De Cora's art is an "art of survivance," where *survivance* is "an active sense of presence, the continuance of native stories . . . renunciations of dominance, tragedy and victimry," I suggest that De Cora's mature focus on abstract design rather than illustration is a purposeful return to the sacred forms of her Indigenous heritage—an acknowledgement of the potentiality of other Native American tribes' sacred imagery and a way to form solidarity with other Native Americans.[60] Despite being forced from their homelands and into boarding schools, De Cora and her students used design to connect to their respective tribal heritages, even while, to outsiders, those designs signaled a general, even stereotyped, "Native" aesthetic.

Finally, in the last chapter I briefly suggest some conclusions from the overlay of these two women's stories. Karen Thronson benefited from the structures of a settler colonial society, and Angel De Cora also gained some social capital through her Yankee connections. Both women found ways to create meaningful bonds between home and heritage, but the legacy and structure of settler colonialism continues.[61]

Nineteenth-century white reformers' efforts to cultivate and "civilize" required destroying both Indigenous nature and Indigenous culture and relegating women to the domestic sphere. Feminizing land and nature helped condone violence against it. As Richard Slotkin notes, it is *violence* that regenerates the myth of the frontier for future utility.[62] This national mythology continues to rationalize pro-corporate racist and patriarchal structures that occlude the problems within the structure itself: the enslavement and oppression of particular people, the rending of Indigenous people from the landscape, and the legacy of inequality and disenfranchisement marring the social and political fabric of the United States.

I use *Native American* in the text to refer generally to the Indigenous people inhabiting North America. When there are historical titles (such as the "Indian arts" program at Carlisle "Indian" Industrial School), I retain the historical usage of *Indian*. I attempt to use the Indigenous name for a people (for example, Ho-Chunk, Kanza), unless specifically referring to the reservation or nation as recognized by the U.S. government (for example, Winnebago, Kaw).

TWO | COMMUNITY AND TRADITION

MAKING A HOME IN KANSAS, 1872–1902

In the Hardanger fjord in the western region of Norway, less than fifty miles from Bergen, cold water cuts through hard land. In a diagonal strip 111 miles long, glacial run-off and North Sea meet between walls of sheared and fracturing granitic layers. The textures of rock and water here are deep and contrasting: layers cut by the opposition of solid and liquid over time. Hardanger embroidery, such as that decorating the bridal crown on display at the Vesterheim Museum in Decorah, Iowa, originated in this region. The embroidered border to the traditional bridal crown, shown in figure 4, demonstrates how the artist creates depth, texture, and separation of line by using positive and negative space in the juxtaposed geometries of swirling sun, star, and cross. This is typical of cut- and counted-thread needlework, which frequently uses geometric patterns, often six- or eight-pointed stars or crosses, generally in white thread on white linen.

Later adaptations made in the United States, such as that by Karen's granddaughter Esther Whitaker shown in figure 5, approximate the look, but in the simpler-to-work mode of crochet. Whitaker crocheted fractal sun stars somewhat like snowflakes, with each loop building onto the next to make a larger and more complex whole. When complete, these sun stars were sewn onto the pillow using loops to create eight points. Similarly, the straw stars that decorate a Norwegian home at Christmas are simple: eight points, bound with red string. (See figure 6.) The red strings tie the blades together to create rays, transforming chaff into a symbol of Christian faith: the star over Jesus's

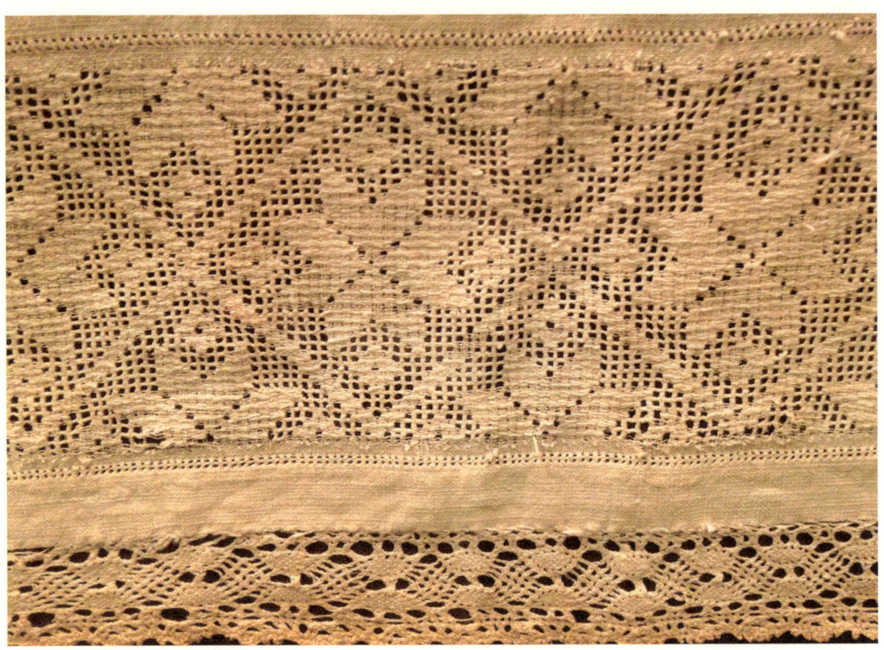

FIGURE 4. Hardanger-style embroidered bridal crown, border detail, eighteenth or nineteenth century, made in the Hardanger region of western Norway. Luther College Collection, Vesterheim Norwegian-American Museum, Decorah, Iowa.

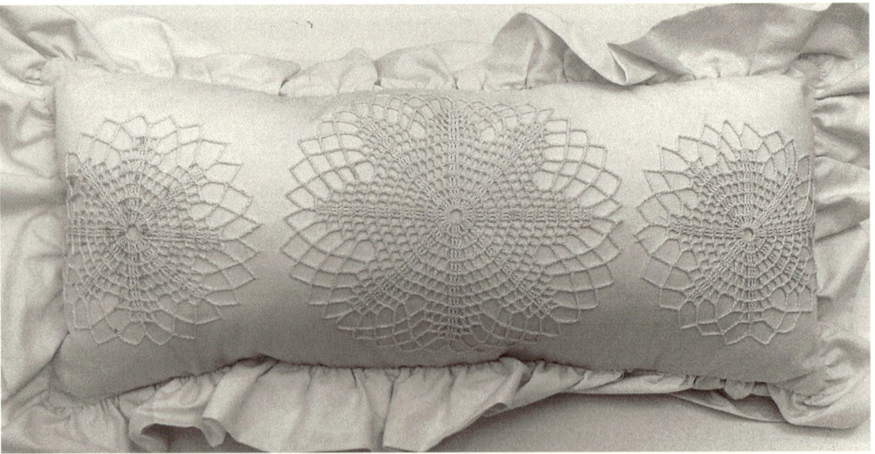

FIGURE 5. Crochet stars mounted on a pillow, made by Esther Whitaker in the second half of the twentieth century. Photo by author.

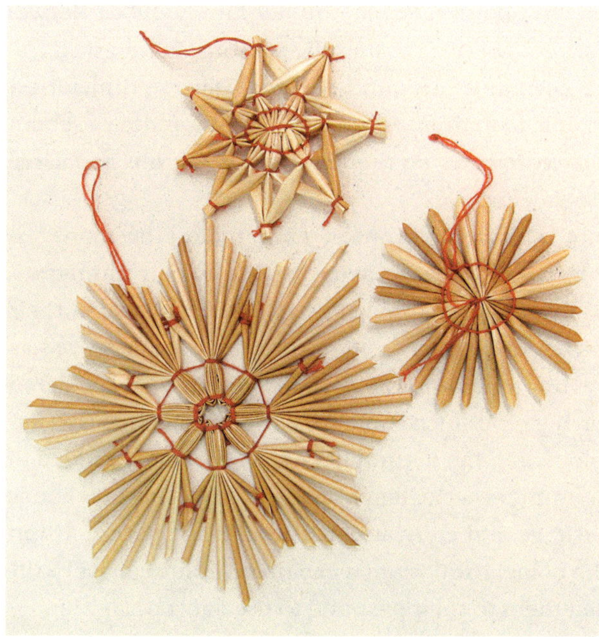

FIGURE 6.
Straw star ornaments, maker unknown. Photo by author.

birthplace. In pre-Christian Scandinavian tradition, stars, also identified as swirling suns and flowers, are fertility symbols.[1]

Domestic arts such as needlework embroidery (*haandarbeide*) and wheat weaving (*hvetevefting)* helped Norwegian women like Karen acknowledge nature and make the new landscape familiar through the filter of old traditions. They did so from within the place they held sway—the home. The geometries of embroidered textiles and woven wheat parallel the imposition of order onto the landscape seen in neatly plowed rows in the soil. Letters written by women from the first generation of Norwegian immigrants suggest that they did not feel loss as the grass was turned over and plowed for wheat; rather, they found beauty in cultivation and in ordering the land into cereal fields, home gardens, and decorations.[2] They created smaller-scale beauty for their homes through neat rows of Hardanger embroidery and wheat strands tightly woven into recognizable shapes. They used these ancient modes of visual communication to honor nature, garner blessings, and ease the difficulties of rural life.

The Thronsons and Seversons experienced great hardship on the Kansas plains, including drought, locusts, and blizzards; one of the latter ultimately cost Mons his life. To deal with nature, Karen and her family did as Norwegians had done for generations: they celebrated the seasons and marked the cycles of human life with decorative arts and designs. Despite difficulties, Karen and her family were able to maintain communal ties, building a school and a church on their property to carry on their cultural traditions and serve as social loci for the Norwegian enclave.

Although no ornaments by Karen Thronson exist today, the many extant examples of embroidery and wheat weaving by Norwegian immigrant women—or more recent ones made by their descendants—speak to their significance. These processes for ordering and decorating a home served as ways to maintain a connection to ethnic roots and traditions. Embroidered geometries and wheat weaving reproduced ancient symbolic references to fertility and a cyclical cosmology, and the natural fiber of wheat corresponded to the fragility of Norwegian immigrant existence on the plains. These activities helped women sustain heritage and cultivate order amid vast nature. Given that women's place was the home, rural women expanded home conceptually through objects that linked them to their past and to the old country.

American land and naturalization policies, along with practiced social norms, allowed Karen and her daughters to maintain their identities and sense of ethnic solidarity, even while patriarchal institutions subordinated the power of women's connection to nature. Karen was able to set up a school and church, and when economically necessary, to return to the well-established supports of the Norwegian community in Story City, Iowa. De Cora, too, found solace in nature and designs derived from natural geometries, although she and her relatives were denied ethnic solidarity and enfranchisement.

Homesteading Hardships

The mixed grasses of Iowa and Kansas bore little resemblance to the fields and fjords of Norway. In contrast, Mankato, Kansas, seems to lie at the crest of a wave amid a mostly calm sea of grass and grain. Trees are few on these plains, especially in the mid- and short-grass areas, except near rivers and creeks or where humans have dug wells to tap the finite aquifers. The wind, with nothing to break it, blows often and strong. The poor soil and extreme weather, along with the isolation of these rural settings, made homesteading extremely difficult. Some 60 percent of homesteaders in Kansas failed to "prove up" on their claims.[3]

When they arrived in Jewell Center, Kansas, in 1872, Karen and her family encountered this ocean of grass, punctuated by the black forms of enormous beasts. What a sight for someone who grew into adolescence among the fjords and valleys of western Norway! Jewell Center was brand new in 1872: the Kanza had just been removed that May, and twenty-seven households (only some included wives) are listed on the official record of residents. The rolls indicate that the Thronsons and Seversons were the only residents in Jewell Center with birthplaces outside the United States. Indeed, this was fairly typical for initial settlement in the West: most early white settlers were Yankees from the East. In Kansas, only 15 percent of its total 316,000 recorded residents were foreign-born in 1870.[4] Isolation was real for Karen, both because of the the small number of immigrants, particularly women, and because of her language and cultural traditions. Like earlier Norwegian settlers, the Thronsons built an enclave of households around school and church to establish their traditions on U.S. soil. Forty miles away, Jamestown already had two United Church congregations and one congregation of the Norwegian Synod. But Jewell Center had no church or school when Karen and Mons arrived: only a stake in the ground marked a future town. To claim their homestead, Mons built a house into a small hill—a dugout—and a similar shelter for the horses. Eleven years later, the family granted two acres of their homestead for the needed school and church.

In settler colonialism, settlers replace already existing communities with their own people and traditions. The Homestead Act and the Fourteenth Amendment helped to spread European cultural traditions over the United States while actively disenfranchising the Indigenous people already there. The Homestead Act, by granting land claimed by the federal government to individuals (which, radically, included women and African Americans), provided a revenue stream from taxable property. Individual Native Americans with land also could be taxed—the only way in which they could be recognized as citizens of the United States. Even then, the individual with an allotment had to be deemed (by Indian agents) "capable" of ownership.

No federal immigration laws existed until 1882, but the Fourteenth Amendment changed the Constitution to give citizenship to African American men, not just to white men of good moral standing, although its interpretation very clearly excluded Native Americans from citizenship. In 1870, the Senate Judiciary Committee stated that "the 14th amendment has no effect whatever upon the status of the Indian tribes within the limits of the United States."

By 1882 Congress had drafted federal immigration legislation to prevent Chinese immigrants from entering the United States and had formed a federal enforcement body. Although the Thronsons and Seversons probably were not aware of how federal legislation benefited them and excluded others, their settlement helped perpetuate unequal immigration and citizenship structures. Their children could go to school and could become citizens, contributing not only to their ethnic community but also to U.S. society—a society they helped form.

On the prairies, social collective organizations, often under the auspices of a church, school, woman's club, or men's auxiliary, provided women with places to socialize and contribute to community causes while retaining aspects of ethnic traditions. The nature of these volunteer groups varied according to their religious denomination or ethnic affiliation, but the women participants generally considered themselves to be exercising what they saw as their duty within their prescribed gender roles: sewing, cooking, and holding social events to garner much-needed funds for the educational and religious infrastructure. Through volunteer organizations, women learned to organize and elect their own leaders, and they gained real authority through their social and economic contributions.[5]

Yet, white women's enfranchisement came at the expense of others peoples' disenfranchisement—elite white women reformers often espoused policies that undermined Native traditions and culture. Whites, whether immigrants building their own churches and schools or Yankees building missions on reservations, promulgated their values and traditions. But Native Americans were prevented from accessing their sacred sites or speaking their languages, and their children were forced to leave the tribe and learn "American" mores.

The General Land Office in Concordia, Kansas, records that Mons and Helge initially each made settlement in August 1872; by September, the Thronsons lived in their dugout. Mons developed the homestead by digging two wells; building a stable and granary; and planting an orchard "to the value of $150." Over eight seasons, the Thronsons raised crops on at least sixty acres. Mons and his corroborating witnesses (his brothers-in-law, Sever and Ole) all list these developments in their respective affidavits.[6] In the records of the Assessment Rolls Value of Taxable Property filed in Center Township in 1877, Mons listed two horses ($125), three cows ($40), two sheep ($3), one "farm implement" ($4), one hog ($6), a wagon ($5), and $15 dollars' worth of additional taxable property, for a total of $198. He claimed $200 Constitutional Exemption—ostensibly for the homestead—and thus paid no taxes, however. Helge had more horses, cows, sheep, and farm implements, for a total taxable property value of $569. He too, exempted $200, and thus was taxed on $369.[7] Mons's patent was granted in 1881, but weather and conditions burdened the family with economic hardship throughout their thirty years in Kansas.

Despite their hope of making money from cereal crops (wheat garnered $2.06 per bushel in 1866),[8] deed records indicate the families' finances did not improve much during their homesteading years. During the thirty years Karen lived in Kansas, wheat prices went down by half: from $1.07 per bushel in 1870 to $0.57 per bushel in 1900. Correspondingly, farm values in Jewell County were low compared to other Kansas counties.[9] In addition, as E. Roy's memoir makes clear, the families experience a plague of constant setbacks: severe weather, grasshoppers, and prairie fires. In addition to the unusually hard winter of 1873–74 and the dry, almost drought-like early summer that followed, the Rocky Mountain locusts came. The great grasshopper plague of 1874 wreaked havoc on Jewell County: the State Board of Agriculture estimated that one thousand individuals required aid out of a county population of 7,654.[10] Although the two families shared their resources, both had to take out mortgages against their initially "free" land; Mons and Karen took out three mortgages before 1886, and Helge took out four between 1883 and 1887 alone.[11] Eventually, when widowed, Karen and Carrie sold both farms, although Karen's brother Ole remained on his homestead into the twentieth century.[12]

Having a homestead and a large family helped the Thronsons and Seversons to find support locally and within both Norwegian and American social structures. As noted, the Thronsons granted two acres of their homestead for a school and a church. Mons and Karen signed a quitclaim deed for an acre to found a school in 1883 (the school's records are extant in the Jewell County Recorder's Office), and after Mons died in September 1884, Karen gave another acre of the homestead to the Evangelical Lutheran Church, in 1885. The institutions of church and school played especially important roles for gathering and community building in rural Norwegian settlements, for Norwegian women especially. Like the family home, these institutions provided places to reinforce individual and collective ethnic identity. The women found that participation in the concentric social circles of home, church, and, for a few, extra-local communities (missions, schools, or literary organizations) provided a sense of ownership and belonging.[13]

Norwegian immigrants maintained cultural traditions by adapting work, worship, and leisure habits from their experiences on Norway's rural and rugged topography to their homes on the North American plains. As most humans do, they used art and decoration as mnemonics to link to traditions and traditional values. They shared material resources, labor, and celebrations, and together they built and sustained a wide community marked by their ethnic heritage. In Norway, landowning farmers (*bønder*) and tenant cotters (*husmenn)* worked the land together and shared cottages. Rather than living in clustered villages, scattered households together comprised a *tun*. These households included not just the nuclear family, but older relatives, unmarried children or cousins, and unrelated laborers.

As work changed with the seasons and labor needs shifted, households adjusted as well. Unmarried children might leave to work at a nearby house (as Karen's daughters and sons did in Kansas), and those who stood to inherit land, animals, fishing rights, or other property waited to marry.[14] Individual household members performed the various tasks necessary for survival, working together with help from neighbors, according to custom. Much labor was gendered: as for Helge and Carrie when still in Landås, women stayed near home while men moved seasonally, depending on fishing or farming needs. Typically, women baked flatbread for the winter during the summer months, in addition to performing daily tasks of dairying, feeding livestock, and cleaning. In fall, both women and men helped harvest grains and potatoes and cut and dried hay. In winter, women worked on indoor projects, including embroidery, spinning, and weaving. Spring, of course, was for planting.

Carrying over these resource-sharing and community-oriented relations from Norway to the United States both benefited families and allowed them to maintain cultural traditions, such as celebrating the harvest with wheat decorations or marking life events with special textiles and accoutrements. These traditions connected art and land, communicating that link visually across generations. For women, building a home was not only about the physical structure: it was about the social relations that affirmed individuals were part of a community. Traditional decorations, like food at a celebratory feast, sustained human bonds and cultural traditions. Harvesting wheat, using it to bake bread, and weaving the straw chaff into forms serving visual and apotropaic purposes honored Earth, nature, and women's roles in creating life and fostering growth.

Preserving Traditions

In the old country, in thanksgiving to nature spirits and to ensure the next year's healthy crop, Norwegians used the last sheaf of harvested wheat to make straw ornaments. Cereal grains are so important for human survival that people around the world use them to honor nature and ensure continued sustenance through various rituals. Wheat weaving is a common practice across Northern Europe, from the British Isles to the Baltic. English-speakers sometimes refer to these decorations as corn dollies, *corn* being a generic term for cereal grains, but barley, rye, and wheat are all used. In Scandinavian traditions, while men brewed the beer, women made the bread and ritual decorations to honor Frigg, the goddess of fertility, weaving, home, and family. As with embroidery and needlework, the fine motor skills required facilitate intimacy between weaver and material, between weaver and nature, and among weavers learning the art together.

In Norway, households shared wheat and its products, from bread and beer to ornaments, with neighbors and with nature spirits to mark the seam of the year: the solstice and return of the sun. Christmastide, like birth, marriage, and death, was a liminal time, and therefore potent: boundaries between the terrestrial and invisible worlds became permeable. Straw and straw ornaments were particularly important because straw, according to widespread belief, helped ward off evil spirits, and the gleanings were harbingers of future successful harvests.[15] Traditionally, beer had to be brewed by December 21 (the date of Michaelmas and the solstice), because like wheat, it was a gift from the land to be shared at this important liminal time. As the sun retreated and other outdoor work was limited, men brewed beer and women wove and cooked indoors. Inside the small house, a mother like Karen would warm water on the stove and keep the oven lit. I imagine Karen multitasking in the cozy kitchen: soaking cereal stalks, their leaves removed, in water, while she kneaded bread—perhaps special Christmas and solstice bread, such as the Santa Lucia rolls that daughters offered to their families as they ritually brought in the light, dressed in white and crowned in candles. The nutty aroma of soaking wheat (have you ever driven past the Malt-O-Meal factory in

Northfield, Minnesota?) mixed with the yeast and cardamom from the bread would welcome anyone who happened into the house.

After the stalks became flexible from soaking, the women and girls would sit together, heads bent over their designs, plaiting the strands into goats, stars, and other shapes. Perhaps they told stories while they did this, each design, each mnemonic, a reminder of values passed on over the generations—passed on as long as there was time to work together. In the United States, immigrants continued these traditions, at least for the first few generations. Brewing beer and bread, sharing it with neighbors by going house to house, often with masquerades, weaving straw decorations from the harvest: all continued to be a very important part of this ritual festivity. As more adults needed and sought wage work to make a living, however, fewer opportunities arose to share in these spaces of work and storytelling.

In Norway, and often in the United States, at *jøl (jul)*, the solstice, or Christmas, the household would gather on straw-strewn floors to protect themselves from bands of ghosts and other such *huldrefolk* as the *oskorei, lussi, julebukk,* and *julegeit*—nature spirits they believed haunted dark winter nights. Cultural historian Kathleen Stokker notes, "too wicked for heaven, but not sufficiently evil for hell, this unruly band of spirits was doomed to roam throughout eternity, but made a particular nuisance of itself during the season of strong winds and storms, whose sounds and devastating effects it imitated."[16] On the North American plains, *julebukking,* the practice of donning costumes and visiting neighbors, was a way to celebrate ethnic identity and reaffirm social ties and bonds essential to the community's economic survival, while also relieving the tensions such close-knit communities often held. Costumes could be as simple as dishtowels with the eyes cut out or shoes that were too big; the point was to upset norms to, ironically, reinforce them. Stokker notes that scant written accounts exist, but oral histories confirm that julebukking continued in the United States at least into the 1930s and 1940s.[17]

The Christmas goat, or julebukk, similarly, is a common straw ornament. In pagan and Judeo-Christian rituals, goats were sacrificed to God; at jøl, families sacrificed a goat because of its association with the thunder god Thor. Thor's month started with jøl, perhaps because his father Odin's alias was Jolnir, and, according to myth, Thor's goats could be slaughtered and eaten, returning to life the next day. Moreover, jøl coincides with the constellation of Capricorn—the goat—whose stellar reign begins on the winter solstice, marking the shortest day of the year and the beginning of longer, lighter days. At jøl, the house needed to be clean: if not, the julebukk could just tromp through the unclean house with its muddy feet, gaining access and enabling it to kidnap a child. To appease and honor these and other nature spirits, and to ensure a good crop and protect the harvest the following year, the best grains from the fall harvest were given to the cows and a sheaf of oats was laid out for the birds. Immigrants told tales of oskorei defiling the Christmas beer with their urine or leading astray or hurting humans foolish enough to venture out on stormy winter evenings.

Other wheat creations used to decorate rural Norwegians' Christmas homes included the crown mobile, very similar to a bridal crown and made of woven rhomb abstractions. Sun stars, rhombs (diamond shapes connotative of wombs), and other abstractions show up repeatedly as wheat decorations, on metal brooches, and in embroidered clothing and linens for babies and brides.[18] The swirling sun and rhombs go back to at least the ninth century. Textile historian Mary Kelly has suggested that the motifs and symbols that women in Norway wove or embroidered on cloths around 1850 for fertility, protection, and peace were meant to honor Frigg and other pagan goddesses.[19] Frigg, married to Odin, is associated with peace, order, and fertility and oversees the home, love, and motherhood. As goddess of home and weaver of peace, Frigg also oversees the acts of spinning and weaving.[20] Pagans honored Frigg at the winter solstice, and later Christmastime traditions regarding fertility and liminality merged with those honoring the Norse goddess. Weaving wheat into geometric rhombs, stars, and hearts was thus doubly associated with Frigg through her role in fertility and creation. These traditions for appeasing nature spirits and Thor through Norway's cold, dark, and snowy winter months with offerings of beer, food, and decorations woven with Frigg's symbols translated easily to the snow-covered windy plains of the American Midwest.

Bridal crowns and embroideries made by immigrants and their daughters also embodied latent associations with fertility, nature, and cyclical time. For pre-Christian Norwegians, the home, as the focal point of family and the human nexus of nature, animals, and other humans, visually and ritually reflected ancestral bonds. Each decoration, linen, and action — especially those that marked significant moments in cyclical time, such as birth, death, and the solstices — demonstrated living humans' readiness to contribute to the mutuality of relation between family members and the extended family of nature and spirits. Thus, a home and all its decorations and rituals reflected belief in the interconnectedness of lives and a line of knowledge that extended on either side of each human life — a line of knowledge that began with foremothers and reached toward descendants.

Although eventually subordinate to Christian symbols and doctrine, Norwegian women continued to use these traditional visual decorations in the space of home to model duty to family and acknowledge the role of community. These visual markers acknowledged the significance of the simple rituals of daily life. Weaving textiles that celebrated nature and the sustenance it provides underscored women's roles, simultaneously honoring nature, supporting the local community, and visually transmitting ancient values. Women necessarily brought these traditions to their church groups and clubs, institutions that created solidarity and helped extend their influence beyond the home.

Traditional items and symbolism merged with those of Christianity: suns, crosses, stars, and even goats. As Norwegians converted to Christianity in the tenth century and embraced Lutheranism in the sixteenth century, old symbols honoring the pagan nature gods took on new meanings, but the connection to land and fertility remained. Norwegian immigrants, like their ancestors, may have outwardly disavowed pagan beliefs, but they carried on ritual practices using traditional symbols with added layers of meaning. Whether the old meanings were conscious or recounted in the new world, the ornaments continued to connect women to the land, old and new.

Folk art historian Marion Nelson, aware that Norwegian and immigrant women often used geometric abstractions in their embroidery and weaving, notes that the earliest historical record of weavers — two women — appear in documents concerning a sixteenth-century witch trial in Bergen. Nelson also notes that the popular tapestry subject the Wise and Foolish Virgins evolved into "two rows of five increasingly similar women," without the figure of Jesus, and that textiles show a preponderance of stepped triangles (goddess skirts), lozenges/rhombs (wombs), and stars (swirling suns).

Although Nelson allows for a "reversion to a more deeply rooted local tradition," he did not connect this abstract geometry (and witch trial!) with pagan goddess worship, as Mary Kelly did in discussing these abstract geometries a few years later.[21] While the artisans themselves may have lost or repressed these associations, the symbols may still have held latent meaning expressing women's daily lives into the nineteenth century. As Kelly relates, most nineteenth-century Norwegian women had no better writing skills than did medieval Norwegian women. Women without written language used symbols such as these on embroidery and other textiles to record their history, beliefs, and points of view. Kelly quotes an illuminating verse from 1854:

> White linen is the paper of [housewives], which
> Must be on hand in great, well-ordered layers,
> Of life, their woes and their joys.[22]

Although the industrialization of the United States excluded women's handwork as fine art, women, including Karen, passed on these symbols and techniques to their daughters and granddaughters as embodiments of renewal and regeneration and rituals for making domestic order, as we saw in the crochet and Hardanger embroidery examples in figures 4 and 5. Vestiges of ancient connections to nature and emblems of connection to a homeland and heritage made them important to Christian immigrant women; specific pagan meanings may have been repressed and forgotten, but handwork with these motifs continued to be of importance, illustrated in turn-of-the-century ladies' magazines and sold in church bazaars.

As noted, Esther Whitaker used the much faster method of crochet to make a lace sun-star in the tradition of her grandmother. Esther's crochet sun star (shown in figure 5) assumes new importance as a symbol of fertility and hope for winter's end given the long, hard winters and uncertain life on the prairie. Karen endured many hard winters and "trusted in the Lord" for a harvest to make it all worthwhile. The stakes were great and circumstances sometimes unforgiving. E. Roy tells how during a three-day-long April blizzard Mons was unable to save his cows; all perished except one who had just given birth and was sheltered near the house, along with her day-old calf. In the winter of 1883–84, Mons had to make a three-day trip for fuel wood: one day over, one day to cut, and one day back. Did he forget the old warnings of the oskorei? Eight miles from home, another blizzard struck. Mons made it to the house by pushing the horses into the wind. He arrived cold and wet. E. Roy writes that Karen put him to bed and warmed him with soup, but Mons did not fully recover: he lingered all summer and died in September 1884.

Karen had no time to mourn—Rasmus was fourteen and Rachel, her youngest of five (E. Roy's future wife), was still just a toddler. The weather did not ease. The winter of 1885–86 was especially severe, with a historic blizzard recorded in January 1886. Karen stayed in Kansas for another fifteen years after Mons died, until 1899, the year her mother also was widowed. The instability of wheat farming may have precipitated the sale of the Thronsons' and Seversons' homesteads, but so, too, did family dynamics and the ages and genders of the children. By 1899, the girls could work, but to do so they needed to live in a more populous town.

Karen sold the homestead in January 1900 for $3,200. In March 1901, she bought four lots near the Skunk River in Ellsworth, Hamilton County, Iowa, for $1,225.[23] Carrie liquidated her property after Helge's death and left Kansas to live with Karen in 1904. Widows could farm on a small scale, focusing on dairying (traditionally women's work in Norway), and could add to their income by taking in boarders, both of which Karen did.[24] After thirty years, Karen, her mother, Carrie, her daughter Rachel, and Henrietta, her sister Thea's daughter, left Kansas for the Story City area, with its larger Norwegian community and concomitant social and support networks: the Norwegian-populated towns of north-central Iowa had well-established Norwegian churches and ladies' aid societies and a need for domestic servants.

The process of making wheat decorations and embroidery persists today, attesting to the continued significance of these symbols of order and ethnicity. Many Iowa Norwegian heritage organizations offer crafting workshops, and books on wheat weaving and embroidery abound. Specialty shops and Ikea sell straw decorations and related textiles. Handcrafts may have been a way for women to "refine" nature and create a home safe and separate from the outside world, thereby participating in the gendered narrative of progress, but they also connected to an ancient, cyclical understanding of the world.[25] For Karen, Norwegian tradition mitigated the difficulties of homesteading in a new land. Ironically, factors associated with industrialization divested women's homemaking and craft of value, and the association of wheat weaving and embroidery with nature, fertility, and the goddess Frigg became obscured—a common story of the occlusion of women's history and the domination of nature. But these symbols and crafts always connoted a connection to heritage and homeland.

Performed ritual and tradition, such as the wheat weaving and embroidery discussed here, help humans interact and engage with, rather than dominate, natural elements. Many Indigenous religions and cultural traditions honor women for their fertility and unique connection to nature. The institutionalization of patriarchy—in religion, government, economics, and culture—has widely suppressed expansive so-called folk knowledge about the world, from understanding ecology to identifying resources for healing. Binding straw into images of stars, diamonds, and hearts might have helped some women to maintain connection to homeland and ancestors and to forge a new one to their new land and communities. Physically manipulating the remnants of fickle crops into familiar, comforting symbols must have provided a sense of control and purpose in the midst of the difficult and destabilizing migrant experience. These items gave rural immigrant women a way to respond to industrialization by expanding their community of relationships through homemade arts, increasingly made within circles of solidarity in church ladies' aid societies and clubs.

THREE | CONNECTING TO HOME

"HER OWN WAY," 1883–1904

Angel De Cora, like Karen Thronson, was an adolescent when she left her homeland. When she was a teacher of Native arts at Carlisle Indian and Industrial School in Pennsylvania, De Cora recounted that as a young girl she had been asked by a "strange white man" whether she wanted to "ride in a steam car."[1] What followed was a lifetime away from her home and community. De Cora merged the aesthetic values of dominant white culture with her own ideas about art. At the same time that her art spoke to whites' racialist ideas and their corresponding demand for "Indian" products and evidence of "progress" in what they saw as an inevitably disappearing race, De Cora affirmed herself and the continued presence of her homeland and heritage. Although the illustrations and designs she created at the turn of the century for *Harper's New Monthly* and the paintings she displayed between 1898 and 1904 in exhibits sponsored by the Office of Indian Affairs at world's fairs were accepted by whites as the work of an "authentic" yet successfully acculturated Indian, De Cora made them in a way that, for her, reformulated what whites saw as "safe." Her work stood as her and her homeland's active, living presence, not as a static, preserved artifact of some generic time and culture.

De Cora's early illustrations for her short story, "Gray Wolf's Daughter" (1899), and the work she presented at the Omaha Trans-Mississippi International Exposition, the Buffalo Pan-American Exposition, and Louisiana Purchase Exposition in St. Louis, exemplify how she negotiated her Native identity in the racist and sexist structure of U.S. society and how within this rigid system she asserted her autonomy and ethnicity by connecting to her home place and family. (Examples appear in figures 7 through 10.) The illustrations reflect her conflicted psychological situation as a métis, educated to live among whites. The tonal style, figures, and "Indian" subjects fulfilled white audiences' expectations for Indigenous art, and the formats she used were ones legible to whites: figural illustrations in popular magazines. Yet the illustrations and paintings also demonstrate De Cora's connection to physical place, namely the rolling hills of her rural Nebraska reservation, as well as her specific tribal traditions and family history. De Cora's biographer, Linda Waggoner, suggests that the prairie scenes that De Cora often used in her illustrations "illuminate warm memories of her childhood on the Nebraska plains after she settled far from home in the east."[2] As a "foreigner" on her own native soil, De Cora worked to meld the values she learned growing up on the Winnebago reservation with the white academic values she learned in American institutions. In effect, her illustrations and paintings (and later, her designs, discussed in chapter 5) reveal her own voice and narratives of her relation to the grassy landscape that was her home.

The Trauma of Displacement and Reform "Success" Story

Although De Cora may have had a somewhat easier time adjusting to white society than some young Native Americans because of her mother's three-quarter French-Canadian Catholic heritage, she was still deeply ambivalent toward her own integration into white society.[3] Collective and personal trauma are not easily forgotten, despite her ameliorative rhetoric. In her experiences and her art, De Cora embodied the conflict between white society and Indigenous culture. She sought to resolve this conflict in her work, but even so, the reality of its wider implications caused her psychological stress, perhaps because she could not acknowledge the structural racism and its limitations as the root cause. Her published compositions and her participation in government exhibits at world's fairs reflect her efforts to reshape and thus reclaim and retain her home through visual means, enabling her to remember and to survive in a system oppressive toward her as an Indigenous woman. Her illustrations and designs demonstrate her ability to adapt forms, using the natural world as a foundational code, quietly refuting assumptions that Native art meant static artifacts as mere market commodities. Without raising hostility or suspicion among whites, De Cora denied the neutral, empty "safety zone," to use Lomawaima and McCarty's term, where "Indian" culture was made palatable to whites.[4]

De Cora was sent to boarding school without knowing where she was going, why, or for how long, an experience she found traumatic, even if later she expressed gratitude for her training. De Cora's 1912 letter to her teacher Cora Folsom, expressing her keen awareness of her particular situation within the larger context of Indian assimilationist policies, is worth quoting at length.

> The rest of the story is what my mother told me when I had returned from Hampton. She insisted that I had been stolen because neither she nor my uncle had been asked for their consent (to be sure the agent may have signed the papers, etc.). Will Harrison's case was the same. His mother or grandparents knew nothing of his going. Both women told me that for weeks and months the two used to weep and mourn together.
>
> I thought it likely my uncle Frank may have had a voice in the matter as he was my guardian and Willie's stepfather, so I asked him then & again some years ago when I was with them, if he had given his consent to the "strange white man." He denied it each time and not only that but he said as soon as he heard I was taken away, he struck the train for Sioux City only to find the train had started on time some days before.
>
> All of this occurred in the "pioneer" days of Indian education when the Indians were loath to give up their young people into the hands of the whites to be trained in ways totally strange to them and I have an idea that there had to be a good deal of just such kidnapping done by schools. I am not laying either cases against Hampton, you understand, but I was told that some of the non-reservation schools went so far as to give as much per head to their recruiting agents and they used to get children by hook or by crook. . . .

She notes that, at the time she was writing (1912), the Indian Office must ask consent and continues,

> I don't see why you or Dr. Frissell [the pastor at Hampton] should think this a blot on Hampton. I am sure my mother and uncle are glad that I got my training elsewhere than the reservation & I vouch that in nearly every case of the same, the kidnapped individual was thankful for the abduction.

> The Winnebagoes are picking themselves up now but for a period they went down to the lowest depths of demoralizations. I am glad I was not with them—I couldn't have done any good. My mother and Willie's mother were the only two Indian women on the reservation that didn't drink. They have led blameless lives but they had to live and see the fearful demoralization go on for years. Mother told me that it was the one bright spot in her life then that two of her daughters were so placed that they didn't have to live on the reservation. Of course I understand that Hampton doesn't want anything like this laid to its door—but it was the turning point in my own case. *I am what I am now (nothing much or useful to be sure) but I might have been worse* had I never left the reservations. [Emphasis added.][5]

While clearly aware, De Cora hesitates to draw a connection between the poverty that such "reforms" made endemic, even as she observes the Winnebagoes "went down to the lowest depths of demoralizations." Her self-esteem suffered because of the reformers' efforts to encourage assimilation delegitimized her cultural community, her identity base. De Cora recognized her low status as a Native among whites, despite her "success" in their world, and she knew she would have been worse off without their support. De Cora wanted to retain her white friends, the only social group she had had since being taken from the reservation, by protecting their feelings. Exemplifying the epitome of white privilege, the reformers put De Cora in the position of having to apologize for their bad feelings about what they did to her and other Native Americans.

Indian reformers believed that art and craft could be a way for Native Americans, especially women, to make money and become independent. Reformers frequently lamented the status of women on the reservation and noted in reports that, to civilize the tribe, women would have to achieve a better position. Organizations like the Women's National Indian Association (founded in 1879) particularly advocated for teaching handcrafts to Native American women to "uplift" them from the long-held stereotype of "squaw drudgery."[6] Although the reports of the Society of Friends consistently included positive notes on the improving "civilization" of the Winnebago, reports also underscored the trope of the needy and abused squaw.[7] Certainly poverty, disease, and despair were unrelenting among the people on the reservation, a result of years of disenfranchising policies aimed at Native eradication.[8] De Cora, born on the reservation, had witnessed the dissolution of communal bonds after removal, most closely in the example of her own father's return to Wisconsin and her mother's abandonment.[9] De Cora's choices were limited by her racial status and gender. She did not want to be "squaw drudge," but she did want to retain her heritage and the values she had learned as a child. She forged her own way, attempting to avoid stereotypes in her representations.

De Cora described her early years on the reservation as ideal. As quoted, she wrote in her autobiography:

> During the summers we lived on the Reservation, my mother cultivating her garden and my father playing the chief's son. During the winters we used to follow the chase away off the Reservation, along rivers and forests. . . . As a child, my life was ideal. In all my childhood I never received a cross word from any one, but nevertheless, my training was incessant . . . a very promising career must have been laid out for me by my grandparents, but a strange white man interrupted it.[10]

Her grandparents' traditions—the path they set for her—were interrupted by U.S. government policies, and De Cora chose a path of continuity as best she could: a path between the false choice of assimilation or systemic poverty on the reservation.

Still, her own path was not an easy one. Reforms may have made the reservation unlivable, but it was home. Living as an assimilated Native American woman was inauthentic to De Cora's sense of self, and her letters and early work indicate this ongoing cognitive dissonance. Folsom wrote that although a representative of Hampton reportedly found De Cora to be unhappy during school holidays on the reservation, "it was not easy to get her [De Cora] out from the stronger of these two currents, but it was accomplished and she was brought back to Hampton where she completed her academic course in 1891."[11]

Nature and landscape were a salve for De Cora, and, in drawing the places that reminded her of her home, De Cora brought her formal training and cultural knowledge together. De Cora told reporters at Mohonk in 1895 that landscape was her favorite subject, and she later wrote that "although at times I yearn to express myself in landscape art, I feel designing is the best channel in which to convey the native qualities of the Indian's decorative talent."[12] Boarding school, and then art school, provided the talented De Cora with opportunities that she otherwise might not have had. She had attended the mission reservation school before Hampton, and she noted in 1895 that "if they had taught me drawing, I do not think I should have run away."[13]

Founded in 1868, Hampton's curriculum initially was conceptualized to raise a generation of disciplined, subservient black workers for the South (Carlisle, modeled on Hampton, had a similar purpose: to cultivate Native American labor). Beginning in 1877, an Indian Department was added to teach home economics, farming, and industrial skills to Native girls and boys. Just like De Cora's experience, students were "recruited" from reservation schools with the "help" of Indian agents. Some of her classes included art, although the focus was on developing manual skills and learning to "see" using the "correct" illusionistic perspective of European art traditions.

After De Cora's graduation from Hampton (one of only 160 total Native students ever to graduate),[14] she matriculated to Smith, where she developed her artistic abilities. After working as cleaning help in the art museum at Smith, De Cora began taking classes with American landscape painter Dwight William Tryon. From Tryon, De Cora learned about expression, tone, and design. Tryon emphasized good draftsmanship, particularly the clearness of line and shade. For him, "[t]onalism was fundamentally landscape art, subdued, profound, and spiritual."[15] Her art took on this tonal effect, and she began to pick up figural commissions and commercial illustrative work.

De Cora then moved to Philadelphia to study at the Drexel Institute of Art, Science, and Industry after graduating from Smith in 1896. Howard Pyle, a well-known illustrator, taught there. He often created illustrations for magazines, was well connected, and liked to use figures to tell stories—he was a very different teacher than Tryon. After her first year of classes at Drexel, Pyle urged De Cora to return to her reservation. He thought that De Cora should exploit her Native American heritage and perspective to appeal to the vogue for Native American art, portraits in particular. De Cora wrote and illustrated "Gray Wolf's Daughter" and her earlier story, "The Sick Child," initially at Pyle's suggestion. These stories demonstrate De Cora's awareness of Native Americans' position in dominant white society—as marginalized, susceptible to disease and assimilation, and yet with rich cultural traditions worthy of preservation.

Ironically, the vogue for Native American portraits partly resulted from the widespread belief that the extinction of Native Americans' way of life—if not of all Native Americans—was inevitable. De Cora subtly countered this fatalistic narrative. Through the reflective young female protagonists in her stories and illustrations, De Cora presented her esteem for nature and independence rather than heavy-handed moralizing narratives about Native Americans that reinforced white audiences' mythologies of a disappearing wild frontier. Even if Pyle did not recognize De Cora's resistance through art, some of De Cora's colleagues did: a peer from Drexel's summer school wrote that

> Angel de Cora—a graduate of Smith College, and a protégé of a wealthy Boston Woman . . . was a genial young woman, ambitious to succeed, but seemingly unable to get away from her native Reservation western life. For example, Mr. Pyle would give the class a subject idea—say "Springtime in the Country." The Indian girl's composition would show a hillside cottage embowered in roses and vines; but far in the distance would always be the wide spaces and open prairies of her native haunts.[16]

In 1897, when Pyle suggested De Cora return to the Winnebago reservation to make studies of her people, Folsom vetoed the idea. Rather, she suggested that De Cora could travel west with her and meet their Hampton friend, Annie Dawson, who was then field matron (a position teaching home economics to women on the reservation, one of the few jobs open to Native American women) at Fort Berthold in North Dakota, the reservation for Hidatsa, Arikara, and Mandan people.

Although these people had traditions distinct from her own, at Fort Berthold, De Cora sketched and photographed for her art. She made many head studies as well as photographic studies of the northern plains (extant at Hampton University Archives). An untitled scene of a teepee, arbor, and wagon on the plains is extant at Hampton University Museum and may have served as a source for illustrations to "Gray Wolf's Daughter" and for paintings exhibited at expositions held between 1898 and 1904.[17] (See figure 7.) The watercolor is about ten inches wide and four inches tall, emphasizing the horizontality of the plains and the wideness of the western sky. Pinks, oranges, and purples meld together to create the grasses, fire-lit teepee, arbor, and wagon at twilight. The fire illuminates two figures within the teepee. A dirt road wends to the arbor, while a horse grazes in the distance. Here is a visual realization of a continuing tension and the desire for home, still elusive for De Cora despite her conventional success. "Gray Wolf's Daughter" captures the

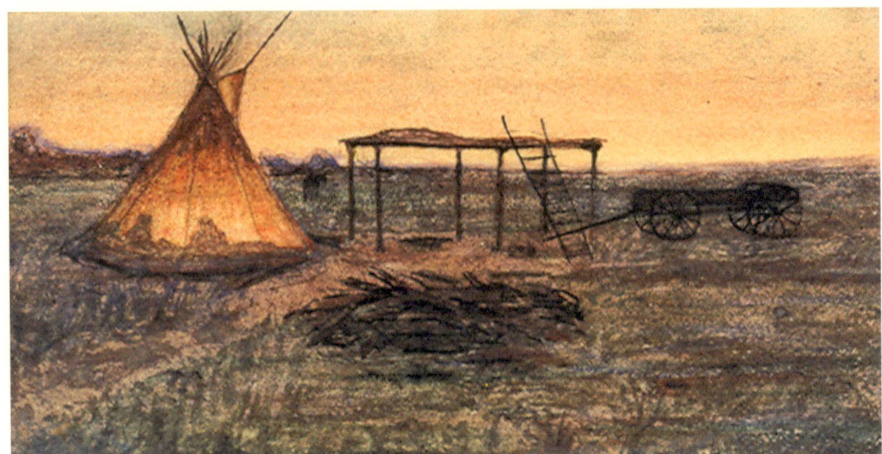

FIGURE 7. Angel De Cora, *Untitled*, ca. 1897, watercolor. Collection of the Hampton University Museum, Hampton, Virginia.

artist's bittersweet cleavage from home, land, and tradition in pursuit of another kind of education, a parting that gives rise to a psychological conflict—the pathos of nostalgia, in its original sense—that De Cora must have felt most of her life.

"Gray Wolf's Daughter"

"Gray Wolf's Daughter," often read as autobiographical, is a story about a young Native girl's choice between participating in her tribe's ways or eschewing them to attend the whites' school.[18] De Cora wrote and illustrated it in 1898–99, a time when she was seeking to make a career in illustration in the East. As in this story about a young girl's ambivalence toward both Native tradition and white ways, De Cora was working through similar feelings.

In the titular illustration, the teenager seen at half-length stands inside a teepee. (See figure 8.) She holds strings of beads in her left hand and her braid in her right. Firelight illuminates the right side of her face as she tilts her head toward the beads. Her dress is beaded with geometric designs, and geometric decorations glow behind her. She seems to be lost in thought, contemplating the choice described in the story: will she leave the ways of the tribe to attend

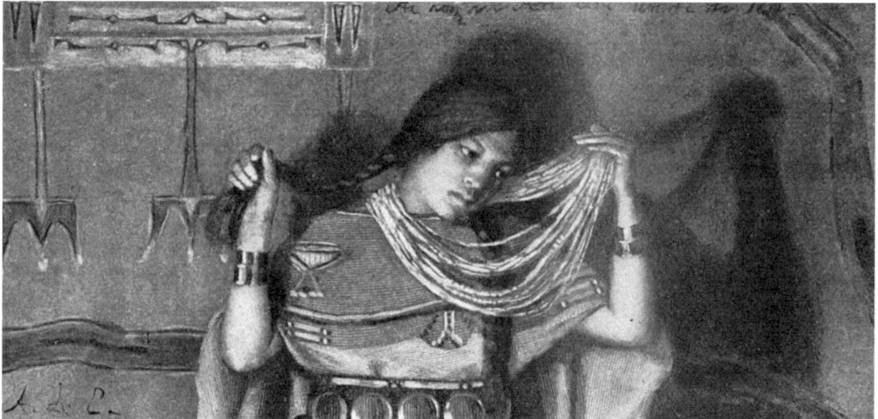

FIGURE 8. Angel De Cora, illustration to "Gray Wolf's Daughter," *Harper's New Monthly,* November 1899, plate 1.

boarding school off the reservation? The short story creates a dilemma around whether she will dance "for the last time" that night with the other girls and raises the question of whether boarding school will lead her to forever wear "white man's shoes" and leave her unable to wear the clothes of her tribe and to dance with her fellow people. De Cora signed the illustration "A de Cora" and used her Ho-Chunk name, Hinook-Mahiwi-Kilinaka, for the byline. Her dual signature, like her métis heritage, underscores the mixing of cultures she experienced.

In the second illustration, Gray Wolf's daughter dances with girls around a fire at night. (See figure 9.) The text indicates that she has decided to dance, feeling bittersweet about her impending departure in the morning. Grass baskets punctuate the foreground. In the story, the beads and silver earrings that Gray Wolf's daughter wears for her dance are stored in baskets and brought out for special occasions. Potawatomi botanist Robin Kimmerer has noted the great significance of baskets to Potawatomi tribes because of their material connection to landscape: grass and wood strips from trees are carefully and respectfully chosen to painstakingly make each basket.[19] Perhaps here, too, the basket, like the other material items (baskets, silver, and beads are transcultural objects derived from early trade), connote connectedness to place through culture and nature.

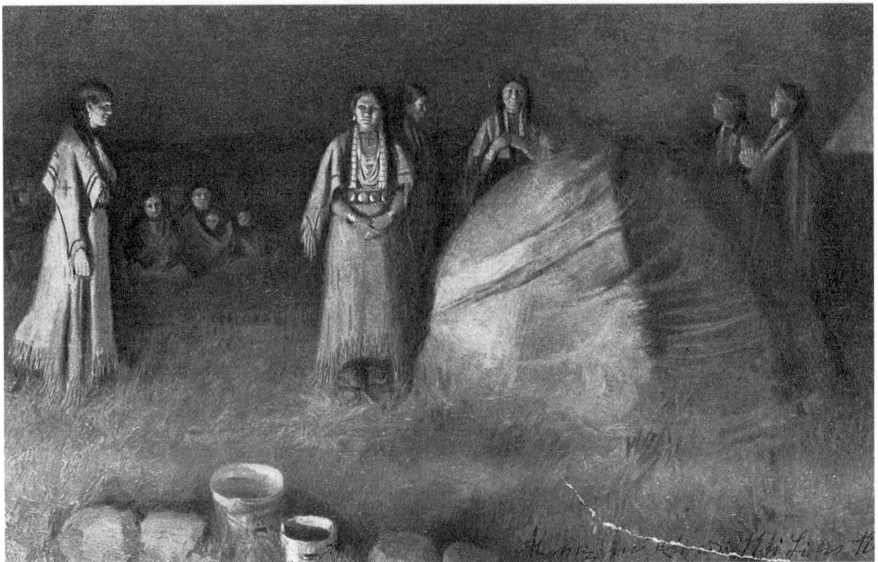

FIGURE 9. Angel De Cora, *Dancing Girls,* illustration to "Gray Wolf's Daughter," *Harper's New Monthly,* November 1899, plate 2.

Both this image and the third illustration for "Gray Wolf's Daughter" situate the young female protagonist amidst a grassy landscape with teepees. In the final illustration, the daughter touches a tree as she stands among the prairie grasses. She looks toward four teepees in the back right of the composition. (See figure 10.) In these latter two illustrations, Gray Wolf's daughter is literally and figuratively connected to the landscape. The baskets are a product of her touch, and she touches the tree. The scenes, night and day, create a contrast paralleled by the contrast of her choice. Nature bridges the night-time tribal dance to her morning exit into the world of whites. The final illustration to "Gray Wolf's Daughter" appears to be unfinished, creating its own compositional division between the top and bottom halves of the frame and, perhaps, underscoring the protagonist's internal conflict. She dances at night, but she still leaves in the morning. From the illustrations it is apparent that Gray Wolf's daughter already possesses knowledge of her clan, its traditions, and their connection to the land. De Cora concludes, "she had always had her own way."

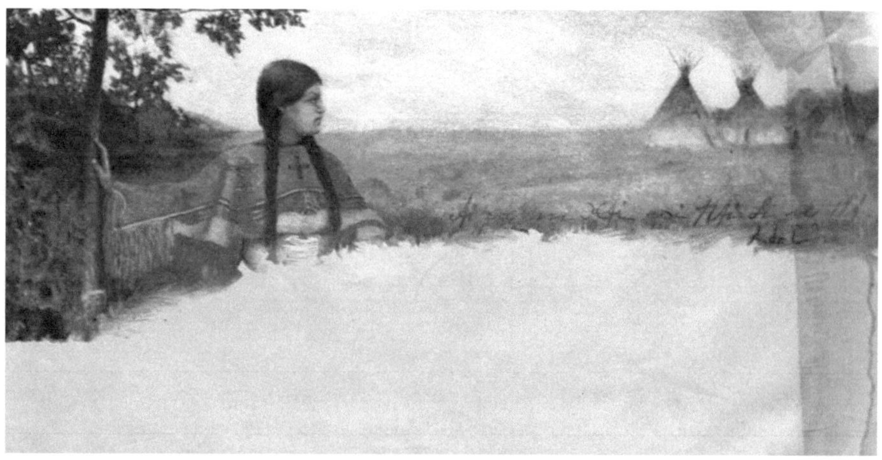

FIGURE 10. Angel De Cora, illustration to "Gray Wolf's Daughter," *Harper's New Monthly,* November 1899, plate 3.

In the first illustration, De Cora's unique designs link Gray Wolf's daughter to the natural world and specifically to De Cora's own Thunderbird clan. The triangular motif on the girl's shoulder is reminiscent of many designs she made using the thunderbird. The three-triangle, horizontal motifs illuminated behind Gray Wolf's daughter are similar to the highly abstracted symbols for the eagle that De Cora refined for Natalie Curtis's 1907 *Indians' Book.*[20] (See figure 11.) De Cora often used variations on triangles and lozenges, a design system that she further developed and articulated in her pedagogy and speeches. Anne Ruggles Gere suggests that the designs, and many of the gestures of De Cora's figures, draw upon the energy and meaning of traditional pictographs and thus translate Native American visual language into forms that whites could "read" even while they preserve the "validity of the traditional entity."[21]

Similar to the sun star and rhombs of ancient Norwegian textiles, geometric abstraction may have recalled the collective memory of long-past traditions. To be sure, white women reformers like Alice Fletcher, Natalie Curtis, and Cora Folsom helped De Cora secure the publications that legitimated her work in a white, male, document-driven world. Initially, Curtis had only commissioned De Cora to prepare the Winnebago page for her book, but the editor

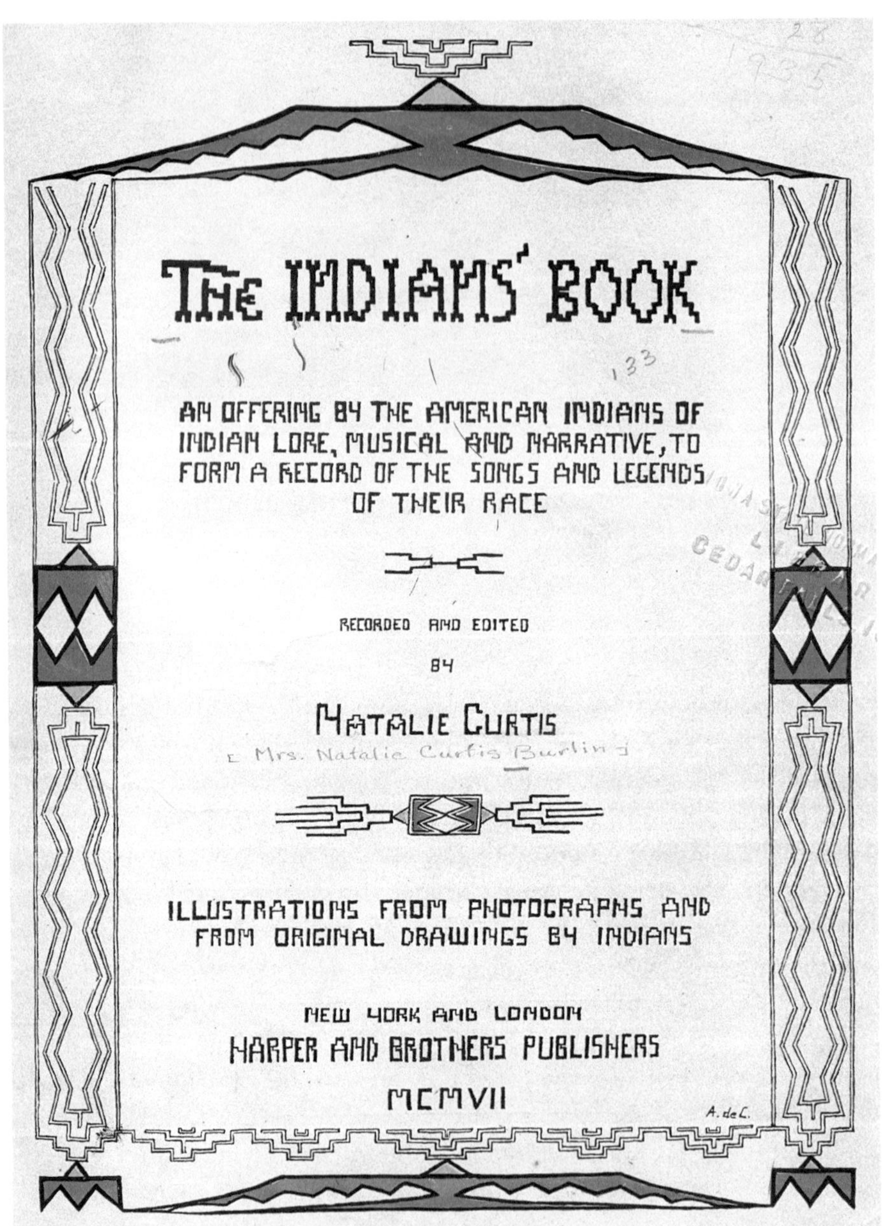
THE INDIANS' BOOK

AN OFFERING BY THE AMERICAN INDIANS OF INDIAN LORE, MUSICAL AND NARRATIVE, TO FORM A RECORD OF THE SONGS AND LEGENDS OF THEIR RACE

RECORDED AND EDITED

BY

NATALIE CURTIS

[Mrs. Natalie Curtis Burlin]

ILLUSTRATIONS FROM PHOTOGRAPHS AND FROM ORIGINAL DRAWINGS BY INDIANS

NEW YORK AND LONDON

HARPER AND BROTHERS PUBLISHERS

MCMVII

A. deC.

FIGURE 11. Angel De Cora, frontispiece to *The Indians' Book,* by Natalie Curtis (New York and London: Harper and Brothers, 1907).

was so impressed by her typography that she asked De Cora to design the lettering denoting each distinct tribe's chapter. Significantly, Curtis took pains to explain De Cora's design iconography to a non-Native audience by including a one-page explanation as a preface to the text. De Cora's title page includes a border where the top and bottom motifs in green and yellow are compressed (widened) eagles (according to Curtis's description). The wings extend horizontally above the tail feathers, and above the yellow beak/head, zigzags seem to indicate its song. On the side borders the eagle motif is repeated, now mirrored. Flowing vertical lines further indicate their song. Curtis made clear that the songs, illustrations, and borders included in her book were all by Native Americans. Thus, De Cora's border and lettering help convey the authenticity of the songs contained therein.

Curtis's book is doubly legitimized: its authenticity is confirmed by Native hands and voices and by its compilation by an elite white woman and its publication by Harper and Brothers, of New York and London, a publisher with an international reputation. The publisher recognized that this authentication made the book more marketable. De Cora's abstract designs were novel for white audiences but still both legible and authentic according to whites' standards; at the same time, the designs creatively expressed De Cora's survivance. De Cora completely reworked the appearance of the words used in ethnographic studies of North American tribes, finding new, representative forms that she expressed through typography of her own devising. Jane Simonsen notes that De Cora appropriated the English letterpress alphabet and transformed it into her own visual language, an appropriation Simonsen suggests, that "marked a crossroads between scientific and artistic production, between Native American ways of designing [viewing, ordering, or seeing] the world and the Euro-American ways of ordering it."[22] As with the earlier illustrations for "Gray Wolf's Daughter," abstraction was a way for De Cora to express *and* protect her own personal connection to what she was creating and even to re-inscribe the power of the English text with Native allusions.

These potentially sacred signs, signifiers of De Cora's identity, retained generically "Indian" echoes for whites. And as we will see, other designs De Cora and her students made include multiple potential meanings in an openness that allowed her and them to straddle both Native and white worlds. In the Curtis volume, this approach gave her space to breathe and express herself while working within the rules of commercial illustration. Whether De Cora intended to subvert these rules through her design is difficult to discern, but Radner and Lenser suggest that implicit coding is not always conscious. Even so, it can still effectively create a sense of individual freedom and solidarity with those who understand. Indeed, they conclude, "ambiguity is a necessary feature of every coded act, [because] any instance of coding risks reinforcing the very ideology it is designed to critique."[23]

De Cora's Work at International Expositions, 1898–1904

"Gray Wolf's Daughter" is about a Native American girl's choice to both dance *and* go to boarding school. It is about the girl's autonomy to choose outsider education to augment the education of her home place. De Cora used her art at a particularly difficult period in her life to build a bridge between her life in the urban East and her roots in the Native grasslands of the West. As she navigated Smith College and art school, she was constantly torn between reservation life and commercial art making in eastern cities. Similarly, paintings at expositions harnessed her nostalgia for the plains, but also fulfilled the expectations of the Office of Indian Affairs and other whites for an Indian art that was both traditional and "industrial"—as evidence of the "progress" of Native Americans under government education and agriculture policies.

The illustrations in "Gray Wolf's Daughter" and De Cora's paintings at expositions show her sustained connection to her tribal homeland even as she uses the realist and tonalist styles then prominent in European and American art academies. The images show her persistent incorporation of the prairie landscape and the dress and decoration of her Ho-Chunk heritage. Nature had long been a way for De Cora to escape the bonds of the white Victorian cultural tenets to which she was expected to adhere and to reconnect with her roots. Still, she did so by using visual and verbal language that appealed to that very culture, even as she included elements that symbolized her being and her connection to her reservation home.

Although she had success with publications in national magazines such as *Harper's*, De Cora was unhappy in Philadelphia. She moved to Boston to study with Joseph DeCamp, Frank Benson, and Edmund Tarbell. There, and subsequently in New York City, De Cora made a meager living as an illustrator, synthesizing the tonalist, realist, and impressionist styles of her teachers. She illustrated Francis La Flesche's *The Middle Five* (1900) and *Old Indian Legends* (1901) by Gertrude Simmons (Zitkála-Šá), and in 1902 De Cora was elected to the National Academy of Design. In her early illustrations she was clearly influenced by her Boston teachers' impressionist style, even while her figures inhabit prairie or woodland landscapes.[24]

Letters to Folsom during this time indicate De Cora's continued unhappiness as she tried to fit in as a commercial illustrator in an eastern city. Her happiest moments were when her cousin Oliver La Mere visited her in New York, "straight from the Winnebago reservation," and when she took a camping vacation with friends: "we had a very primitive time of it but it was what I wanted & needed." Art and nature were still an escape for her. In this letter from 1902, De Cora also mentions that she will

> make a fresh trial for your St. Louis affair what do you say about it. I have a subject started and a canvas now that I feel robust & determined I feel sure that the next thing will not look so *sick & morbid*. I don't know why the Gov't should put a hundred dollar value on that panel piece for it was only twenty five dollars that I attached to it in my mind.[25]

The illustrations she made, along with her stellar reputation and references from Hampton, helped De Cora gain national attention and additional commissions. She was asked to exhibit her paintings and designs at multiple world's fairs.[26]

The Office of Indian Affairs (renamed the Bureau of Indian Affairs in 1947) enlisted De Cora to show her paintings and design work in its Indian Schools exhibits at three fairs: the 1898 Trans-Mississippi International Exposition in Omaha, the 1901 Pan-American International Exposition in Buffalo, and the 1904 Louisiana Purchase Exposition in St. Louis. The Indian schools' exhibits were under the purview of the U.S. government, via the OIA. Government exhibits stood opposite the sensational spectacles of the midway, and the contrast served to underscore the fairs' aims: to make money; demonstrate the superiority of white, middle-class American democracy and capitalism; celebrate American industrial, commercial, and technological progress; support U.S. policies; and shape the future of U.S. education, which would tell the American story as one of Manifest Destiny enacted by white settlers.

De Cora was an example of a "successful" Native American woman, educated by whites. She fulfilled white expectations and exemplified the transformation narrative by conforming to "modern" industrial U.S. society, while also suggesting "traditional" Native American symbolism in her art and design. As we have seen, the demand for Indian arts coincided with reformers'—particularly white women reformers'—promotion of Indigenous handcrafts to free Native women from their presumed "squaw drudgery." Native American handcrafts also assuaged white guilt by preserving ("safely," of course) what was assumed to be, or soon to become, extinct cultural traditions in the wake of "necessary" civilizing progress. This contrast of the uncivilized and doomed "blanket" Indian against the "progress" of Native Americans who participated in reformists' ideals in education played out visually at the spate of world's fairs held in various U.S. cities at the turn of the century. De Cora's paintings and illustrations were safe because they read as authentically by a Native artist—trained by whites—and were therefore legible to whites.

It is widely understood today that world's fairs promoted colonial governments' expansion and power abroad as well as their control over internally colonized people (in the United States, Indigenous Americans). Fairs in colonizer countries (Great Britain, France, and the United States) legitimated this power and control by displaying technologies and the apparent superiority of white, western ingenuity to millions of visitors and armchair tourists who read about them in newspapers and magazines.[27] As displays of colonial power and ingenuity, fairs promoted the values of capitalist nations both via displays and in their organization: all three of the fairs mentioned were organized by corporate bodies of local businessmen who saw an opportunity to profit by facilitating large-scale, government-subsidized spectacles. The 1898 Trans-Mississippi Exposition paid 92.5 percent return back to its stockholders; the Pan-American and Louisiana Purchase organizers similarly sought to make such a profit.[28] In addition to the entrance fees to exhibits and animal shows, posters, postcards, and various other souvenirs were printed and sold in the thousands to Exposition visitors. The corporate organization of these fairs underscored the apparent superiority of capitalism and its attendant middle-class consumer culture and the "natural" subservience of inferior workers.

At Omaha and St. Louis, the United States celebrated its interior westward expansion, while the Pan-American Exposition was meant to celebrate the Americas' (specifically, the United States') abundance and external dominance in the western hemisphere. At each of the fairs, the U.S. government subsidized its own exhibits. For the 1898 Exposition at Omaha, Congress made

$40,000 available for the Indian exhibit as part of the Indian Appropriation Bill; for the Pan-American exposition, Congress appropriated $500,000 for government buildings, which included the Indian exhibit.[29] In comparison, the Louisiana Purchase Exposition had *initial* total capitalization at $15 million (coincidentally, the same amount originally paid for the Louisiana Territory).[30] Government exhibits at the fairs emphasized a moral (and assumed racial) superiority through the display of new inventions and the utility and commodification of items for the home. Indian schools' exhibits were part of the overarching narrative of progress and white European superiority and inevitable hegemony. The exhibits therefore showcased industrial arts and handcrafts that sufficiently acculturated Native Americans were able to make, ostensibly because of their education at U.S. boarding schools. These exhibits reinforced the assimilationist goals of reformers and underscored the role of U.S. schools, generally, and Indian boarding schools, specifically, in developing a working class for the U.S. industrial economy.

The Indian schools' exhibits were in marked contrast to the nostalgic spectacle of the "Indian congress," a feature at every exposition, often advertised as "the Last Great Congress." The goal of these "congresses" was not to uplift, but rather to collect and provide ethnographic "fact" regarding uncivilized people, before they disappeared, and to contrast them with those Native Americans who had been successfully civilized. In effect, they put people on display. Relying on racist pseudoscience, the congresses and villages of other Indigenous people of the world set out to provide a visible "timeline" of human progress and white superiority. William McGee, the anthropologist charged with organizing the ethnological displays for the Louisiana Purchase Exposition, explained that the contrast between Indian village and Indian school told "two living stories. It presents the race narratives of odd people who mark time while the world advances, and how savages [are] made, by American methods, into civilized workers."[31] While three million visitors are estimated to have gone through the Indian school exhibits at St. Louis in 1904, even more people gawked at the Indian villages outside.[32]

At all the fairs, midway booths and Pike displays (midways offered amusements, while the main thoroughfares, or "Pikes," were lined with exhibits) exploited and confirmed racist stereotypes and white settlers' nostalgia for the "frontier" (be they internal frontiers or faraway occupied territories such as the Philippines) that they had conquered, "developed," and "civilized." The

Indian congresses also were meant to showcase the "reality" of how "primitive," yet-to-be civilized people lived. In outdoor encampments, Native Americans dressed in their traditional clothes and were required to enact "rituals," make crafts, and generally be on display for the mostly white tourists who consumed the spectacle. At the 1904 exposition in St. Louis, the Indian congress included more than five hundred individuals, and it was crowned—literally situated above it on a hill—by a Model Indian School, manifesting fulfillment of the "White Man's Burden" to uplift savage races. The Model School was part of the corporate-sponsored anthropology section organized by McGee and was separate from the government exhibit. The students at the school had no choice but to be present. Other Native Americans participating in these congresses were solicited by Indian agents. Participants had their travel expenses paid, but they were not paid a wage. The organizers' rationale for not paying participants was that they would make money by selling objects and photographs.

The report to the Secretary of the Interior regarding the success of the exposition at Omaha described the Indian congress as "the strongest, most original and most interesting feature of the exposition." Summarizing the national mythology believed (and reproduced) by many white people at the time, the report concludes:

> It is the last opportunity of seeing the American Indian as a savage, for the government work now in progress will lift the savage Indian into American citizenship before this generation passes into history, and the onward march of American civilization and American industry will wipe off the maps of the United States the Indian reservation and wipe off the face of the earth the reservation Indian.[33]

No doubt its critical success at Omaha influenced future fair organizers to include the congress at their own expositions.

Objects in the ethnology buildings complemented the stilled "past" represented in the Indian congress: here static artifacts illustrated white anthropologists' "researches into the origin, the filiation, the customs and institutions of wild and barbarian tribes still existing, or of whom we have authentic records."[34] Holes in white organizers' idea of the inevitably of "progress" are visible in hindsight: Commissioner of Indian Affairs William Jones lamented that while the progress of Indian farming was something the OIA adamantly wanted to showcase (a success "outside of school work"), "the office was prevented from doing so by a disappointing lack of response to its attempt to obtain necessary materials."[35]

De Cora's work was displayed in the government exhibits at all three fairs. The government buildings at the Pan-American Exposition were frequently praised in reviews for their organization, Indian displays, and marvelous inventions, although the Office of Indian Affairs was not generally mentioned by name.[36] While the Indian school exhibit received little press (an example from Mary Hart: "In a dark room in this same part of the building the government schools make a novel exhibit of their work by means of the biograph and phonograph . . ."), the Indian Congress and villages of "Eskimos" and "Africans" were frequently cited as must-sees.[37] Edward Brush wrote nothing about the OIA exhibit in the government buildings at the Pan, but he did write multiple paragraphs on the Indian congress:

> For white people of all classes and nationalities the red man possesses a remarkable fascination. His history, revealing so much of injustice and double dealing on the part of the white settlers, brings us face to face with the question of his future, and it is sad in some respects to think that whatever civilization may have in store for him his life as a wild child of Nature has about come to its end. The young Indians of the far West today have no chance left to make names for themselves as warriors, as their forefathers had, for the tomahawk is being made into a hoe, the wigwam is being discarded for the house, and instead of engaging as of old in the buffalo hunt they receive cattle from the government.[38]

In the exhibits for the OIA, government officials sought to balance expectations for the Indian trope with evidence of the reform policies' successes. As described in Rand McNally's guidebook to the Pan-American Exposition:

> The front line of the exhibit of the Office of Indian Affairs is marked at one end by the life-size figures of an Indian woman and child; at the other end by a warrior, with battle-ax and shield ready to defend his home. Between these stand a case containing specimens of some of the native arts, industries and foods. . . . Back of this line are cases filled with examples of the schoolroom and industrial work of the different government schools scattered from Carlisle, Pa., to Chemawa, Ore., and

> from Phoenix, Ariz., to Oneida, Wis. This part of the exhibit includes several models. One, from Chilocca, Oklahoma, of a house made by Charles Blackeyes, of the Seneca tribe, is finished completely within as well as without; the doors and windows open so that one can see the wainscoted rooms. A four years' course in sewing is shown, beginning with simple hemming and cutting of patterns through the different stages up to the completed costume. . . . Behind the school exhibit is a space set apart by a screen of grillwork made by the Indian students at Hampton Institute, Va. All the articles within this enclosure are the handiwork of Indians who are either in school or are working for themselves at their respective avocations. The central object in this room is the mantel. The woodwork was done at Haskell Institute, Kan., from a design by Angel de Cora, a young Winnebago artist, who also furnished the oil painting.[39]

At the Pan and the other fairs, De Cora's contributions notably were not exhibited in the Fine Arts or Women's buildings. Native women's art had been on display in the Women's building at the 1893 fair in Chicago, and De Cora's male teachers, Tarbell and Tryon, had multiple works on display and were mentioned by name in reviews of the 1901 exposition.[40] De Cora was not invited to exhibit as an American artist, or even, as a woman artist. Her status was clearly identified first as that of a successfully assimilated Indian pupil of white "civilization."

The OIA had three goals for their segment of the 1901 exhibition (goals that clearly are part of the displays at Omaha and St. Louis, as well), including to show "native ability" and "the methods used for training Indians in US schools" and "to present examples of the use [the Indian] makes of this training to express in forms intelligible to us his artistic feeling and his power of workmanship."[41] For the 1898 and 1901 expositions, Alice Fletcher had been asked to find former boarding-school students to showcase these components. She, along with Omaha writer Francis LaFlesche, already knew De Cora from their time on the Nebraska reservation and at Hampton.[42] De Cora's artistic presence could visually underscore a national story of the gains made by Native American students trained by whites. Moreover, the subject matter of her work confirmed the demand for portraits of "traditional" Indians and their home environments — the very same fantasies that were on display in the live tableaus of the Indian congresses.

At the Omaha expo, De Cora contributed three paintings — probably two portraits completed while at Fort Berthold and the painting *Medicine Lodge* (whereabouts unknown). Commissioner Jones noticed De Cora's work at the 1898 exposition and knew her illustrations for LaFlesche's *The Middle Five* and Zitkála-Šá's *Old Indian Legends*. Jones asked her to design a mantel and settee to go along with paintings for the 1901 expo. De Cora contributed *Fire Light* to complement her interior design of a hearth fire with thunderbird rising from the flames.

Fletcher's description of the 1901 exhibit is quoted in the government report that Jones made to the Secretary of the Interior. The description was widely distributed in McNally's guidebook as well. Fletcher described De Cora's contribution thus:

> Miss Decora has combined the native symbolism of fire with our own tradition of the fireside. Upon the space below the shelf, in low relief of red wood, is a conventionalized "thunderbird," the plumes of its wings flashing out into flames. On the side uprights, and in a band around the upper part of the mantel, making a frame for the central painting, are conventionalized forms of the sticks used in making the "sacred fire" by friction. The scene of the picture painted by Miss Decora is on the rolling prairie, at sunset, suggesting the hour of gathering about the hearth; off to the left is a cluster of Indian tents, each one aglow from the bright fire within; while in front, a little to the right, against a background of golden clouds, stand a pair of lovers, the beginning of a new fireside.[43]

The *Fire Light* painting, like the one in Hampton, probably is based on photographs that De Cora made on the plains at Fort Berthold, North Dakota.[44] This "rolling prairie" landscape is also reminiscent of the rolling hills of De Cora's home on the Winnebago reservation. Instead of portraits that might have fulfilled whites' nostalgic and exotic fascinations, De Cora focused on landscape and how the landscape, in its combination of teepee, fire, and thunderbird, was a home.

As with many artists, De Cora selected design elements from her experience and from the world around her — this included symbolic, metaphorical, and social aspects of life: features of her social, physical, and metaphysical landscapes. The design and her painting complemented each other and illustrated the theme of home — a theme that resonated with whites and their ideals of feminine and Indian domesticity (they are on a mantel and settee!), to be sure—but De Cora's choices are more complex than mere illustrations of living as a Native presence in a white space. They indicate that this is *her* landscape, *her* conception of home: replete with fire, family clan motif, and the prairie grasses of the plains home landscape she also illustrated in the "Gray Wolf's Daughter." And like Gray Wolf's daughter, De Cora would have *her* own way.

At the Pan-American Exposition, De Cora's installation exactly fulfilled the expectations of the Office of Indian Affairs and of white viewers more broadly. In a world where most whites—even reformers like Folsom, Curtis, and Fletcher—saw Native American cultures as inevitably doomed in the wake of "progress," De Cora's "Indian art" was an "authentic" (read: made by a "real" Indian) reminder of cultures (bittersweetly) bound for extinction due to the righteousness of "civilization." But her work also resisted the presumption of static "preservation" of a "traditional" artistic past.

De Cora was aware of the prescribed contrast between these fairs' stories of an uncivilized, doomed past and destined progress. But her idea of progress was much more nuanced and particular to her own needs than those of the reformers. De Cora thought about how she could learn from the traditional arts and crafts she saw women making in the villages.[45] She was not nostalgic for something perceived in decline: she was inspired. Her work lives and breathes in her recontextualization of specific elements of her home and her past, even while, on the surface, a teepee and a thunderbird signaled "authenticity" to whites. In the extant documentation of the 1904 exhibit, what are probably her paintings hang above the display of a Winnebago wigwam. (See figure 12.)

As we have seen, land and place are significant to an individual's personal and communal identity and conception of home. In Wisconsin, Iowa, and Nebraska, differing conceptions of land were major factors in the dynamics between the Ho-Chunk nation and the U.S. government. De Cora's own migrations were a direct result of the removal of her forebears, her subsequent forced matriculation to a boarding school, and her own desire to escape the poverty and insularity she witnessed on her reservation. While most of her work after 1899 was commissioned or commercial, De Cora still had sufficient leeway to inflect her compositions with personal details that often included her clan symbol, women protagonists, and the prairie landscape. Her illustrations and designs both fulfilled white expectations and allowed her to retain her connection to both work and home.

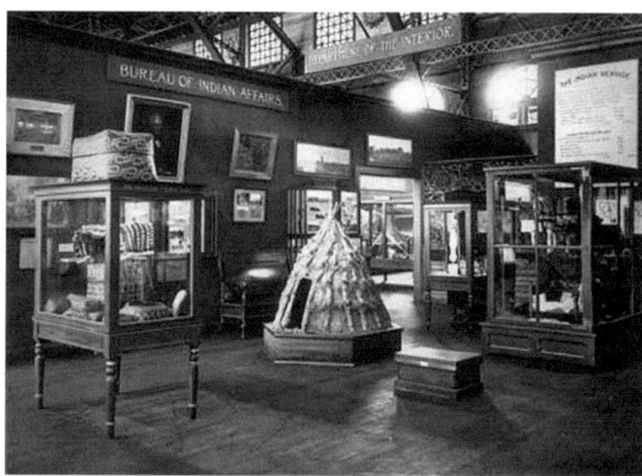

FIGURE 12. Photo of the 1904 Louisiana Purchase Exposition, St. Louis. Record Group 56, Records of World's Fairs, NARA, Washington, D.C.

In "Gray Wolf's Daughter," the symbols on the young woman's dress and teepee read as an index of "Indianness" for whites interested in the subject. But for De Cora, they had personal meaning. "Gray Wolf's Daughter" appealed to white readers through its fashionable tonal illustration technique and "Indian" subject, as well as through the legitimacy gained from appearing in a national magazine. By including the abstract designs and prairie landscape, De Cora might have been inviting whites to share her home figuratively, but she also was connecting to it from afar, bridging the dissonance of her varied experiences.

De Cora tapped into a long history of Native women artists' unique visual creations, particularly in design. Communing with animals, invisible beings, and other natural forces allows humans to partake in the whole of the earth's ecology. Sacred images, such as thunderbirds and underwater panthers, became abstracted and frequently appear abstracted on objects created by Great Lakes and Plains people, including Ho-Chunk, to aid in this communion and communication. Sacred images and symbols could be applied to any manner of object, imbuing it with important spiritual function. In Plains warrior cultures, shields, drums, and shirts particularly can hold protective powers.

Women often play a role in creating these important objects. Plains women typically use a geometric visual language and incorporate abstract forms distinct to and owned by the individual maker. These designs share some conventional motifs, assembling basic units into a variety of creative combinations. Because many of these designs belong to the individual creator, meaning is held by that creator.[46] For example, the iconography of sacred thunderbirds and underwater panthers on woven bags made by Anishinaabe, Potawatomi, and Ho-Chunk people often reflect dreams and can serve protective purposes. In their abstraction, the images become symbolic, but they retain a certain opacity because the dream itself is only fully known to the commissioner and those to whom he or she relates it. Ruth Phillips notes that "the semi-hidden meaning of motifs in Winnebago woven bags can be seen as representations of moods and feelings in the weaver's life."[47] While the abstraction of panther or thunderbird is widely recognized as such, the personal meaning behind it is known only to a privy few. It retains its sacredness in abstraction.

At the international expositions, too, De Cora contributed tonalist landscape paintings that fulfilled white viewers' ideas about the Indian frontier, but she kept them free of cowboys and narratives of Indian victimhood or white superiority. She also increasingly moved toward greater abstraction. Design motifs in "Gray Wolf's Daughter" and the design for the settee and mantel at the 1901 exposition symbolically place De Cora among her people and her family, just as the landscape provides a familiar setting. In the decoration of the settee and mantel, modern domestic objects, De Cora provided enough visual information for Fletcher to "translate" the iconographical meaning of the symbols for whites reading the guidebooks and government reports, establishing the required authenticity. Here, too, however, these symbols probably meant more to De Cora, and commodification was beside the point.

Through the layers of her landscapes and abstract designs, De Cora protected her identity from superficial commodification. De Cora's apparent success in dominant white society was very much inflected by her Ho-Chunk aesthetic values and the experiences of her forebears, and her own traumas could be ameliorated by images and design that provided her with a window to home, a mnemonic of her past, a piece of the whole of her tribal identity that was mostly emptied of such meaning in white consumer society. Living in the East within the institutions of dominant society necessitated that De Cora accommodate consumer demands and make a living as best she could as a single, female "foreign" artist. Land and family—clan—were De Cora's inspiration, because for her, and for many others, they form the basis of Native American culture.

De Cora was enlisted to participate in these exhibits as a former student and "civilized" success story, but she retained her own voice in the choices she made to represent her home. As an artist and teacher at Carlisle, De Cora increasingly focused on design to express herself and to provide her students with accessible links to their own pasts. Even when pushed to illustrate figures, De Cora focused on landscape and designs that linked her to her home. She, like Gray Wolf's daughter, would "have her way."

FOUR | NORWEGIAN WOMEN CRAFTING CONNECTIONS IN IOWA, 1904–1912

Karen Thronson and her daughters settled in Iowa and Kansas in an era when white women's economic role in the United States generally was shifting from producer to consumer. Although Norwegian immigrants established communities as rural ethnic enclaves, Karen Thronson and her daughters, like their peers, adopted notions of female behavior that aligned with Anglo norms for women in an industrialized America, even while maintaining other Norwegian cultural traditions. Whereas on the farm women's contributions were essential to its functioning, modernization increasingly relegated women's work to the home, and wage labor took on more economic importance. Still, their ethnicity, supported by their membership in the Norwegian Lutheran church and the wider Norwegian immigrant female community, mediated these "American" mores.

Norwegian immigrant women used their folk knowledge to adhere to tradition while also accommodating to American consumer society. They distinguished their clothes and home with handmade items in traditional patterns, and they also found ideas for modernizing techniques and applications in printed magazines, specifically *Kvinden og Hjemmet* (The woman and the home). This magazine provided an extra-local, virtual community that appealed both to cultural heritage and Americanization. Women also formed local face-to-face organizations to hold onto tradition and find autonomy outside of their own domains, forming church ladies' aid societies to make and find fellowship outside of the home.

As we have seen, Norwegian immigrants across the Midwest established tight-knit communities around Lutheran worship and education. As women and men ideologically differentiated their work between the private domestic sphere and the public sphere of production, women's primary responsibilities increasingly centered on homemaking, childcare, and buying products to make those labors more efficient. Some women, including rural Norwegian women, continued to engage in subsistence activities, and the separate "spheres" were not as rigid in practice as in prescribed social mores; they also necessarily varied from urban to rural settings and across classes.[1]

Since industrialization fundamentally transformed the household economy by making it increasingly reliant on earnings from wage labor, some women also had to work outside the home, as would be the case for Karen's daughter Rachel. Still, generally women's unpaid responsibilities, such as needlework and cooking, were stripped of economic significance and instead viewed as moral, spiritual, and thus volunteer, activities.[2] Ladies' aid societies used this model, such that women made things to benefit the collective, usually the church. In so doing, the women collectively gained economic power within gender norms of the day. At the same time that more urban middle- and upper-class white women promoted and revered the idea of the home, reproducing gender roles by publishing ideas for homemaking in magazines and other "public" print media, they also engaged in reform movements geared toward assimilating women whose ethnic traditions or class or both challenged their elite idea of feminine values: Native American women, incarcerated women, and immigrant women.[3]

For Norwegian women, textiles especially were a way to express connection to their heritage and to assert status by showing their skills in embroidery and household money management. In the nineteenth century in both Norway and the United States, lace collars, apron borders, bonnets, napkins, scarves, runners, and other items could be used for special occasions and to show off one's needlework abilities. Increasingly, traditional designs were added onto more "American" modernized dress and accessories or adapted to simpler techniques such as crochet. While rosemåling (ornamental flower painting), traditionally done by men, only rarely continued to be made in the United States (until its renaissance in the 1940s, as later generations of Norwegian Americans sought connection to their roots),[4] embroidery and needle arts maintained their utility and significance.

Techniques evolved to accommodate new American needs and desires. Women still embroidered, but interest in fitting in culturally with American norms was increasing, particularly among second- and third-generation immigrants. Hardanger patterns and design — even if not the technique itself — especially grew in popularity with homemakers, even those not of Scandinavian heritage. In the first quarter of the twentieth century Hardanger designs showed up on aprons worn with American dresses and on table borders and pillows. For Norwegian immigrants, Hardanger sent a message of Norwegian ethnicity, even as it was transposed to crochet or assimilated onto American products. The technique and its association with international refinement, as well as the spectacle of rural exoticism, was further disseminated in magazines like *Ladies' Home Journal*; in *Kvinden og Hjemmet*, more practical hybrids of design and makeability were provided to interested readers who read their heritage into it as well. Immigrant women shared designs and patterns through the virtual community of magazines, and they made clothing and decorative pieces for their churches, working together in local ladies' aid societies. Both virtual and real spaces of community allowed Norwegian American women to hold onto tradition while situating themselves relatively autonomously in an economy (and in congregations) that otherwise routinely devalued women's contributions.

Virtual Communities: Magazines, Hardanger, and Crochet

Kvinden og Hjemmet, printed in Norwegian and Danish and published in Cedar Rapids, Iowa, between 1888 and 1947, used an established Euro-American medium (printed text) to bridge Scandinavian and American cultural norms. In the Scandinavian Midwest, women shared information through *Kvinden og Hjemmet*. With little time for leisure and socializing on isolated farms, magazines brought immigrant women together virtually. *Ladies' Home Journal* and *Kvinden og Hjemmet* were contemporaries. The *Journal* began just five years before *Kvinden og Hjemmet* and with a similar name: *Women at Home*. In 1883 its name changed to *Ladies' Home Journal and Practical Housekeeper*; by 1886, it was simply *Ladies' Home Journal*.

The magazines were similar in their scope of features, although the substance of those features varied slightly to accord with their readerships. They both were published monthly (*LHJ* became quarterly in 2014), and, in the first few decades, their regular features included advice columns, letters from readers, special interest current events, short stories, home remedies and recipes, child care and health, fashions and clothing, and handwork designs and patterns. The demand for magazines such as these — magazines that provided a model for a woman who could "make" her home by being both consumer and a nurturing wife/mother/homemaker — is indicated by the fact that in 1903 the *Journal* was the first American magazine to reach one million subscribers.[5] By comparison, at *Kvinden og Hjemmet*'s peak circulation, between 1904 and 1910, the magazine sold almost 83,000 copies in North America and abroad.[6] In 1895, an annual subscription to *Ladies' Home Journal* was one dollar; *Kvinden og Hjemmet* was forty percent less: a reader in the United States paid sixty cents for a one-year subscription. Both magazines reinforced the domestic identity of the "modern American woman" as consumer.

In their articles and advertisements, *LHJ* and *Kvinden og Hjemmet* provide insight into what was in demand, respectively, by white, mostly urban, upper middle-class American women and by aspiring middle-class, mostly rural, Norwegian American women at the turn of the century, as well as what advertisers and editors sought to sell to these respective audiences. For example, advertisers in *Kvinden og Hjemmet* include companies marketing home remedies, sewing machines, and clothing pattern books; realty companies with land for sale in Iowa, Minnesota, and Wisconsin; railroad ticket agents; and companies offering packaged travel excursions to visit Norway. Ads in *Ladies' Home Journal* included home remedies, clothing pattern books, sewing machines and baby carriages, and even art, including a few ads for "Indian" art, reflecting the trend around 1900 described in the previous chapter.

Generally, *Ladies' Home Journal* had content that would have appealed to elite white women and to those aspiring to the elite — a more urban and wealthier woman than those reading *Kvinden og Hjemmet*. *LHJ* was larger in format, folio-size versus *Kvinden's* slighter ten-inch height. *LHJ* featured colored covers and double-page spreads of photographs of national and international locations, gardens, and other illustrations to accompany its articles. The articles on lace and textiles for the years 1901 to 1908 present international styles, including Italian, Flemish, Eastern European (Hungary and Bulgaria), and Scandinavian techniques and designs. Designs are often quite ornate and technically advanced. The articles generally describe the style and design of a particular lace or how to wear it or use it, rather than offering a how-to. *Kvinden og Hjemmet*, on the other hand, focused on how to make *and* use particular items, such as a table covers, doilies, lampshades, pillow covers, children's sweaters, and, at Christmastime, decorations such as stars, flowers, and angels made of tissue paper, foil, wire, and fibers.

Magazines like *Ladies' Home Journal* and *Kvinden og Hjemmet* emphasized prudence, thrift, economy, and industry for every woman, virtues exemplified by crafting and handwork. By making and consuming, immigrant women participated in their native and adopted cultural communities. Women connected to their homelands through design and connected to their new homes by adapting and exchanging those designs within an industrialized consumer society. Even as one page of a nineteenth-century ladies' magazine promoted the machine age and its products, the next page might display handcrafts, themselves intimate objects that express personal, rather than prefabricated identities. Making a house comfortable (especially a dugout or one made of sod or planks) was a way for immigrant women to show "the stabilizing force of family had arrived."[7] Creating lace borders for curtains, planting kitchen gardens, or binding straw: each action was a small step toward imposing order on the unruly landscape. In new places, women had to figure out how to use different materials and adapt to the available resources. Making things for her home—homemaking—was a way for her to assert her authentic self in a space of her own making. The results were hybrid objects, such as American purses and pillow shams that mimicked Norwegian Hardanger embroidery.

At the turn of the twentieth century, the Hardanger style was emblematic of Norwegian needlework and design. The squares and stars of Hardanger spread in popularity among immigrants in the United States outside the Norwegian communities, perhaps because of Yankee elites' nostalgia for "simpler" times, and many early twentieth-century American ladies' magazines attest to Hardanger's popularity by including patterns and articles about it.[8] At the same time, these magazines advertised new machine-fabricated products and shared American trends in making a home efficient by learning how to cook, sew, and use everyday materials to make decorative, functional items. Women used the Scandinavian designs to decorate dresses and other functional objects and to reinforce their ethnic identities and express themselves; some also used them to enhance their income.[9] In *Kvinden og Hjemmet*, women shared traditional patterns adapted to consumer-friendly household items. Printed serials showed how Hardanger and similar but simpler crocheted and knitted work could be modified to create an American home.

Hardanger embroidery is difficult and generally was only used to decorate important items of clothing for special occasions, such as christenings or weddings. Crocheting, tatting, and cut-thread needlework are techniques used to make lace, albeit in very distinct ways. Indeed, crochet and tatting use hooks and shuttles; "true" lace is generally made with finer threads using a needle. Knitting and weaving were important skills for clothes making, and crochet and tatting, like embroidery, were used decoratively. Throughout the decades of its publication, almost every issue of *Kvinden og Hjemmet* contained the haandarbeide (handwork) section. Regardless of the end product's function (whether doily, pillow, tablecloth, or purse), many of the patterns and illustrations were designs of simple six-or eight-pointed stars, flowers, or other fairly basic geometries. Many of these, in turn, are crochet patterns (*heklemønster*).

Hardanger embroidery was featured about yearly throughout the magazine's run, with a peak of three articles about it in 1904 (August, April, March) and two in 1905 (March and October). Crocheted table doilies from 1894, a filet crochet purse from 1917, and a child's knitted sweater from 1923 provide just a sampling of the range of items for which *Kvinden og Hjemmet* provided star design patterns very similar to Hardanger designs. (See figures 13, 14, and 15.) The combination of traditional design and patterns for stylish things exemplifies the objective of the magazine. Ida Hansen, the founder and for fifty years the editor of *Kvinden og Hjemmet*, was clear that her goal was to introduce Norwegian American women to American styles. She wrote to her readers in 1908,

> Wherever we women turn, we are facing something new, which we must learn to understand as fast as possible if we are to feel at home in this country. Language, which many believe is the most important matter to learn, is hardly as important as understanding the customs in the new society. And to understand it in such a way that is only possible if the information is transmitted in our own language.[10]

In a paper given at a conference of the Textile Society of America, Laurann Gilbertson and Karen Olsen provided an important synthesis of how patterns for Hardanger and quilts in *Kvinden og Hjemmet* brought Yankee American ideas to Norwegian- (and Danish-) speaking women. Gilbertson and Olsen conclude that between 1900 and 1930 the Hardanger patterns in *Kvinden og Hjemmet* were adapted for items not traditionally used in Norway but that were then popular in American households, such as doilies and pillows.[11] Gilbertson and Olsen relate that national women's magazines printed designs for

Haandarbeide.

Benævnelser som forekommer i Heklemønster.

Lm. — Luftmasker eller Kjædemasker — en lige Rad af Løkker, hver ny trukken igjennem den foregaaende med Naalen. Fm. — Fastmasker — en Maske paa Naalen, stik Naalen igjennem en Maske, tag Traaden om Naalen og træk den igjennem, saa der er to Masker, træk saa Traaden igjennem begge disse. St. Stav eller Pind — Maske paa Naalen, slyng Traaden om Naalen, stik Naalen gjennem en Maske og træk Traaden gjennem saa der er 3 paa Naalen, tag op Traaden og træk gjennem to af disse, tag op Traaden igjen og træk gjennem de næste to. D. St. — dobbelt Stav eller Pind hekles paa samme Maade, kun slynges Traaden to Gange om istedetfor en; Traaden trækkes gjennem to ad Gangen ligesom i forrige. T. d. St. — tredobbelt Stav eller Pind som de foregaaende, men med tre Slyng om Naalen

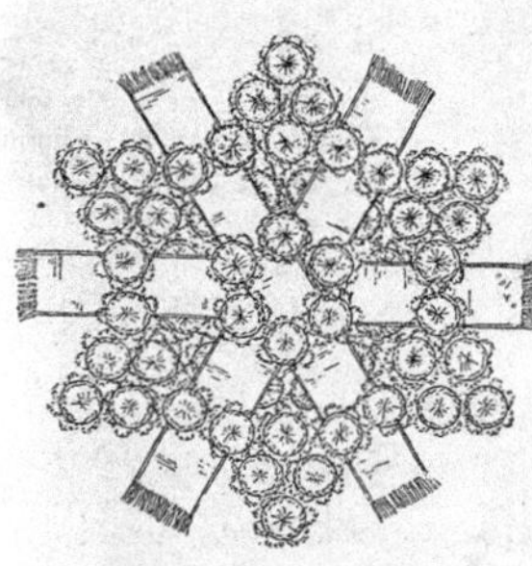

Tidy eller Tæppe.

(Se Ill.)

Det stjerneformede Tæppe, som Ill. viser, er dannet af heklede Stjerner eller Hjul og Silkebaand. Stjernene syes sammen som Ill. viser, og man passer at lade Aabninger blive, hvor Baandene passere gjennem. De to illustrerede Hjul, hvortil Prøver er indsendt af Bertha Halvorsen og Mrs. Magdaline Krog, New Hartford, Iowa, kunne begge passe til dette Brug. For et lille Stoletæppe maa man dog have mindre Hjul eller hekle dem af meget fint Garn.

Den ene Stjerne er tydelig nok; men den anden ser noget utydelig ud, og skal vi derfor forklare, at efter den inderste Runding er heklet, dannes der to Rader Blade, heklede med Stave, begge Rader hekles til den indre Runddel; men saaledes at Spidserne af Bladene i underste Rad kommer midt mellem Bladspidserne af øverste Rad.

Prøve til den i dette Hefte illustrerede heklede Blonde er indsendt af Olufine Thue, Hoodsport, Wash. Nogen nøiere Beskrivelse over denne nette Blonde er vist overflødig, da Ill. tydelig viser Mønstret.

For „Kvinden og Hjemmet.

Gulvmatter.

Jeg vil fortælle, hvordan jeg fornylig lavede en rigtig pen Gulvmatte af gamle tykke Klæder. Af de mindst slidte Dele klippedes Strimler omtrent 2 Tommer brede. Knaphulsting syedes rundt om paa begge Sider med kulørt Uldgarn. Længden af Strimlerne maa være den forønskede Størrelse af Matten. De, som skal være tvers over, bør være kortere. De væves ud og ind, (over den ene og under den anden). Det hele fores og paa Enderne sættes Fryndser af Uldgarn.

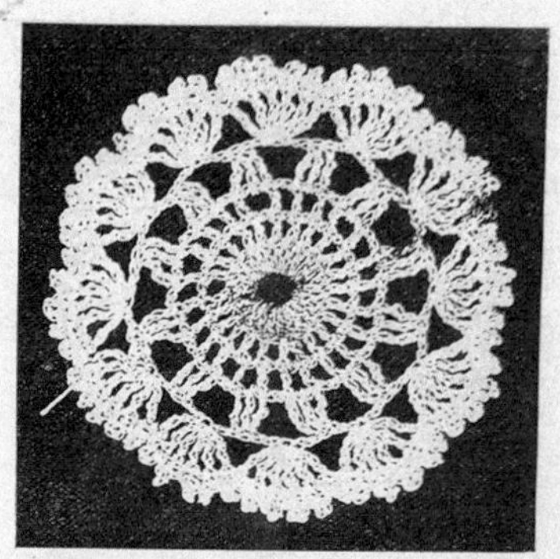

Tynde Bomuldstøier kan ogsaa benyttes paa samme Maade, kun med den Forskjel at Strimlerne maa fores og Kanterne brettes ind, naar det syes med Uldgarnet.

J. Schow,
Perley, Minn.

Heklet Fotografi eller Billedramme.

(Se Ill.)

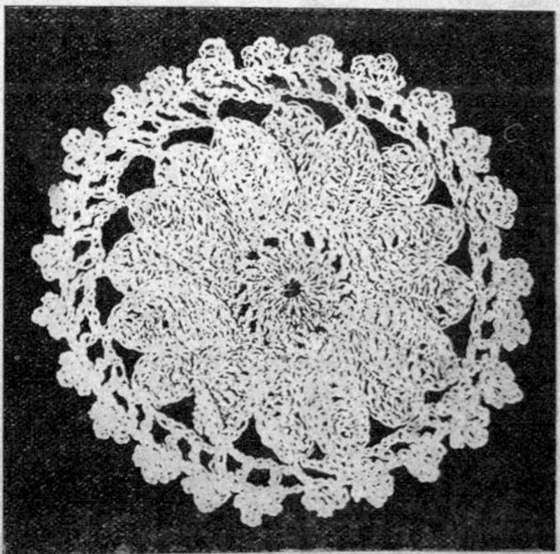

Rococo Hekling er noget af det nyeste i Heklearbeide og skiller sig fra det vanlige Heklearbeide deri, at man bruger Molds, Forme af forskjellige Faconer, som man overhekler og fæster sammen, saa de danne sammenhængende Mønstre. Den her illustrerede Ramme er en Prøve paa denne Slags Arbeide, idet de smaa Hjul og Tungerne ere heklede over Forme og derpaa føiet sammen, men man kan ligesaa godt hekle Rammer efter dette Mønster uden Forme, da disse endnu ikke ere at faa kjøbt allevegne.

Heklet af grovt cremefarvet Bomuldsgarn ser en saadan Ramme paa Afstand ud som Træskjærerarbeide. Man kan ogsaa bronzere eller forgylde Rammen eller visse Partier af den.

I alle Tilfælde bør Rammen hekles af grovt Garn for at faa Udseende af at være udskaaret, og strækkes over en glat Ramme af Træ.

Hjulene hekles først og hekles sammen, eftersom de hekles, til man har den rette Størrelse for Rammen, saa hekles Tungerne omkring og tilsidst den indre Kant. Mønstret er jo tydelig nok i Ill.

FIGURE 13. A page from *Kvinden og Hjemmet,* February 1894, illustrating and providing a pattern for a crocheted doily.

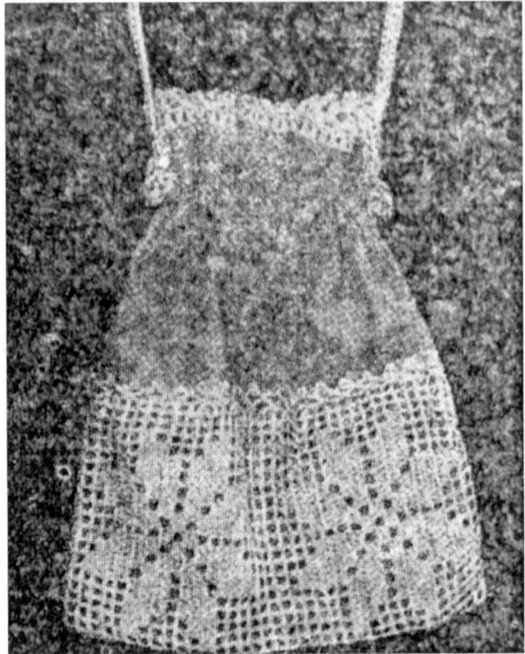

FIGURE 14. An illustration from *Kvinden og Hjemmet,* June 1917, showing a filet crochet purse.

collars and cuffs and aprons using a style of Hardanger embroidery, adapted to Victorian or Edwardian taste. The materials suggested for working such patterns were also humbler than the traditional white on white linen. For example, a lamp rug in the September 1901 issue required: "ground fabric of fine white Grenadine (28 double thread) and embroidery of light and dark lilac Filofloss silk together with fine gold thread (2 strands)."[12]

The first Hardanger embroidery patterns appearing in *Kvinden og Hjemmet* were for doilies, a mainstream middle-class Victorian decorative household item, in the August 1898 issue; the crocheted doilies predate these. Similarly, many later issues offered patterns for decorative household items, including doilies, tablecloths, runners, lamp rugs, tea cloths, tray covers, pillows, and trims, although not always in pure Hardanger but, rather, using other techniques.

The inclusion of Hardanger in *Ladies' Home Journal* in May 1901 and its frequent appearance in *Kvinden og Hjemmet* in 1904 and 1905 coincide with an increase in its popularity—and status—after the embroidery was displayed at

6 Kvinden og Hjemmets Mønstertidende.

Haandarbeide.

En varm, strikket Dragt for en lille Gut. (Ill. 1.) Hertil medgaa 8 Ounces firedobbelt Germantown Zephyr

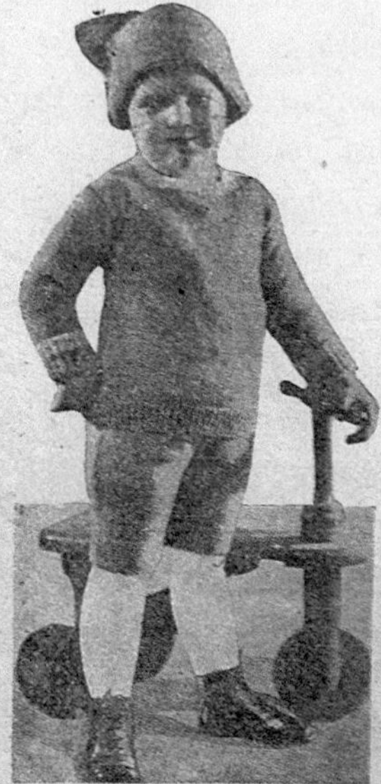

Ill. 1.

Garn og et Par Amber Strikkepinde, No. 4½.

Modellen var udarbeidet i Blaat, med Krave og Ærmelinninger i Lyseblaat. Længden fra Skuldre til Folden er 16 Tommer; Ærmet, med Underærme og Linninger iberegnede, er 13 Tommer, og over Brystet er den 10 Tommer. 13 Masker maaler 2 Tommer, og der er 9 Omgange pr. Tomme.

Sweater: Slaa op 78 M (Masker) til Ryggen.

1. Omg.: 1 r (ret), * 1 r, 1 v (vrang), gjentag fra *, afsluttende med 1 r.

Gjentag denne Omgang 15 Gange til Borten eller Striberne; fortsæt saa med Overdelen paa følgende Maade:

1. Omg.: Strik ret.
2. Omg.: 3 r, 72 v, 3 r.

Gjentag disse 2 Omgange, indtil Arbeidet maaler 14½ Tomme fra Begyndelsen, afsluttende med Mønstrets 2den Omgang.

Skulder: Strik 22 r, vend.

2. Omg.: 19 v, 3 r.

Gjentag disse 2 Omgange, strikkende frem og tilbage paa 22 Masker for 1½ Tomme; luk jevnt.

Levn 34 af de 56 tilbageværende Masker paa en extra Naal for Nakken. Paa de 22 Masker, som er tilbage, strik det andet Skulderstykke ligesom det første.

Halslinning: Med Lyseblaat eller kontrasterende Farve strik r frem og tilbage til en Tomme eller 6 Striber; strik saa ½ Tomme paa de første 7 Masker, luk. Strik saa af 20 af de Masker, som er tilbage paa Naalen, og strik ½ Tomme paa de tilbageværende 7 Masker.

Forstykket: Følg Beskrivelsen til Ryggen, indtil man har 13½ Tomme fra Begyndelsen, del derefter Maskerne for Skuldre og Hals paa samme Maade som før, kun med den Forskjel, at hver Skulder strikkes til 2½ Tomme i Stedet for 1½; ligeledes strikkes 1½ Tomme paa de 7 Masker til Halslinning i Stedet for ½ Tomme.

Ærme: Slaa op 68 M.

1. Omg.: Strik r.
2. Omg.: 3 r, 62 v, 3 r.

Gjentag disse 2 Omgange, tagende af ved begge Ender af hver 10de Omgang, indtil man har 60 M tilbage. Fortsæt uden at tage af mere, indtil Ærmet maaler 10 Tommer. I næste Omgang strikkes * 1 r, tag af; gjentag. Der bør nu være 40 M paa Pinden. Strik nu 2 Tommer efter Beskrivelsen for nederste Del af Rygstykket, derefter 1 Tomme med Lyseblaat og luk.

Sweateren kan let gjøres større ved at anvende grovere Garn eller Pinde, følgende samme Beskrivelse, eller ved at slaa op flere Masker og saa strikke i Forhold dertil.

Knickers: Slaa op 66 M for nederste Del af venstre Ben. Strik r frem og tilbage 2 Tommer; og øg i begge Ender af hver 4de Omgang. Strik saa ind de 2 Mønsteromgange (strikkende først r, og, vendende tilbage, 3 r, saa v, saa nær som de 3 sidste, der strikkes r), fortsæt at øge følgende Beskrivelsen, indtil man har 96 M paa Pinden. Strik 1 Tomme uden at øge, derefter tages der af ved Begyndelsen af hver Omgang, indtil der er 90 M paa Pindene.

Tag nu af ved Enden af Pinden i hver 4de Omgang, indtil man har 72 M tilbage, og afslut med en Omgang r. Derefter strikkes der paa følgende Maade:

1. Omg.: 12 r, vend.
*2. Omg.: 9 v, 3 r.
3. Omg.: 24 r, vend.
4. Omg.: 21 v, 3 r.
5. Omg.: 36 r, vend.
6. Omg.: 33 v, 3 r.
7. Omg.: 48 r, vend.
8. Omg.: 45 v, 3 r.
9. Omg.: 60 r, vend.
10. Omg.: 57 v, 3 r.
11. Omg.: 72 r.

Strik r frem og tilbage 1 Tomme og luk jevnt.

Det høire Ben strikkes paa samme Maade, indtil den sidste Aftagning er gjort. Afslut med en Omgang af r i Stedet for v; derefter strikkes paa følgende Maade:

1. Omg.: 3 r, 9 v.
2. Omg.: 12 r.
3. Omg.: 3 r, 21 v.
4. Omg.: 24 r.
5. Omg.: 3 r, 33 v.
6. Omg.: 36 r.
7. Omg.: 3 r, 45 v.
8. Omg.: 48 r.
9. Omg.: 3 r, 57 v.
10. Omg.: 60 r.
11. Omg.: 3 r, 66 v, 3 r.

Fuldend med en Tomme af r og luk.

Efter at have presset hvert Stykke nøie, sys Sømmene sammen over Skuldrene og Halslinningen sys til.

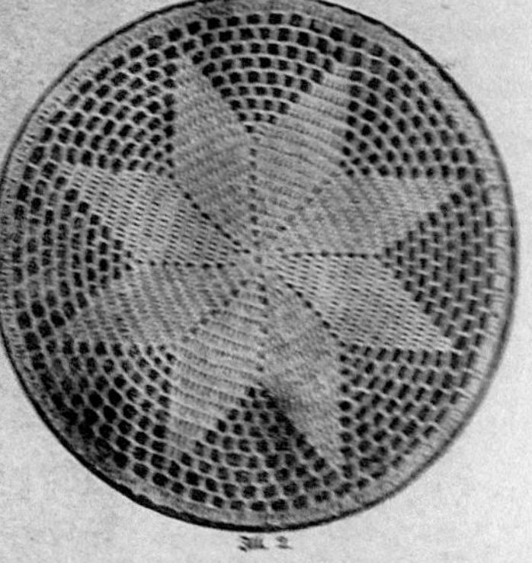

Ill. 2.

Sæt Ærmerne i, sy os Siderne til Underærmesømmene. [illegible]

FIGURE 15. A page from *Kvinden og Hjemmet*, January 1923, illustrating and providing instructions for a knitted children's sweater.

the International Expositions in Paris in 1900.[13] Just like expositions and fairs that promoted Native American "industrial" arts, so too, this international exposition introduced Hardanger to the world as fashionable, exotic, and nostalgic.[14] Brita Skåltveit's embroidered apron was displayed and subsequently met with wide acclaim. The European "peasant," like the "Indian," was an exotic trope to many urban Yankee elites. In July 1908, a two-page spread in *Ladies' Home Journal* included "Needlework of Foreign Peasants" and "New Designs in Swedish Needlework," implicitly relating the two. In that spread, the six-pointed sun star is elaborately expanded into a crocheted coverlet. (See figure 16.) Below the photograph and a detail, "A Swedish Bedspread in Star Pattern" designed by Cecilia Swenson is explained: "As a handicraft crochet work offers a wide field for both the pattern-maker and the worker who merely copies. Among the best designers in this work are the Swedes and Norwegians."[15]

Ida Hansen had emigrated from Norway just three years after Karen Thronson, in 1870. She too, was a young woman of seventeen when she arrived. She understood how difficult it was to travel west, get married (she married publisher and immigrant Niels Frederick Hansen at 22), and live in the strange landscape of Iowa. Hansen was able to build onto her husband's business and create a successful magazine, *Kvinden og Hjemmet,* of her own, one that connected her to fellow Norwegian American women, to Norway, and to her new more industrialized home. Like Karen Thronson and Ida Hansen, many of the immigrant women in Iowa came from the Hordaland and Hardanger areas of western Norway. Therefore, readers probably already had some experience with, or more likely, were familiar with the look of Hardanger needlework. Understandably, they would want to have the fashionable and comforting look of Hardanger, even if they did not have the time or skill to make it.

Karen and her daughter, Rachel, as farming women, probably had little time or money for the intricacies of Hardanger.[16] Rachel did not learn it, but a photograph from around 1880—before her return to the Norwegian cultural center of the Story City area—shows how Karen displayed her needlework skill and her heritage in the lace collar of her dress. Her hairstyle, like the photograph itself, connotes her new American status. (See figure 17.) Immigrants sent photographs along with letters across the Atlantic to indicate their new "American" status in dress and style.[17] At this time, women's clothing mostly was either homemade or custom-made by a local dressmaker. Custom-made clothes allowed Norwegian American women to combine newer elements with

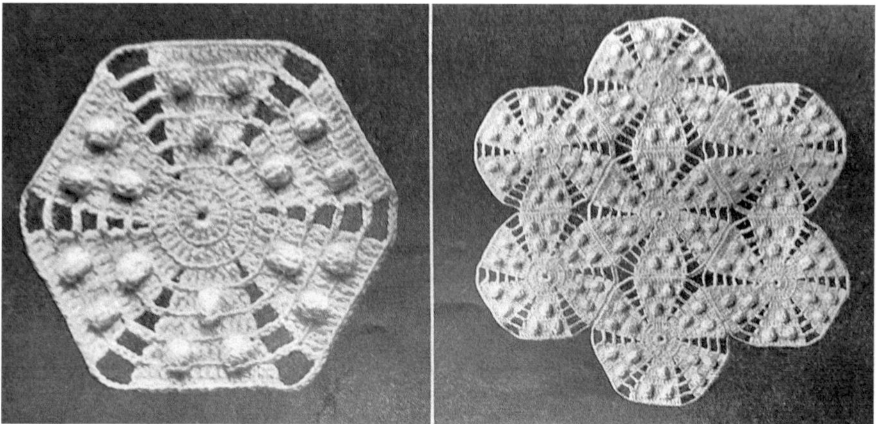

FIGURE 16. "A Swedish Bedspread in Star Pattern, by Cecilia Swenson," *Ladies' Home Journal,* July 1908, illustrating a crocheted star coverlet. In part, the caption reads, "As a handicraft crochet work offers a wide field for both the pattern-maker and the worker who merely copies. Among the best designers in this work are the Swedes and Norwegians, a Swedish woman having designed and made this beautiful star coverlet."

the older silhouettes they still favored. Here, Karen retains a full and cuffed sleeve, a style from the late 1860s, but the way the sleeve attaches at the shoulder is indicative of the 1870s (in the 1860s the seam would have been lower on the shoulder). The short standing collar with lace added is typical of the 1870s—and she wears a bow at her neckline, which was common then. In Norway her hair would have been covered, but here it has an austere center part. This photograph was a pendant to a portrait of Mons. Like so many Norwegian immigrants, the pair sat for portraits to be able to send visual assurance of their well-being back to family in Norway.

The lace on Karen's collar approximates Hardanger and was a link to her past as well as a visual assertion of her own skill. Many such examples exist in collections of Norwegian American immigrant material culture, from the Story City Historical Society to the Vesterheim Museum in Decorah. In Norway, clothes signaled a person's home region. They also signaled class. One of the first things immigrants to the United States did was to adopt U.S. clothing styles, although details and accessories—like embroidered borders and lace collars—announced their specific Norwegian heritage. Wearing or displaying

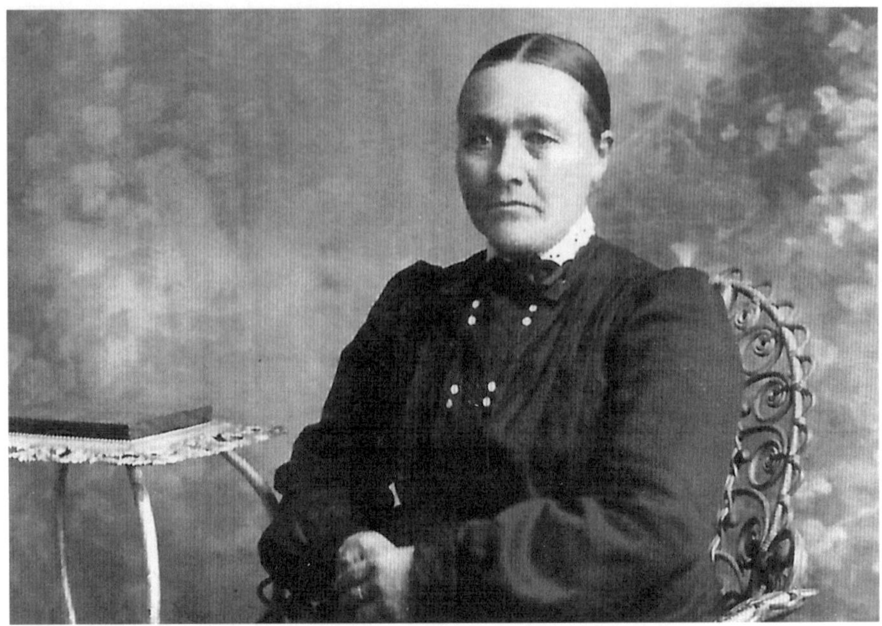

FIGURE 17. Karen Severson Thronson, ca. 1882. Photographer unknown.

fine things decorated with lace—cutwork, tatted, or crocheted—affirmed identity. For Norwegian women, such decoration made a home; for others, perhaps, the work was more nostalgic. As Ida Hansen and her readers indicated, like so many Norwegian American women, they wanted to fit in while maintaining the comforts of tradition.

As we have seen, lace making and Hardanger were a visual mode for demonstrating recent immigrants' heritage and hand skills; by the 1940s, busy women—many second- and third-generation immigrants—had adapted traditional patterns like stars from the intricate embroidery into crochet, thereby retaining a connection to the past in patterns, but simplifying their making. Around the turn of the twentieth century, as the first generation of immigrants saw their grandchildren born and raised in the United States, "a national awareness developed among the Norwegian-American people. . . . For many immigrants any object of Norwegian origin acquired symbolic significance relating to nostalgia, roots, identity, and ethnic pride."[18] Rachel Abbott summarized in her study of Scandinavian immigrants in Utah: "the relationship between land and the people who live on it is a reflexive one: the land influences and affects how people live and what objects they produce, and those objects, in turn, reflect the land and affect how people use the space around them."[19] Rural women made designs from the natural phenomena around them (stars, flowers) and ancient symbols of fertility and women passed down to them; elite women co-opted those designs, finding needlework an area of autonomy in an increasingly closed and gendered society.

Women used design to identify with other Norwegian immigrants, even while techniques were modified to accommodate busy lives and the consumer culture of the modernizing United States. The anthropologist Henry Glassie suggested that abstraction helps many people combine and restructure ideas that may seem contradictory, synthesizing and restructuring the "old" with what is new and available in the world.

> The person faced with conflicting models within his community calls upon his ability at analytic abstraction and breaks the old and new forms and functions apart; he need not accept the new or retain the old, he is free to develop new things that are neither completely new or completely old, which involve, perhaps, a complex formal synthesis, a restructuring of the form's hierarchy of functions.[20]

The shift from Hardanger to crochet suggests the shift to a consumer and increasingly industrialized economy, but women still retained the essence of ancient sun stars and nature's geometries in crochet. As Gilbertson and Olsen relate, "*Kvinden og Hjemmet* provided patterns for New World textiles in the language of the Old Country and for a significant number of women."[21]

To be able to approximate its style in different techniques through similar designs probably appealed to many frugal and busy housewives and working mothers, women who may not have had the time for the painstaking work of Hardanger proper, but who still desired its look and associations with ethnicity and skill. Rachel's daughter Esther said that she had never properly learned how to tat or make lace; however, she inherited a tatting shuttle, and she, her sisters, and her daughters all practiced simple forms of embroidery, knitting, and crochet in the 1940s and 1950s. Esther's crocheted star is very similar to the bedspread pattern from *Ladies' Home Journal* shown in figure 16. Its design reflects connection to the maker's Norwegian heritage, and its technique expresses an American homemaker's efficiency and utility in the application of that heritage. As a pillow, like other items in *Kvinden og Hjemmet*, it falls between "peasant" and "refined" for the "modern" woman's middle-class

American home. In the mainstream *Ladies' Home Journal*, crochet, peasants, and Scandinavians are connected, and Scandinavian women are deemed "some of the best designers" for such a "peasant" handcraft.

Magazines like *Kvinden og Hjemmet* provided a connection to the homeland, becoming a fading memory, while also teaching how to acculturate to a new country. Although such nostalgia was not explicit in its articles or features, Langeland concludes that *Kvinden og Hjemmet* was a source of strength in hard times, "like a surrogate mother or aunt" from the "old country," providing the ways and means for "harmonious adjustment."[22] Readers' letters and poems conveyed the pain of immigration and the comfort women took from the journal. A farm wife wrote to the magazine in 1905 to express that "[the magazine] brings comfort to the hearts of tired and depressed mothers in this vast country so filled with sin and misery."[23] The magazine fulfilled immigrant women's need to connect to other women and their old home by providing old-world patterns adapted to new-world situations. As one Norwegian farm wife put it in 1917, *Kvinden og Hjemmet* was there for her, even when "grasshoppers and hail have ruined seed several times and the Indians have many a time frightened me by their sudden appearance."[24]

Historian Glenda Riley suggests that the need for female companionship to deal with the physical and emotional hardships of rural settings was great and that rural women were "domestic artisans" whose production entailed social networking.[25] Indeed, the legitimization of this companionship in print and church communities was what Native Americans such as De Cora were prevented from enjoying. For Norwegian immigrants, women's creativity was necessary to organize the natural resources available to them into a home. Processing raw materials for the house was a significant component of female labor on a homestead, whether making corncob rolling pins or straw stars. Immigrant women used their creativity to transform available natural resources into a home and to connect to the new land and to each other.

Real Communities: Church Ladies' Aid Societies

Although needlework was traditionally utilitarian, working women read magazines to learn how to imitate the fancywork enjoyed by wealthy women in cities, and many crochet and embroidery patterns translate original folk designs of fancywork like Hardanger embroidery. With the rise of industrialization and the separation of gendered public and private spheres, handwork, particularly fancywork such as lace making, became a safe domestic or economic activity for elite women; working women had time for the simpler crochet technique. An article in *Ladies' Home Journal* suggests a clear distinction between fancywork and crochet, where the author states that it is "not exactly correct to consider it [tatting] lace."[26] Lace fancywork became a pastime for elites—and if necessary, a way for well-to-do widows to find some respectable sources of income. Some elite women, like Lady Marian Alford in England, used print media to promote needlework as an art rather than a lesser-valued craft.[27] She did so to align elite women with the purviews of men; fancywork versus crochet or art versus craft distinctions signified class and power: the separation of handwork and handcrafts as being for women, and as distinct from the male "fine" arts, also served to reserve "art" as an intellectualized profession for men.

Elites viewed handcrafts as a moral good, for elite white women as well as for the working class and "inferior" cultures. At all class levels, handcrafts kept women busy in a mutually reinforcing system of oppression within an industrial society that exacerbated class and gender separation. Ladies' magazines advertised Indian art and featured handwork for similar reasons: such work could profitably keep women occupied in their relegated sphere, while reflecting a general nostalgia for what seemed a simpler, premodern past. Women reformers unselfconsciously co-opted "folk" designs for their own purposes, while rural women aspired to bourgeois consumption and elite tastes by making Hardanger doilies and crocheted pillows, retaining traditional patterns but adjusting product and technique to adapt to busy American lives and shifting gender roles. *Kvinden og Hjemmet* helped Norwegian American women transform Hardanger motifs into crocheted doilies and pillows, acknowledging their new American landscape in the process.

Like the virtual community forged by reading and corresponding through magazines, church ladies' aid societies also served connective social and cultural functions for immigrant women. Both social spaces connected women through making. Aid societies helped rural women maintain social connections and support by expanding their social circles from home to the local church and by increasing female autonomy through collective activity. As in the pages of *Kvinden og Hjemmet,* women built communities by sharing advice while piecing quilts, crocheting, cooking, and planning fundraisers.

Magazines and aid societies created intimacy among women concerned with homemaking and connected those women to other women in similar situations.

By selling or gifting handmade objects, Norwegian American women could build networks and increase their social and, at times, economic power. Ladies' aid societies were an important mechanism for rural women not only to socialize, but also to participate and make decisions within their communities. Although women were not allowed to vote in church business (or in U.S. elections until 1920), the money they collectively amassed gave women power to decide which church projects they would help finance. In many cases, the ladies' aid society provided the funds to build the church itself.[28] This power was in addition to the mutually reinforcing kinship ties and neighborhood economic exchanges in which rural and immigrant women participated.[29] Women folded their interactions into the networks of kinship and ethnic bonds—such as church community—rather than keeping accounts. Therefore,

> women could exercise more control over social relationships within their kin-groups and neighborhoods than in the domain of the market and public life. Rural women conducted the activities of visiting and mutual aid that sustained local social networks, which strengthened their position in their families and community as well as enabling them to provide for their families' needs.[30]

Women contributed to the "civilization" of the frontier by building community and infrastructure through organizations like ladies' aids.[31]

After returning to the Story City area in 1901, Karen and Rachel promptly joined Immanuel Lutheran Church in Story City. Story City had—and still has—a large Norwegian American population. Even after moving to Ellsworth Township, ten miles down the road from Story City, they did not find themselves alone. Between 1890 and 1900, the population of Story City grew 123 percent, and it continued to grow for the next twenty years, from 536 residents in 1890 to 1,591 tallied in the 1920 US census.[32] Norwegian immigrants in the United States during the nineteenth century were by far the most rural of all immigrants, and they retained much of their heritage by maintaining a rural and small-town existence into the third and fourth generations.[33] In particular, Norwegian immigrants built churches and schools, ideally staffed by preachers and teachers trained in and sent from Norway, to maintain their faith, language, and heritage.

As we have seen, Karen tried to do this in Mankato; in Story City, such institutions already were well established. San Petri and Immanuel were two sizeable Norwegian Lutheran churches in Story City; two much smaller congregations of Lutherans also met in Ellsworth Township at the turn of the century.[34] In the summer of 1898, forty-six men voted to split from San Petri because of doctrinal disputes, and they formed Immanuel's congregation.[35] The minutes from Immanuel's 1902 annual meeting, held on Monday, January 6, show that "Mrs. Thronson with her daughter" along with "Miss Larson" (who is listed as part of the Thronson household as a servant in the 1910 census) were approved as members of Immanuel's congregation.[36]

Karen saw church as an important part of her life, as indicated by the gift of some of the family's Kansas land to the Norwegian Evangelical Lutheran Church. For many Norwegian American women, social networking was absolutely one of the benefits of church membership.[37] Norwegian Lutheran Church ladies' aids (*kvindeforening*) were organizations where women could make friends and foster the mission of the church by making objects for sale. Aids organized the mutual assistance that Norwegians revered and on which first generation immigrants in particular relied. The aids facilitated sharing by women (and sometimes bachelors) of the goods necessary to survive on the plains by sourcing needed equipment, childcare, and food. Aids raised money with auctions (the church bazaar), suppers, and picnics, money that could be used to purchase items for the congregation, such as pews, stained glass, or artwork for altars, and to fund missionary activity or other charitable projects. Women gathered at ladies' aid meetings to make traditional as well as fancy textile handwork that they could sell. Meetings generally were held once or twice a month, usually in one of the members' homes. They lasted hours and included a meal, which children and men often attended. Girls had their version too, known as the *pigeforening,* the "Busy Bees," where they practiced their fancywork and devotions. In addition to the money made from selling their work, women paid dues to the society of five to twenty-five cents a month at the turn of the century.

Immanuel Lutheran, where Karen and Rachel Thronson were members, had a kvindeforening from at least 1906 and a pigeforening from at least 1904. Names of the organization's officers were recorded since 1909. Both organizations were mentioned variously in annual meeting records, mostly to discuss the amounts given to the church. Budget records from 1918 show that the ladies' aid gave one thousand dollars that year to purchase new windows, flooring, carpet, dishes, and tables for the church. In 1929, their support of two hundred dollars to defray the costs of laying sewer is mentioned in the annual meeting minutes.

With the exception of officers, no individual women are named in extant records; however, Karen and Rachel probably were involved. Rachel owned a Norwegian Hauge Synod Bible, debossed "Rachel Trohnson, 1905," that she must have used for devotions at church. Karen also was active in the church community, pledging a little each year. Records show "Mrs. Trondsen" gave two dollars in 1904 and 1906; in 1908 she increased her pledge to three dollars. The church pledge rosters in the first decade of Immanuel's existence are not very long—it contained fewer than one hundred individuals in any given year before 1914. Most pledges ranged between two and eight dollars. A few men had the means to pledge fifteen or twenty dollars. Some individuals only pledged fifty cents. Karen's pledge amount coincides with her status as a widow and her reduced livelihood. That she was only ever listed as "Mrs. Thronsen" (or Mrs. Trondsen) also indicates her elder status.[38]

Second Generation Acculturation

Shared faith and language around Story City helped Karen Thronson and the women in her family maintain their Norwegian heritage and establish their economic independence. Even as they retained some of the traditional norms of Norway, the women born in the United States necessarily adopted modern American customs to contribute to the household. Economic necessity prompted new designs and products and new labor models. In turn, these helped Karen's descendants learn about and exercise political power.

After moving to Ellsworth, Karen was head of the household and for much-needed income took in some boarders; she also undertook some dairying.[39] Dairying in Norway was women's work, and as Handy-Marchello and Lagerquist have discussed, the impact of this kind of women's economic contribution was very important to households, especially in years when crops were poor. Also once in Ellsworth, Rachel and her cousin Henrietta contributed to the household by seeking work outside the home. Early letters and immigrant accounts indicated that the pay for servants could be fairly good, especially if a woman spoke some English. Johan Reiersen indicated in his *Pathfinder for Norwegian Emigrants* that female domestic servants could earn six to eight dollars per month or even one dollar a day as a washerwoman; she could make money sewing clothing, as well. Ole Rynning advertised the rates for a domestic servant as $1.50 to $2.00 per day in the 1840s.[40] As second-generation Norwegian Americans, Rachel and Henrietta would have been well equipped to be servants and cooks, since they could speak English. They were able to transition from rural to industrialized modernity by working within the expectations of their class and gender. Although, as was typical, these unmarried women contributed to the household by gaining wage-labor employment, as well as by providing domestic assistance in their mother's or another relative's home, women ultimately needed to marry to be valued as contributors to society. Once in the domestic sphere, they could "freely" participate and demonstrate their enhanced status — now as domestic consumers.

Rachel Thronson met her future husband while employed as a cook at the "clubhouse," a boarding house near Iowa State University in Ames, Iowa. According to E. Roy's memoir, he had been an Iowa farm boy who wanted to go to college. Although his parents objected "for different reasons," in September 1907, he left Batavia for Ames, a distance of 130 miles, taking three trains and walking. He immediately sought a room and work. Near the college, he saw a sign for the YMCA. The YMCA had no rooms available, but when he registered at Central Hall the next day, the YMCA secretary told him that a new club was being organized "down the street." This was the "clubhouse" where Rachel and Henrietta were both cooks. E. Roy recounts that as he settled in at this new boarding house, meeting the other men, he also met the "girls" who had come to care for the new arrivals. He recalls meeting the women as they set down their suitcases. Henrietta had a bad leg, and she fell. Even though E. Roy caught Henrietta, he later joked that it was Rachel for whom he "fell."

E. Roy recounts his homesickness and waxes romantic recalling conversations with Rachel in the clubhouse kitchen. She gave him emotional and physical support by creating a "home" for him with her cooking and conversation. He praised her abilities, and he especially praised her efficiency and good service, writing that the steward of the club asked Rachel for advice because she managed the kitchen so well, serving thirty-eight to fifty men a day. The second year at Iowa State, E. Roy indicated that most of the same men stayed together again, but in a different house, which they called "The Alamo." By the second Christmas, E. Roy professed his love to Rachel. One and a half years later, on September 6, 1911, E. Roy and Rachel were married in Jewell, Iowa, just three miles from Ellsworth. Rachel was twenty-eight years old. E. Roy was three months shy of twenty-four.

By the second generation, Rachel's generation, most immigrants had fully adopted American cultural norms, adding them to their own. Language, foods, and fashion trends mixed. A photograph of Rachel and E. Roy beside a horse and buggy on their honeymoon shows Rachel in an American-style wedding dress. This "lingerie" style was very popular from 1900 to about 1910. Women made them from purchased or handmade laces sewn together and often layered over very lightweight white cotton. Rachel had jettisoned the traditional regional clothes that in Norway would have communicated status and region of origin but that in the United States simply stood out as different. Rachel knew both English and Norwegian; her daughter Esther, however, communicated only in English.

Marrying outside the community further indicates the second generation's willingness to look beyond the immigrant enclave. Interestingly, Rachel's more recent immigrant status was viewed askance by her future husband's family, the Campbells and Parretts, who had immigrated to Virginia as Scottish Presbyterians in the eighteenth century.[41] After their wedding, E. Roy and Rachel moved to southeast Iowa, just west of Fairfield, to a farm in Packwood. Rachel contributed to the household by selling cream, butter, and other things she and the children made on the farm. They became members of the rural Cross Lanes Presbyterian Church. Their acculturation facilitated the family's social mobility. Their farm increased in value, and Rachel's daughters became teachers; their daughters became teachers, shop owners, and lawyers. Historian Sara Egge suggests that the increasing numbers of young women working outside the home as servants, teachers, and store clerks in the early twentieth century contributed to softening attitudes toward female suffrage.[42] Indeed, while Karen's and Rachel's views on suffrage are unknown, once Rachel's daughter Esther, born in 1915, came of age, she voted in every election.

After her daughter married, Karen Thronson and her mother, Carrie Severson, continued to live in Ellsworth until Carrie died in 1916. In 1917, Karen had Rasmus, her first born, help her sell the property. Filed in Hamilton County, Iowa, the deed is notarized in Minnesota, where Rasmus then lived.

After selling her small piece of land, Karen made crafts and cooked traditional foods with her grandchildren on Rachel's farm. Esther remembered eating lefse, a traditional Norwegian flatbread, and salted cod with Karen, making cutout paper chains, sewing, and doing needlework—grandmotherly traditions she continued when she had grandchildren.

An anecdote my mother told me reveals how the shift from farm to wage labor among women and their corresponding busyness required many women to put off teaching traditional skills and making until later in life. When she came home after a long day at work to find Grandma Esther cutting out paper dolls with my brothers and me, my mother said, "Is this something you learned to do in your retirement?" (Esther had been a teacher.) Grandma replied, "My mother [Rachel] may not have had time to do this with me, but my grandmother [Karen] did." Grandma Esther taught us how to quilt and crochet and how to enjoy lefse with butter and sugar. These activities we did together evenings and weekends.

Karen made handcrafts on the farm with her daughters and granddaughters, and through these activities and those of making with and for her church, she mediated between old and new, past and present, tradition and industrial modernity. Women worked, and their handcrafts changed, reflecting shifts in status and cultural identity. They conformed to the expectations of U.S. consumer culture, with the idea that future generations would benefit.

Church was a place to build social community through making. *Kvinden og Hjemmet* was a virtual community where women shared *how* to make. Ladies' aids and magazines helped often isolated women to gather and connect. These communities provided information and helped immigrant women acculturate, domesticate, and order their land and lives in their new (to them) territory. By combining old-country traditions—whether Hardanger or crochet—in items sold at ladies' aid church bazaars, the women in these communities adapted to the needs of their new place, furthering their descendants' potential according to the dominant values of U.S. society.

FIVE | CREATING SOLIDARITY

DE CORA AT CARLISLE, 1907–1914

While teaching at Carlisle Indian Industrial School between 1907 and 1915, Angel De Cora made a community of her classroom and sought solidarity in the Pan-Indian movement. As ladies' aids societies and *Kvinden og Hjemmet* were to rural Scandinavian women, De Cora's Native students and others with whom she could engage ideas became her community. She increasingly focused on design because it allowed her and her students to explore making art that complicated the "traditional" handcrafts sanctioned by government officials for Indian education. Although she often used the rhetoric of white reformers — the racialist idea of a "natural" Indian artist — she did so to inspire her students and find solidarity within the Pan-Indian movement.[1] Still, she taught and developed specificity of design, designs that individuals synthesized from their own tribal heritage. In this way, she and her students found some autonomy within the stereotyped and discriminatory parameters of the white market and official curriculum. Through design, De Cora sought to contribute to the Pan-Indian movement by demonstrating that Native Americans were "natural" artists. She also showed that Native artistry and skill were not based in mimicry or copying, but rather were enriched by patterns and traditions "peculiar to each tribe." Through her teaching and her focus on complex design, De Cora Indigenized the curriculum and found a sense of community within the structures of dominant white society.

Natural Design

Before accepting a teaching position at Carlisle, De Cora published and exhibited at the national level, working closely with white professionals in government, academic, and commercial settings. Reformers had used her as an example of a government success story because of her positive academic and commercial reputation in mainstream white America. After exhibiting design work at world's fairs, such as the thunderbird mantel and settee, De Cora increasingly focused her work on integrated, functionally decorative designs: borders, typography, and images that could be applied onto consumer products, in line with the wider Arts and Crafts movement.[2] Her later work shows a preference for natural forms in various stages of abstraction, from prairie grass, eight-pointed stars, and thunderbirds to zigzags. Abstract images can hold multiplicities of complex meaning. De Cora found that design could encompass both the values she learned during her youth in Nebraska and the skills she acquired from academically trained teachers: art for art's sake and functionality freed from the western illusionistic way of viewing and representing the world. De Cora's transition from realistic and tonal illustrations to design during her teaching years at Carlisle coincides with her heartfelt desire to raise the status of all Native Americans. She promoted the Pan-Indian movement because she genuinely believed that design was a major contribution that all Native Americans could make to "American" culture by accessing a collective knowledge.

Design for De Cora was an extension of and evolution from her earlier interest in landscape. Like landscape, Native design was "natural"—and feminized. For De Cora, the Indigenous *woman* is a designer who goes outside, "drawing her inspiration from the broad espects [*sic*] of Nature. Her zig-zag line indicates the hills in the distance, and the blue and white back ground so usual in the Indian color scheme denotes the sky. . . . She makes her color contrasts under the glare of the sun, whose brilliancy makes even her bright tones seem softened into tints." She believed "animal forms, and symbols of human life" should inform design work.[3] De Cora's research at ethnographic fairs and her observations of her students led her to note that such animal forms and landscape geometries were common, especially among Plains artists. While nature inspired De Cora, she and her students modified it, distilled it, and made it their own, rather than copying it.

De Cora used the Carlisle magazines and newspaper to feature her own and her students' design work and to promote her belief in Native Americans' contribution to design. Students published their art and design in the *Indian Craftsman,* first published in 1909, showcasing their "natural" skills. Below realistic illustrations of animals such as eagles and bears, teepees, and warriors, was a byline identifying the image as "by an Indian" or "by a Sioux Indian." Abstract designs bordered photographs, poems, and stories "not only *about* Indians, but *by* Indians," as the tagline proudly proclaimed on the magazine's front page. In the back of each issue were explanatory advertisements for handcrafts and rugs available for purchase from Carlisle. The border of interlocking crosses around the advertisement was credited: "THIS BORDER IS AN ORIGINAL ONE — MADE BY A STUDENT OF OUR NATIVE INDIAN ART DEPARTMENT."

The magazine promoted original art and design for consumption, just as the mainstream Arts and Crafts movement commodified functional art and design. In fact, due to confusion and conflict with Gustav Stickley's national magazine the *Craftsman,* the school was obliged to change the name of its magazine to *Red Man.*[4] *Red Man* continued to advertise itself as "about and by Indians" and to show Native art made by Native students for sale. The original choice of the title *Indian Craftsman* reveals De Cora's aspirations to fulfill goals similar to those of Arts and Crafts artists, who wanted to make aesthetic and useful objects that benefited society.

Before the magazine was born under De Cora and Dietz's tutelage, the school newspaper, the *Arrow,* had showcased De Cora's work and philosophy. Soon after she began working at Carlisle in 1907, it printed her motifs and lettering along with her speech to the National Education Association, "Native Art." Multicolored (although printed in black and white) interlocking crenellations surround a photograph of Carlisle students in class. Punctuating this header are two embellishments on either side, comprised of prairie grasses that extend diagonally from a right triangle, underscoring Native connection to both art and nature. (See figures 18 and 18a.) Similarly, the embellishments and borders around the front-page photographs for the *Arrow* from July 19, 1907, show gradations of abstraction. The frame around the photographs of the new Leupp Art Building (paid for by revenue from the Carlisle football team), is comprised of dynamically expanding zigzags that run both vertically and horizontally. On either side appear geometrically decorated hummingbirds

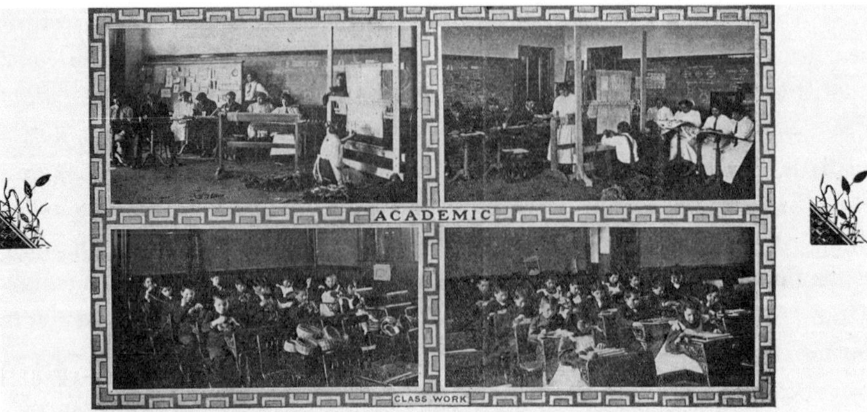

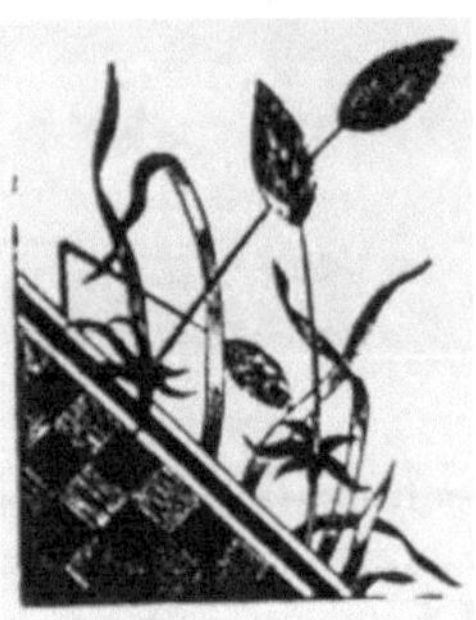

FIGURES 18 and 18a.
Angel De Cora, decorative header to an article reprinting text from her 1907 speech "Native Art," before the National Education Association; the *Arrow,* August 23, 1907.

within encircled eight-pointed stars. At the bottom, between the photographs, a woman weaves a basket (figures 19 and 19a). The front-page design and illustration demonstrate De Cora's synthesis of realism and abstract design and her ideas about the role of Native women as *artists*.

A few years into De Cora's tenure at Carlisle, the *Philadelphia Inquirer* picked up her rhetoric on how Native American design contributed to (white) American society and how it could be commercialized. De Cora clarifies how abstraction allows expression of different meanings for different tribes. The reporter writes:

> Angel DeCora firmly believes that Indian designing has a high commercial value and if properly studied and understood would be very popular in the general market. . . . "[T]he hand that first welcomed your ancestors is again extended and within it lies a latent talent. As every race has contributed its art to America, so this is the Indian's contribution."

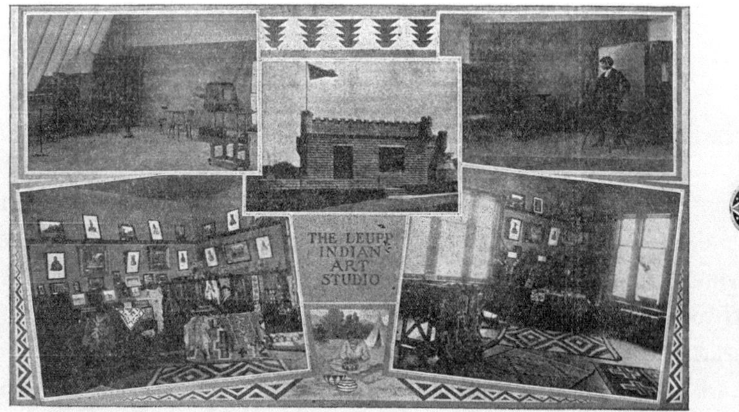

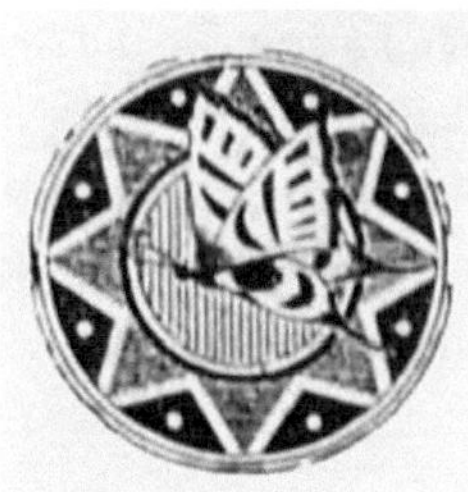

FIGURES 19 and 19a.
Angel De Cora, decorative header to an article in the *Arrow,* July 19, 1907.

The reporter goes on to paraphrase and quote De Cora on the tribal specificity of symbols.

> Indian art is distinctive, points out Angel DeCora, and should be preserved and developed as American art. "The nature of Indian art is formed on a purely conventional and geometric basis," she explains, and continues: "The simple forms that were used to denote objects, revealing the influence of the Indian's daily life by his surroundings, were of the most commonplace geometrical forms. The triangle, the square, the rectangle were all popular shapes, as well as the straight, the wavy, and zigzag lines. A series of triangles in a horizontal row may stand for a line of hills with one tribe, while with another a chain of mountains or clouds. A single figure of the triangle stood also for wigwam with most of the tribes that build that style of a habitation. . . . Each thought or object called for a new device."[5]

The suppression of culture that De Cora herself had experienced and the effects of which she witnessed among her students galvanized her to vocalize and visualize a Pan-Indian aesthetic and ideal similar to the integrated design philosophy of the Arts and Crafts movement. The reformist ideals of the Arts and Crafts movement, which tried to introduce beauty into workers' lives so they could make aesthetic and useful objects that morally uplifted society, was mirrored in public schools' early art education curricula that focused on the individual student's aesthetic faculties.[6] De Cora hoped elevating Native artists through original functional design would bring her people and all Native Americans solidarity and freedom within white society. In her position at Carlisle, De Cora again had firsthand experience of reformers' ideas about Native education and was in a position to undermine the rigid and racist precepts. Superintendent of Indian Education Estelle Reel's *Course of Study for the Indian Schools of the United States* (1901) suggested a gendered, industrialized education, where art was only taught for the production of craft and to develop manual skills. But during her time at Carlisle, De Cora repeatedly asserted that her students and all Native Americans were original artists.

Native Art Education

De Cora was hired by Commissioner of Indian Affairs Francis Leupp in 1906, shortly after his appointment in 1905. In light of other reformers' efforts, he sought to "progress" Native American education toward a commercialization of Native culture that appealed to white consumers who were, by then, able to romanticize Native Americans rather than see them as a threat.

Inspired by Hampton's educational program for African and Native Americans, Carlisle Indian Industrial School had been established by Captain Richard Henry Pratt to "kill the Indian, save the man." But Pratt took a notoriously hard line when it came to assimilation. His ideas about Indian education were in stark contrast to the ideology employed at Hampton and the relative sympathy shown by Cora Folsom and her supervisor, Samuel Armstrong, who held that, within the school's reform-minded goals, Native American and African American students should retain aspects of their respective heritages.[7] Leupp's approach was more like Armstrong's, while Pratt tolerated nothing that was not European-American in origin. Under assimilationist policy, Native American students' hair was cut, their languages suppressed (often violently), and their religion replaced with Christianity; no aspect of Native culture was encouraged.

Pratt's hard-line approach fell out of favor after the election of Theodore Roosevelt and Leupp's appointment. Leupp believed in "improvement, not transformation" although, for him, improvement meant commodifying aesthetic heritage by assimilating to the economic standard of industrialization. Leupp preferred that "improvement" occur on reservations, at day schools, but he recognized the potential for inculcating industrial self-sufficiency at boarding institutions like Carlisle. Especially in the context of the growing market for Native American goods, Carlisle could inaugurate his philosophy of "improvement, not transformation"—"improving" Native capacity to produce for white consumers.

Following Leupp's appointment, Carlisle's newspaper the *Arrow* ran extracts from his first report on Indian Affairs. These extracts underscored his views on the significant role of industrial arts in improving Native Americans by including them in the U.S. economy. The second volume of the Carlisle *Arrow* from 1906, quotes Leupp:

> I have no sympathy with the sentiment which would throw the squaw's bead bag into the rubbish heap and set her to making lace. Teach her lace-making, by all means, as an addition to her stock of profitable accomplishments; but don't set down her beaded moccasins as merely barbarous, while holding up her lace handkerchief as a symbol of advanced civilization. . . . The Indian is a natural warrior, a natural logician, a natural artist.[8]

Leupp sought a balance between preserving Native traditions—what were seen as essential and inherent to the "race"—and "improving" those traits to conform to the realities of industrial society. If the Indian is a natural warrior, logician, and artist, then those skills could be put to profitable use.

Lace making and beading together were held up as productive and useful activities for women in American society to occupy their time. For many whites, handwork—both Native Americans' and rural white women's—was seen as part of a disappearing historical past, something quaint and worth collecting. Nostalgia for pioneer wagons and survival based on resourcefulness and efficiency coincided with the nostalgia for buckskin-wearing Indians and the Protestant work ethic that undergirded the American frontier myth.

Both represented a lost time, and handcrafts stood in for that seemingly simpler era of real, unalienated labor. "Preserving" and selling Native traditions paralleled the contrasting display of acculturated Indian skills in the OIA exhibits and of the soon-to-be extinct "savages" in the Indian congresses.

As we have seen, in the pages of the *Ladies' Home Journal* "primitive" or "peasant" crafts became both examples for middle- and upper-class white women devising their home décor and talismans of escape from the alienation of modern mechanization; emulating such crafts helped women preserve status within the only sphere open to them: the home. This can be seen in the course of the so-called "Indian craze," supported by female philanthropic groups, such as the Women's National Indian Association and Indian Industries League, ostensibly to elevate the "squaw" from drudgery. But the focus on Native artistry as "craft" reinforced white and Native women's gender roles by rendering their creative work less valuable than men's "fine" art and wage labor.[9]

De Cora's work and reception contravened this pattern. Leupp had actively sought out De Cora to teach Native arts at Carlisle. At Carlisle, as in the Indian schools exhibits organized by the Office of Indian Affairs, De Cora could be held up as exemplary: She was a visible alternative to Pratt's views, an example of an Indian artist whose work was marketable, a woman who was nationally renowned, yet humble (and therefore unthreatening), and who was respected both within the artistic community and among the well-heeled reformers of the day. Although Native products were advertised nationally in mainstream ladies' magazines, they were not necessarily held up as anything more than commodities. De Cora's art, on the other hand, was sought after by well-connected women like Fletcher and Curtis and printed by mainstream publishers. By promoting the Native *woman* as an *original* artist—that is, one producing "high" art rather than "low" handcraft—De Cora decoupled Native American arts from the female-gendered domestic labor so devalued in wage-labor society. Simonsen suggests that

> De Cora infused domestic production with new cultural imperatives. Native American crafts should be legitimated not just as commodities that supported white consumers' needs or a therapeutic recovery of premodern values but as an avenue to a specifically Native American identity. . . . De Cora embraced work as a tool for creating Indian identity

while redefining domestic production as having both cultural and economic value.[10]

As Indian Commissioner, Leupp built on the educational precepts established by prior Commissioner of Indian Affairs Thomas Morgan (1889–1893) and Superintendent Estelle Reel. An experienced educator, Morgan published *Studies in Pedagogy* (1889), a textbook for public schools, and served two terms as vice president of the National Education Association. Morgan often spoke at the Lake Mohonk conferences, and as an ordained Baptist minister he corroborated the Protestant-capitalist ethic promoted by many reformers. As commissioner, Morgan pursued a standardized approach to Indian education and set out his ideas for a national compulsory system in his pamphlet *Rules for Indian Schools.* (First appearing as an appendix to the Commissioner's annual report in 1890, the document was revised and disseminated in 1892 as *Rules for Indian Schools with Course of Study, List of Text Books and Civil Service Rules.*)[11]

Morgan believed that public education was integral to "civilizing" through assimilation[12] and that the purpose of government education was to prepare

> Indian youth for assimilation into the national life by such a course of training as will prepare them for the duties and privileges of American citizenship. This involves the training of the hand in useful industries; the development of the mind in independent and self-directing power of thought, the impartation of useful practical knowledge; the culture of the moral nature, and the formation of the character.[13]

Morgan's ideas were grounded in theories about the social role of public education and the ongoing debate surrounding the role of art education, especially in the public-school curriculum. Training in art theoretically helped "uncivilized" students develop motor skills, concentration, precision, and, of course, moral sensibility. Initially, art education in the standard public-school curriculum focused on having students copy from life or pictures to promote visual acuity, improve hand-eye coordination, and develop skills needed for semiskilled labor. Art instruction was considered important for students' moral development as well, making it useful as part of the larger project of using U.S. schools to create a laboring underclass of immigrants and Native Americans.

Copying and drawing were also common features of Indian art education and were highlighted in Thomas Morgan's proposed curriculum. Following the standards set in other public schools, he deployed drawing to help Native students fine-tune motor skills and assist them in learning to write. Drawing, seen as the foundation for all other hand-related activity, was widely taught in art departments at normal (teacher training) schools and at universities and was the most commonly taught art skill in public grade schools. Reel, Superintendent of Indian Schools from in 1898 and until 1910, had not included drawing in her program for Indian schools, however, even though it had been a major component of previous Indian school curricula.[14]

Lentis argues that while public school art education changed over time to incorporate models based on child development theories, Indian education continued to maintain a highly structured, old-fashioned system that disallowed Native students' freedom or flexibility and focused on morality and the motor skills and dexterity necessary for industrial workers. When art was taught it was not so that Native American children could become artists and creative free thinkers, but rather so that they would become effective producers of manufactured goods. Lentis maintains that in Indian art education, "drawing . . . was a tool for improving industrial skills, not for developing the ability to make fancy pictures or express one's own creativity. . . . Native children had to learn how to draw and see things from a western perspective that did not take into account their Indigenous knowledge or social and natural environments."[15] The curriculum assumed Native Americans should not be artists—and perhaps that they were not capable of creativity, expression, and freedom of thought.

When William Hailmann became Commissioner of Indian Affairs in 1894, he moved to incorporate ideals of expression and "beauty" into Native art education to connect students to their new American schools and values. Yet Hailmann remained interested in the moral component and industrial potential of art education. In Reel's *Course of Study* and in practice at the boarding schools, industrial ability was the core of instruction, with production of a useful, saleable object the end goal. In Reel's proposed curriculum, "children needed to be taught a disposition of mind in order to fit into the white world." This required learning the "proper" way to see (ostensibly, the western academic ideal of illusionistic realism) and performing practical exercises that eliminated inaccuracy, impulsiveness, and negligence.[16]

In Estelle Reel's first report as superintendent she stated that "[i]ndustrial training should have the foremost place in Indian education, for it is the foundation upon which the government's desire for the improvement of the Indian is built."[17] In Reel's curriculum, Native students were not asked to draw for the sake of developing aesthetic taste or creativity. Art education for Native Americans implicitly confirmed their expected low status as laborers producing objects conforming to the tastes of white American consumers. Reel's curriculum focused on learning service skills and making saleable handcrafts. Girls were expected to learn the "crafts" of basketry, weaving, beadwork, and pottery, while boys learned industrial arts, including printing and woodwork. In her *Course of Study,* Reel presented a curriculum affirming Native Americans' role as processing and supplying goods (beadwork, rugs) for a white market; the students were not taught in a way meant to promote ingenuity or intellectualism. Although Commissioner Leupp was less austere in his approach to Indian education, he, too, believed that commercializing Native arts as an industry was an excellent means by which to "transform" the Indigenous student into a productive member of white society.

Many issues of *Arrow,* Carlisle's newspaper, and later of its magazines *Indian Craftsman* and *Red Man,* had articles reporting on agriculture, the arts, and what Reel, Leupp, and other reformers considered Native Americans' inherent virtuous traits, which they believed would help them assimilate into the U.S. agricultural industry.[18] Although the "Indian" artist was identified as such, the figurative images, more so than the designs, seem to mirror white reformers' ideas. A print (dated 1910) by De Cora's then husband, William "Lonestar" Dietz, for the *Indian Craftsman* illustrates white reformist ideals for Indian education and Native art education especially.[19] (See figure 20.) In this image, a woman in braids and buckskin beads her knee-high moccasins. In the distance are teepees and horses. Interestingly, the design on the woman's moccasins shows the thunderbird motif with extended vertical line also present behind Gray Wolf's daughter in De Cora's earlier illustration (shown in figure 8). The frontispiece by Dietz to the *Indian Craftsman* from May 1909 shows a Native American woman making a basket. (See figure 21.) She kneels, attentive to her task. A few southwestern-style pots sit behind her. She wears a simple shift dress and shawl, and her hair is bound in two ponytails. Significantly, no landscape is depicted; Indian and products—beaded moccasins and baskets, products Leupp and Reel approved for Native women to make—are the subjects here.

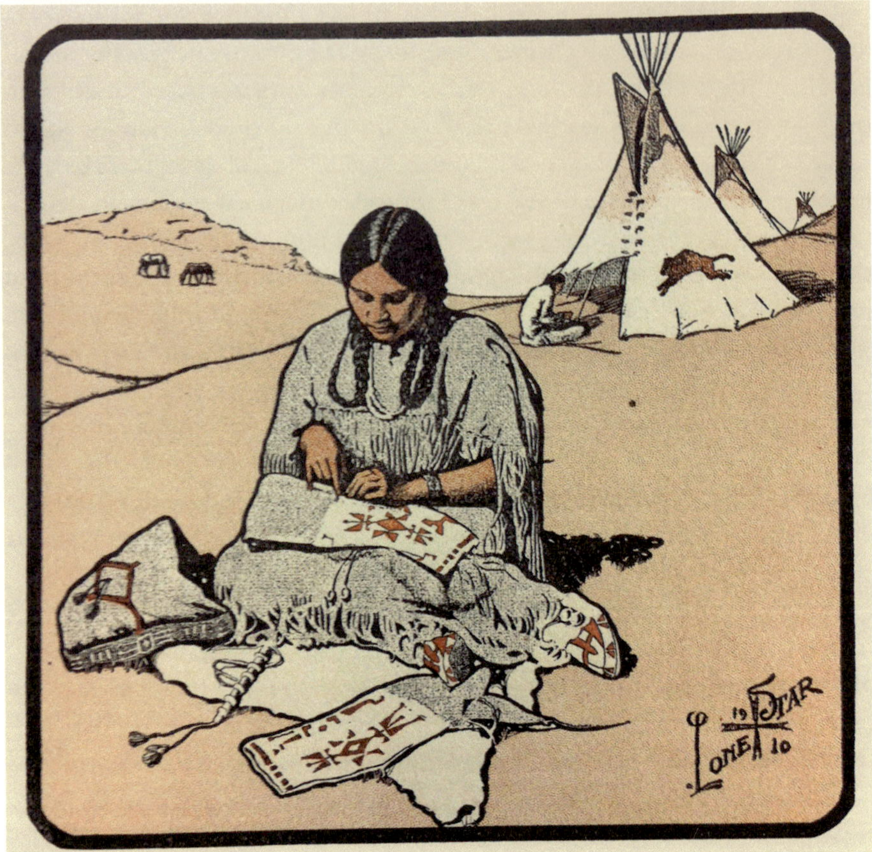

FIGURE 20. William “Lone Star” Dietz, cover design, *Indian Craftsman,* 1910 (woman beading moccasins). Cumberland County Historical Society.

Most of Dietz’s extant illustrations for *Indian Craftsman* and *Red Man* show idealized Native American women, a craftsperson, or a Native American man as agriculturalist, all in accord with the reformers’ ideas. Women are shown making baskets, weaving rugs, beading, and cutting hide; men are shown plowing rows in a field, harvesting wheat, and hoeing among cabbages. Indeed, Deitz’s cover design showing a woman beading is directly copied from a photograph, probably of De Cora.[20] The woman in the photograph is indoors, sitting on Navajo rugs like those often displayed in the Leupp art studio. The designs Dietz added seem to have come from De Cora.

VOLUME 1, NUMBER 4 ONE DOLLAR A YEAR

THE INDIAN CRAFTSMAN

MAY, 1909

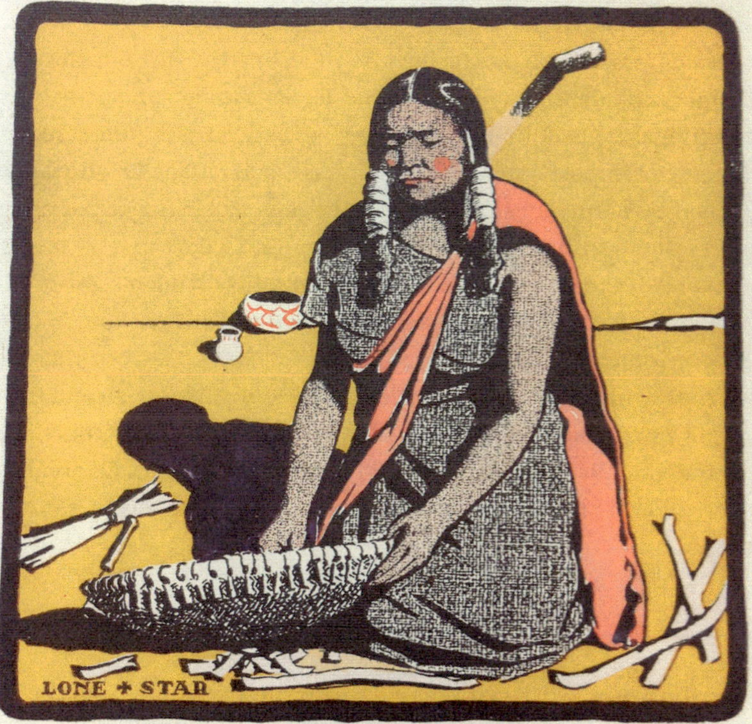

THE CARLISLE INDIAN PRESS

U. S. INDIAN SCHOOL, CARLISLE, PENNSYLVANIA

FIGURE 21. William "Lone Star" Dietz, cover, *Indian Craftsman,* May 1909 (woman making a basket). Cumberland County Historical Society.

Deitz's literal illustrations reinforce the white racialist and gendered norms for Native American art using realist stereotypes that conformed to Reel's unified curriculum for government Indian schools. Reel, too, homogenized tribal specificities into a stereotype of Indian art that was reproducible and marketable. Lentis has further argued that the crafts as taught in the Indian schools were rendered "safe" *because* they were appropriated as commodities. Homogenized and aestheticized, divorced from functionality and individual and tribal expression, "Native industries were thus beneficial pastimes through which students could be trained in making valuable use of their hand skills and their unoccupied moments": never would a Native student sit idle while they had "profitable work" to do.[21]

But for De Cora, design was flexible. As envisioned by De Cora, design could provide modern adaptions of traditional forms through the artist's creativity and originality. In a highly structured society, artists were (are) freer to work outside of imposed norms. De Cora's students made broadly appealing work valued by both educated Native Americans of various tribes and white audiences, thus fulfilling the tenets of Indian art education as it was then conceptualized. At the same time, the designs that students made in class and published in Carlisle's printed journals allowed them to connect with their respective homes and heritages in multiple ways. De Cora systematized geometric patterns and categorized designs by general location and tribe. She also empowered students with a flexible pedagogy that gave them space to connect individually to those places and a choice in how they combined motif and color, allowing them to design in ways that corresponded with their own traditions.

Indigenizing the Curriculum

Although the works by Dietz discussed correspond generally with the reformers' conceptions of Indian art education by explicitly illustrating gendered production in a realist style, many examples of work by De Cora and her students broaden and complicate conceptions of what Native American art could be. De Cora resisted mere vocational training and stereotype and allowed her students to pursue tribal specificity and their individual heritages.

At Carlisle De Cora drew out her own and her students' repressed connections to their homelands. De Cora noted that when she first began teaching, her students were so traumatized by institutionalized cultural repression that she felt she was addressing children of an "alien race."[22] To accommodate their needs, she adapted the standard art education curriculum to allow her students room for creative expression. As she herself used art to connect to her own home, she tried to help her students mend the trauma of separation from their homes.

In her classroom, De Cora asked her students to excavate memories of their homes and heritages by relating to images of nature and place. She recounts in a speech titled "An Effort to Encourage Indian Art," given at the Congrès International des americanistes in Québec in 1906, that

> I endeavored to recall to my pupils' minds, the days of the old life and to send them back in imagination to the time when their grandmothers, and their fathers and mothers produced the native art-work. But . . . I found that I had to manufacture my Indians. I advised my pupils to try in every possible way to learn something of the Indian lore of the past, and the best that I could do, for these Indians who were transplanted from all contact with their own people, was to refer them to the Reports of the Bureau of Ethnology.[23]

De Cora's use of "transplanted" is illuminating. Home was a place to situate the being and becoming of her students. De Cora took students outside, and she showed them pictures and photographs of the peoples and places from which they had come. She sought to inspire them to remember what they already knew, to access their memories of place and their talent, to unearth communities of relationships that had been repressed, never replaced. De Cora stated that "[al]l the invironments [*sic*] and motives that inspire the art of a race just at this particular state of development have been taken from them."[24]

De Cora used the geographical model of Franz Boas (whom she met in 1907) to help her form culturally based stylistic categories of design that she could use as a foundation for teaching her students.[25] Boas held that culture should be understood as varying according to geographic differences. De Cora applied this idea by actively incorporating images from ethnographic collections to demonstrate general design types and, more importantly, to unlock her students' memories. She ordered photographic books from the Bureau of American Ethnology for her classroom. William Henry Holmes, the bureau's director, sent her many volumes and also offprints relevant to the study of Indian art from the bureau's *Annual Reports* and the *Report of the United States National Museum*.[26] Just as she had done at the international expositions and at Fort Berthold, De Cora continued to watch, and sometimes photograph, women at work at reservations in Albuquerque and Omaha and at Winnebago reservations whenever she delivered speeches near those places.

De Cora used these materials to teach a more flexible way of seeing the world than the one she had been taught in school. Although Indigenous handcrafts appealed to white Americans because they fit into a nostalgic nationalism for Indians and the frontier, they also provided her and her students with media onto which they could safely inscribe designs with personal meaning. In her address to the audience gathered at Lake Mohonk in 1908, De Cora specifically explained how she used her summers to visit women on reservations to learn from them. In her speech, she toed the line, offering that their designs could be applied to "jardinières, teapots, finger bowls, lamps, and vases of all shapes," curtains, purses, and opera bags, but chastised the meaningless application of pansies to towels.[27] She also iterated that her department at Carlisle broke with the "regular routine" by not studying European classics in art; rather, she stated, we "take the old symbolic figures and forms which we find on beadwork, pottery, and baskets . . . then we create designs according to these old established methods and apply them to the products of the workshops of the school."[28] Privately De Cora commented on the worthlessness of the trinkets she (and her students), of necessity, made. In letters to Folsom, De Cora often described little pieces she made that sold well as "foolish"; she denigrated the commercialization and chastised herself for participating in it. But such use of their symbols allowed Native artists to forge a real connection to the design and meaning presented.

In De Cora's curriculum, students were discouraged from copying; rather, they were encouraged to elicit their "natural" cultural symbols by going outside and by looking at ethnographic photographs. They were then given scope to synthesize the information and their experiences in drawing. In 1911, De Cora explained her method of teaching design to other well-educated Native Americans at the first gathering of the Society of American Indians (SAI):

> [T]he study of fundamental systems was followed by the combined figures, made up of two or more of the elements of design, then the still

> more complex figures made by repeated use of two or more of the elements of design. Under this analytic system we have studied the various tribal styles, the Arapahoe system which represents the tribes of the mountainous regions, the Winnebago system which treats of the forest and lake country; the Navajo which presents still another style showing the character of desert country.[29]

Examples of her students' work from around 1910 show exactly this pedagogical approach. De Cora's categorizing of symbols, while general and seemingly based on European epistemological models, is grounded in *places.* Initial geographical and tribal generality provided a foundation on which students could build as they continued to learn more about themselves and their heritages and to develop more particular designs as a result. As De Cora said in the same SAI speech,

> [t]he Indian pictured the broader aspects of nature, such as sky, clouds, hills, lakes, rivers, trees and rocks in symbolic figures of geometrical shapes, so the general character of the country had much to do with each tribal scheme of symbolisms.[30]

Moreover, De Cora retained drawing as an essential component to her art instruction at a time when it explicitly was *not* included in the curriculum for Indian education. In fact, she changed the course description to emphasize the importance of individual and specific Native design.

> Drawing: Freehand drawing is given throughout the course. Most Indian pupils come to us with some pretty definite knowledge of drawing already fixed in their minds. For such pupils the aim of the teaching work here is to systematize that knowledge, to eliminate anything of an impertinent nature, and to strengthen and add to that which is of real value. One of the aims in teaching drawing to Indians is to standardize, perpetuate, and give to the world at large the priceless decorative designs peculiar to the race.[31]

Here, values of individuality and specificity are clearly articulated: De Cora allowed and promoted each of her students' individual cultural expressions as Native Americans and "added" to it, even while signaling the rigidity and homogeneity ("to systematize" and "eliminate anything of an impertinent nature") that might appeal to reformers. Certainly, De Cora promoted the idea that the Indian inherently was more connected to nature—a racial stereotype—but she cultivated this idea in order to rationalize her pedagogical system to whites.

The view of Native Americans as having an inherent affinity to both art and landscape, and an ability to synthesize the two, was iterated at multiple levels at Carlisle. Teachers, students, and Leupp consistently trotted out this apparent truism. Second graders from Miss Optskey's class wrote repetitious summaries of a "field trip" to the school's art studio. Lorenzo Miguel, Peter Thomas, and their classmates wrote "they learned it from nature," and "Miss De Cora is their able teacher. They do not copy but get it out of their Heads."[32] Clearly, what De Cora wrote she also preached in classes at Carlisle. Not much student work survives from De Cora's tenure at Carlisle, but what is available at the Cumberland County Historical Society demonstrates De Cora's philosophy of *seeing* nature and abstracting its forms. In addition to the expected still lifes, students made studies of trees, leaves, berries, and flowers, in pencil and watercolor. Two students further abstracted details from nature for a butterfly design in watercolor.[33]

Although on the surface it appears that De Cora enacted Leupp and Reel's curriculum of Native arts, she provided avenues for subversion of white expectations and opened doors for individual expression, tribal specificity, and, through them, connection to homeland, renewed identity, and self-definition for her students. Take, for example, the contrasting art lessons for rendering butterflies at Hampton and under De Cora's tutelage. A photograph taken at Hampton, clearly staged, shows teenaged female students apparently using watercolor to faithfully reproduce the butterflies pinned to their desk easels. (Lentis notes the lack of water jars and the rigidity of the students' postures.)[34] (See figure 22.) In marked contrast, De Cora had her students *design* butterflies, cut stencils, and use the stencils and watercolors to study color. (See figures 23, 24, 25, 26, and 27.) Examples of such butterfly designs by Eunice Bartlette and Lillian Rice, two of De Cora's female students, are extant at Cumberland County Historical Society. The stencil template was cut by Bartlette, and the yellow butterflies are labeled "*Study in Color Harmony* by Lillian Rice." The darker butterflies are unlabeled, but they may very well be Bartlette's.

Like De Cora, both Bartlette and Rice grew up in the Midwest: Bartlette probably was Anishinaabe, and Rice was Lakota.[35] While not much is known

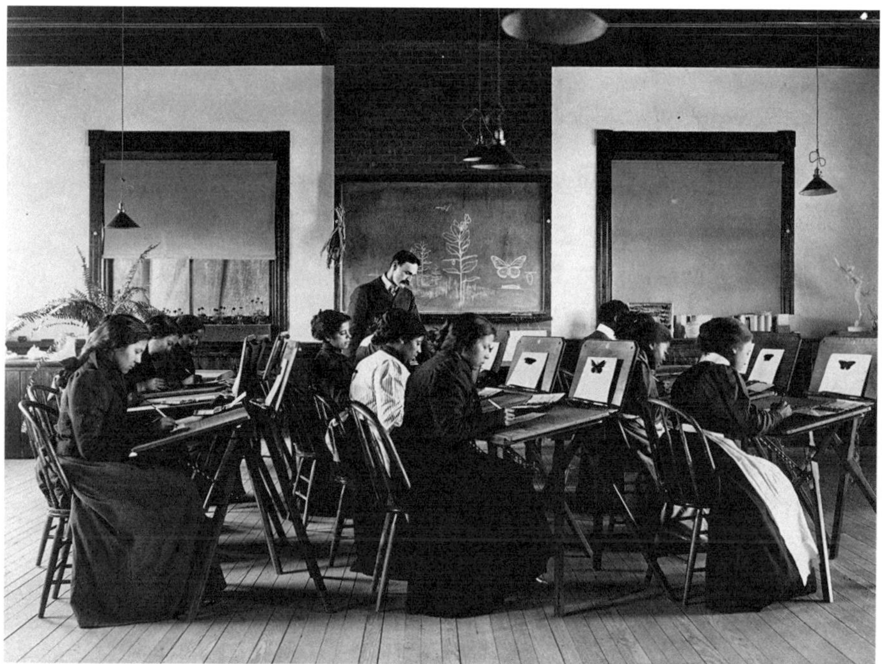

FIGURE 22. A photograph showing an art lesson on painting butterflies held at Hampton Institute ca. 1899–1900. Frances Benjamin Johnson Collection, LOC, LC-USZ62-127364.

about Eunice Bartlette, Lillian Rice was a teenager from the Rosebud Reservation in South Dakota. She attended Carlisle late in her teens, matriculating there in 1910. Born in 1891, she had been orphaned at a young age. Her mother died of starvation, and her brother died of tuberculosis. According to Shope, Rice's daughter remembers stories her mother told of her relatives' deaths by starvation when, following the Fort Laramie Treaty (1868), her tribe was kept in government camps and provided little by way of food rations.[36]

While painting watercolor butterflies apparently was something of a standard art lesson in Indian schools (perhaps De Cora adapted a lesson she herself had learned at Hampton), Shope notes that butterflies are significant to Lakota and Dakota women, especially for medicinal purposes and for their symbolic implications of transformation.[37] Referencing butterflies' healing potential to someone like Rice, who had been traumatized in multiple ways,

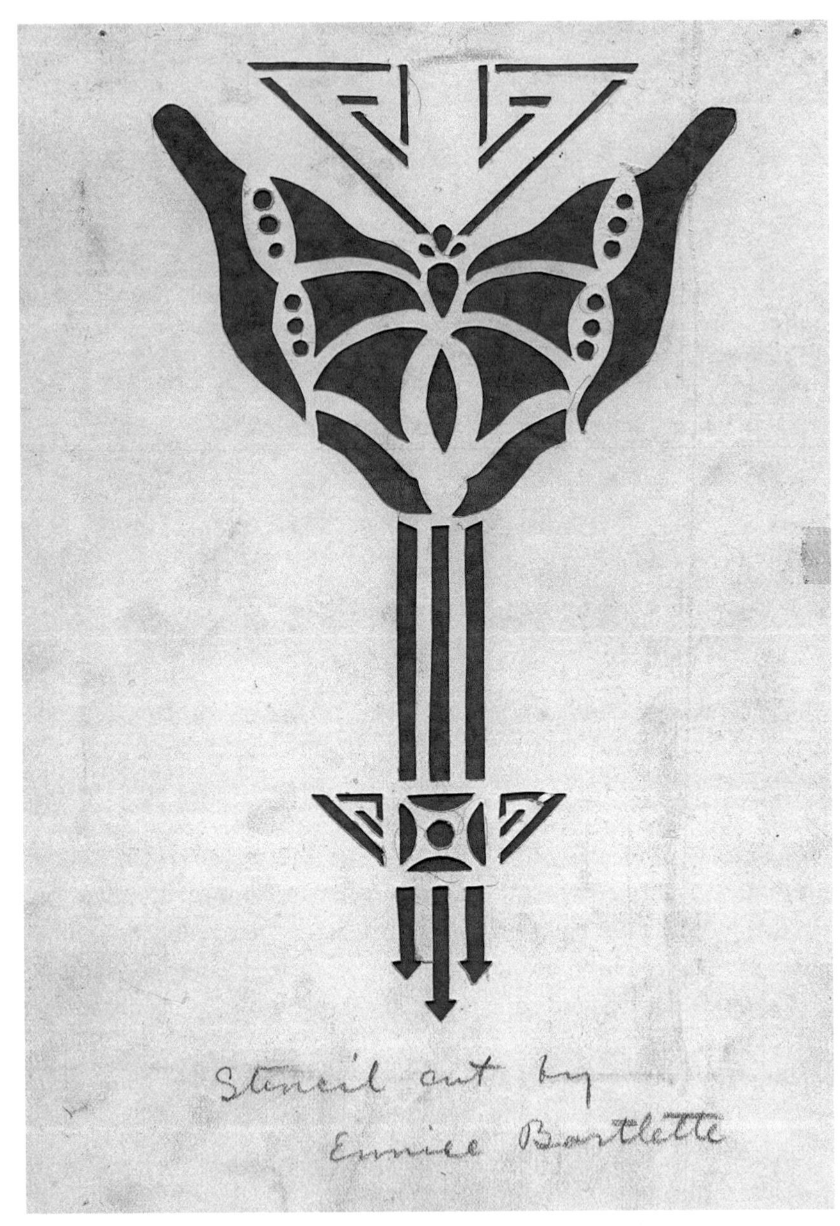

FIGURE 23. Eunice Bartlette, stencil template, ca. 1910. Cumberland County Historical Society.

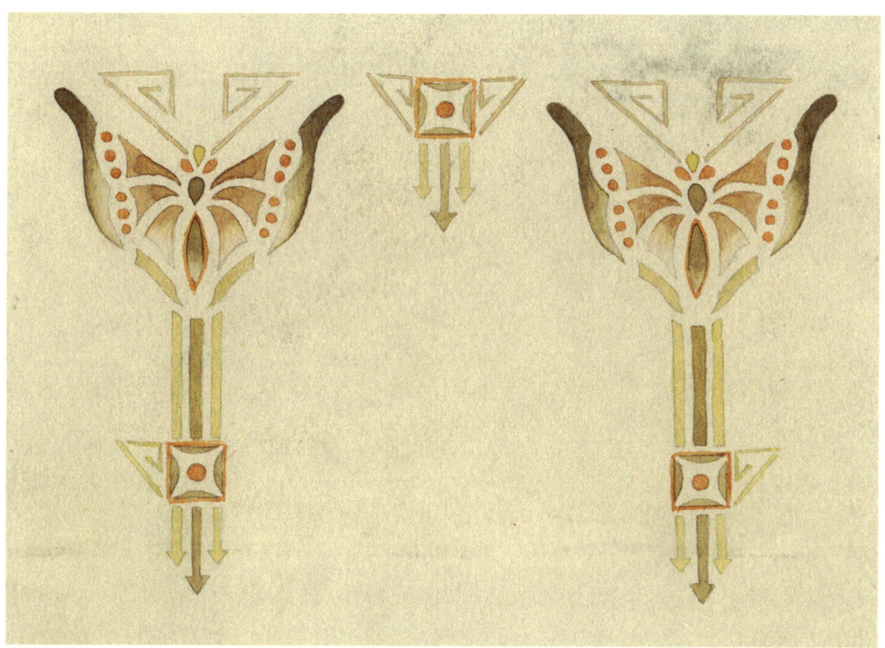

FIGURE 24. *Butterflies,* possibly by Eunice Bartlette, watercolor, ca. 1910. Cumberland County Historical Society.

seems purposeful. Her daughter recalled that Rice continued to apply butterflies (not pansies!) to her handwork throughout her life, embroidering them on towels and other linens.[38] Likewise, although color theory was a regular component of the standard art curriculum, the colors De Cora's students employed were those traditionally used by their own tribes and may have been personally meaningful to each student. In the two extant butterfly watercolor designs, Bartlette's is orange-red, yellow, and black-brown. Rice's study is yellow, orange-red, and green with black outlines. Crosses with circles in the middle punctuate a vertical column made up of three downward-pointing arrows. Although in both works the colors have faded (it is probable that the orange was red and the brown was black), it is striking that red, black/brown, and yellow appear in both, in addition to the crosses and butterflies. These symbols and colors are important in Dakota-Lakota cosmology.

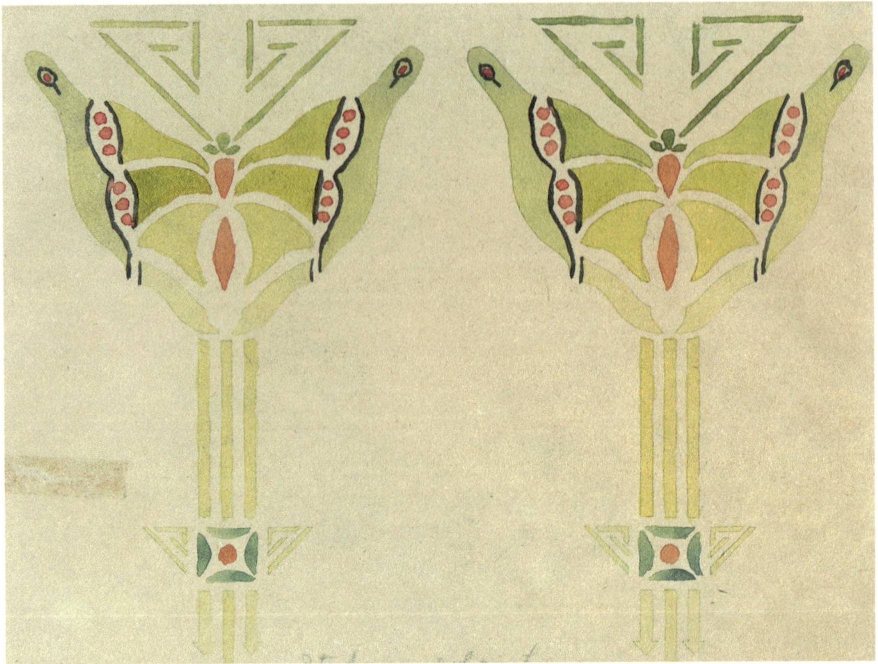

FIGURE 25. Lillian Rice, *Study in Color Harmony,* watercolor, ca. 1910. Cumberland County Historical Society.

In contrast to the western color wheel based on Newtonian optics (where blue complements orange and red complements green), the colors on the Native American color wheel relate to elements of the cosmos; thus sacred, their relations are ordered according to their cosmic meanings. Colors are associated with directionality, and taken together, they form a richly meaningful wheel. For many Dakota and Lakota tribes, red symbolizes the east wind, sunrise, birth, spring, and beginnings generally. Yellow is a symbol of light and the sun and its radiant warmth and is associated with the south, summer, and growing. Black corresponds to the shadow side, the dream world, the west, and autumn. West, where the sun sets, is where light and warmth fade to black night. White is north and winter, reflecting the season's cold, harsh conditions, snow, and ice.

Sacred colors and directions on the wheel also relate to sacred beings, such as the thunderbird—or, in the examples here, perhaps, a butterfly—who influence human lives. The wheel is depicted as a cross inside a circle. Envisioned as a three-dimensional sphere, the wheel contains the four colors of red, black, yellow, and white; in addition are the sky direction blue, the earth direction green, and the center direction. The center, or seventh direction, is metaphysically both within the individual and representative of the axis mundi, connecting all other elements. In these students' designs, the circle inscribed in the cross at the base of the butterfly design may reference this wheel; the arrows point down to earth; above, the butterfly offers healing.

Interestingly, an anonymous student stencil preserved at the Cumberland County Historical Society also seems to illustrate these ideas, but transposes the cross for the butterfly. Two blue crosses made of eight rectangles each stand atop elongated columnar bases made up of quadrilaterals, triangles, diamonds, and squares. The bases fade from yellow toward green, emphasizing the mix of blue and yellow used to make green (figure 26). The four directions, the sacred wheel with its extensions toward sky and earth, and the concomitant interconnections between all parts seem here to be abstracted in shape and color.

A design by Meskwaki (Fox) student Cora Mae Battice shows four orange-red, elongated repeating diamonds that mirror each other with isosceles triangles winging out from the bottom diamond (figure 27). Below, squares decreasing in size complement the horizontal upper border of triangles punctuated by post-and-lintel rectangles. The color scheme is gradations of red with yellow, fading into orange. Like the artist who created the butterflies, Battice may have abstracted these geometric designs from her own physical and metaphysical landscapes. Shope relates the patterning to other Meskwaki traditional arts, and the red diamond iconography is potentially recognizable as otter backs or, perhaps, abstracted human bodies.[39] As it is for Dakota and Lakota, color is highly symbolic for Meskwaki as well. Two colors are especially important: green, signifying the creator, and red, signifying the Meskwaki people, the red-earth people.[40] Red can also signify joy and affirmation and is traditionally used on positive occasions to represent ideas of renewal and life.[41] Each clan in Meskwaki also has its own distinctive color. For example, the Thunder clan is yellow, the Bear clan, green, the Fox clan, red. This example from 1910 was made halfway through Battice's time at Carlisle. She attended school there from 1906 to 1916 and probably had many classes with De Cora.

De Cora cultivated her students' interest in designing rather than copying,

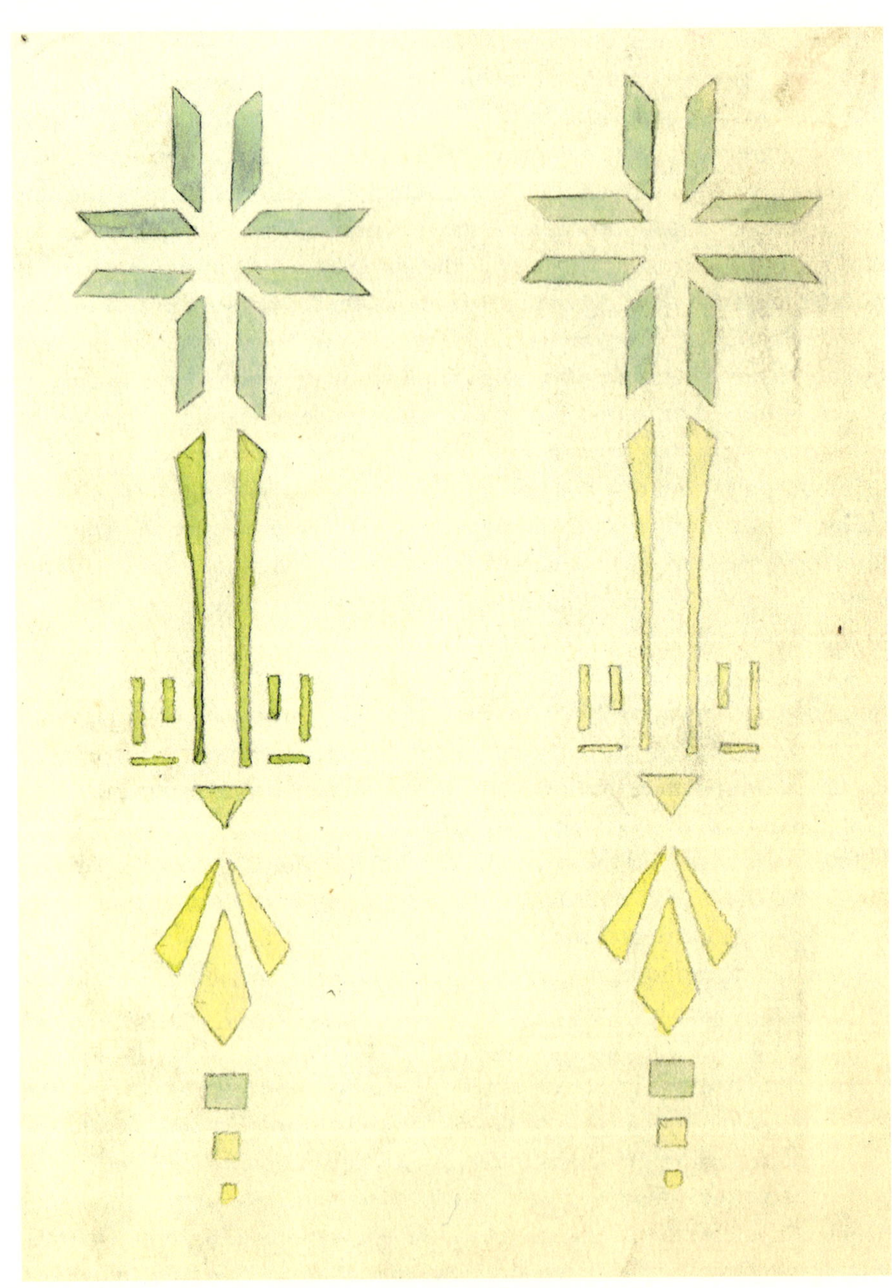

FIGURE 26. *Four Directions Design in Blue and Yellow,* watercolor, ca. 1910. Artist unknown. Cumberland County Historical Society.

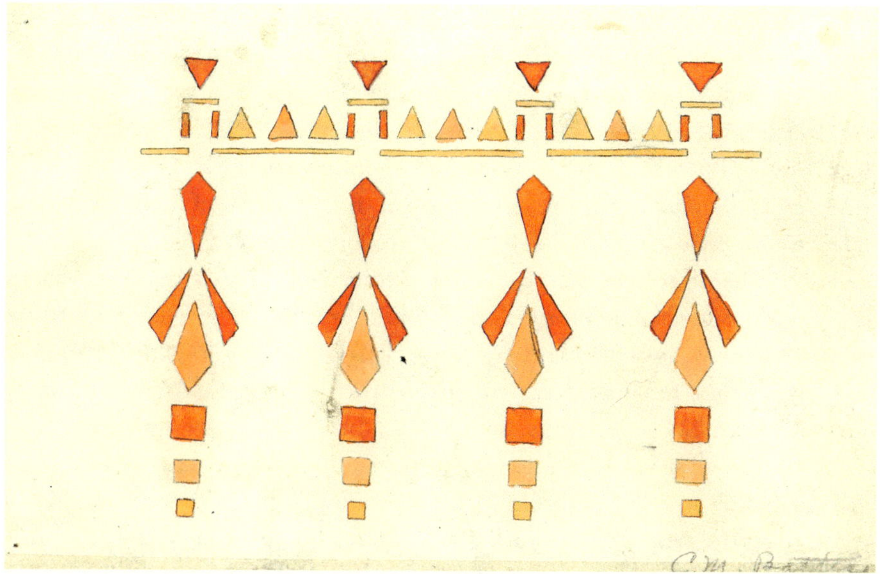

FIGURE 27. Cora Mae Battice, *Geometric Study of Color Harmony*, watercolor, ca. 1910. Cumberland County Historical Society.

and she allowed them to use colors meaningful to them. Although seemingly ambiguous to nonacculturated people, these abstractions and colors could represent and preserve ideas that would be easily and widely understood by people within the culture of those using them. Thus, as Shope suggests, "[t]ribally specific symbols serve as abbreviations for the belief systems . . . thereby made available to students."[42] Certain colors and symbols portrayed not only actual natural organisms (a butterfly) or landscape features, but also supernatural entities that inhabit and are embodied within the natural forms. They connected individuals, traumatized by assimilationist policies, to their distinct homes and heritages. De Cora also emphasized the sensitivity of Native women to nature and, in particular, the women's awareness of natural color harmonies. She stated:

> [Native women's] bold touches of green and red and yellow she has learned from nature's own use of these colors in the green grass and flowers. . . . [S]he makes strong color contrasts under the glare of the sun. . . . [T]his scheme of color has been called barbaric and crude.[43]

De Cora wanted her female students to express themselves in art as she had seen Native women do on reservations and at the fairs and as she herself attempted to do. Venturing outside was one way she sought to inspire them and refresh their memories of home and heritage. In the spring of 1907, De Cora took three of her female students ("winsome Indian maidens") on a field trip to Mount Holly. A short feature in the Carlisle *Arrow* describes their adventure: "They wended their way through a thick undergrowth and deep forest, to a spot described in tradition as 'the place of solitude.' . . . [T]hey gathered roots and various fruits known only to the Indian mind . . . ."[44] What used to be Mount Holly Park is now a conservation area in Cumberland County, Pennsylvania, fewer than ten miles from where Carlisle Industrial School was located. Pine and oak trees shade trails, while huckleberry, blueberry, and mountain laurel compete for rays of sunshine closer to the earth. Several creeks and springs, babbling over mountain rocks, flow down into a wetland.

Although the article set the outing within a romantic frame of "Indian lore," the trip exemplified De Cora's attempts to create community through art and experiences with nature. Articles suggest that De Cora led outdoor outings with gusto.[45] These outings were reported as "Indian" in their makeup—reinforcing the trope of Native American's inherent connection to nature. De Cora did not merely take students outside to copy or perpetuate stereotypes, however. She believed in drawing and design as a way to see the world, a way to elicit connection with one's culture; for her students, it was a way to rebuild through creative expression what they had lost.

Not only did De Cora take her female students outdoors on field trips, but in addressing the Madison, Wisconsin, women's club in 1914, De Cora maintained that Native American girls must pursue higher education. This was in contrast to the typical Indian school curriculum aimed at simply training students for labor. De Cora lamented that at Carlisle Native American girls received only half-day courses in academic subjects, with the remainder of the day devoted to domestic industries of baking, washing, and sewing. She discussed the resulting lack of opportunity in many of her talks on Native art between 1907 and 1914, focusing on her expertise in Native American design and its potential for widespread application to household items.[46]

The designs developed by De Cora and her students adapted Native American motifs for industrial settings and markets. But at the same time they restructured physical landscape into something symbolic, melding it with their worldviews *about* that landscape and thereby retaining the sacred and specific meanings of a specific tribal heritage. De Cora declared that

> I have taken care to leave my pupils' creative faculty absolutely independent and to let each student draw from his own mind, true to his own thought, and as much as possible, true to his tribal method of symbolic design. No two Indian drawings are alike and every one is original work. . . . What is more, the best designs were made by my artist pupils away from my supervision.[47]

Clearly, De Cora allowed for her students' autonomy to remember and to solve their own problems, not merely to create objects for market demand. She provided them with space to breathe.

Although De Cora believed in the role of education to develop young Native adults, development for her was more complex than mere industrial skill. Heritage and personal and intellectual experiences mattered: education was holistic. De Cora asserted that any advancement of Native Americans' position in the United States must follow practices allowing them to express their "natural" Native cultural traits: including that of designer. De Cora advocated for the racial distinction of Native Designer because she linked both "Native American" and "good design" to the natural world.

Design facilitated De Cora's ability to connect with students from a variety of tribal backgrounds and to guide them in producing functional items for white consumers. De Cora taught her students more than just basketry, beading, or rug weaving, but her students continued to make these products and market them to white consumers. At Carlisle, De Cora and her students showcased work in weekly exhibits and competitions, as well as in the publications the *Arrow, Indian Craftsman*, and *Red Man*.[48] Print was another medium, like baskets and rugs, that could bear individualized designs. While De Cora and her students' application of designs to newspapers, journals, and household items was in accord with the educational reforms of the day, their approach did not preclude individual expression and connection to nature. Thus although designs abstracted from nature were explicitly applied to consumer culture, mass media, and domestic handcrafts, the designs were rooted in Native American understanding and connection to nature and the land.

Safe Resistance

Although she espoused "natural" Native talent in design and acquiesced to marketing it, at Carlisle De Cora was resolute in preserving her autonomy as an artist and a teacher. In 1906, De Cora was living in New York, and her letters to Folsom during her years there clearly indicate her unhappiness. When she was visited by Indian Commissioner Francis Leupp and offered a position at Carlisle, to begin in early 1907, De Cora must have seen it as a way to escape the urban commercial artist box that she had stepped into. Furthermore, she wielded some power because of her previous successes and fame: she could teach how she wanted. Curtis wrote in 1912 that "Miss De Cora said she would only accept this position with the understanding that she would be allowed to develop the native art in a characteristic manner and be left quite free to apply this art to such industries as proved practicable."[49] Later, Curtis suggested that De Cora was even more adamant about her freedom, writing that she had said "I will take a Government position on one condition only . . . and that is that I shall not be expected to teach the white man's way, but shall be given complete liberty to develop the art of my own race and to apply this, as far as possible, to various forms of industries and crafts."[50] Already, De Cora was thinking about expanding how her future students, other Native Americans, and whites, thought about Native arts.

In 1911, De Cora explained to the Society of American Indians that she credited Native Americans with two languages: sign language and abstract symbols, or design.[51] She did so to promote — again — the inherent connection of Native art making with *being* Native American. She used this Pan-Indian racialist language because it was what was available to her as she worked within the dominant white cultural system. I have suggested that De Cora's designing was resistance, a form of coding. Whites are on the outside of the tribal system of knowledge; they do not deserve, nor are they *allowed,* to know the potential multiplicities of meaning that Native abstractions of motif and color might convey.

Charles Eastman, a Dakota physician born in Minnesota and educated in Boston, was an influential proponent of preserving Native rights and culture. At the SAI conference, he responded to De Cora's speech on Native art and design by suggesting that it was important for Indian art to retain its particularity to distinct tribes. He suggested that, to be effective, art had to be specific to tribal traditions and meanings. In other words, one's place and *being*—identity—may not be fully situated in a universal aesthetic. He confirmed that while the general might be understood by other Native Americans and whites alike, specificity itself adds to the potential for sacredness in symbol.[52] After additional commentary from Horton G. Elm, who asserted the need for Indians to assimilate—"to identify with every interest and phase of American life,"[53]—Sherman Coolidge (Arapaho) tellingly used a joke to remind his colleagues about Native Americans' distinctive use of humor, often missed by whites. Coolidge noted that "the race has a reputation for being too serious. [Laughter.] We want to assure them [whites] that we are not quite so serious."[54]A Pan-Indian aesthetic was safe for a white audience, but as with ironic humor, specific meanings behind motifs and colors could make such abstractions safe in their ambiguity—and still individually specific—for those who could identify such coding.

Whether or not conscious or intentional, De Cora was savvy, and she could be a smart-aleck and ironic. She expressed sarcastically in 1906 that repression of Native traditions "would have discouraged me too if I had been successfully CIVILIZED."[55] De Cora taught categories of Indian designs inspired by her students' tribes, and she did so to assist students' connections to their respective heritages. De Cora lambasted asinine copying. She left students to their own creative independence to draw "from their heads." She allowed her students opportunity for specificity and individuality. In a place of rigid rules and boundaries, such manifestations, as she modified them—from butterfly lesson plans to the idea(l) of the natural Native designer as particularly female—became parodies of the rules and tropes of white expectations.

Leupp, too, wanted teachers to instruct pupils in Native industries in ways that accorded with students' own tribal affinities, thereby making more authentic pieces for white consumers. His and other reformers' very sincere belief about the benefits of Native participation in industrial production are not ironic, however. As well as she could, De Cora worked within white society while maintaining the vivacity and value of her being as an individual, a woman, and a Native artist. She used her role as a teacher to show her students that they, too, were creative and Indigenous beings of worth, part of a community of Native Americans.

De Cora helped her students expand their worlds and see anew. She provided lenses for viewing their individual tribal heritage and showed them how to put that heritage into a larger context of Pan-Indianism for a white audience. Shope concludes that "[t]he nuances in the symbol systems . . . would be the empowering elements for the students," and that De Cora used "symbol systems to teach about cultures through these concise, subversive forms of discourse: teaching worldviews through the arts."[56] Hers was a worldview formed in and by conflict with the dominant ideology of reformers and settler-colonists; it is a worldview that emphasized the importance of humans acting in harmony with nature, understanding the reciprocity and necessary balance of men, women, plants, animals, and all creatures in the world. Through her actions and art, she modeled this holistic view, contra the "American" ethos.

However layered and multifaceted De Cora's illustrations and designs, in a commercialized display setting they were empty of individual, expressive meaning for most whites because the meaning they carried was outside dominant norms. Still, De Cora consistently maintained that Native Americans as creative individuals were not emptied, and that she and her students were not a cultural dumping ground. She told a crowd in Québec to "Go to [a Native American] if you think it worthwhile, and get his story. After he has given you what you want, don't think that what he gave out has left a vacancy in his spiritual nature for you to fill with your own ideas."[57] She derided lessons meant to produce "brown Caucasians." Rather, she sought to allow her students to transform their memories of nature through a Pan-Indian culture. Even if later merely applied to household items for sale, such as lace, curtains, or teapots, the designs would be their own.

De Cora's attempts to both accommodate and undermine white values through design reflect her idealism and autonomy. De Cora asserted her government education and Yankee female connections to communicate with and tap into multiple communities. Although her letters indicate that she never found teaching to be cathartic, design allowed De Cora both to reconnect with her specific cultural roots and to appease with a decorative nod calls for "Indian" authenticity as expected by whites. She brought tribal specificity and sacred nature together in her and her students' design work. She helped her students find a place in a white-dominant setting by promoting their connection to their cultural memory and heritage. It is clear from her students' work and her writings that De Cora believed that Native American students could access their shared "Indian" heritage, which included an innate connection to nature, and transform it into universally appealing and uplifting design that could be both functional and therapeutic. Through her pedagogy, De Cora helped to mend the cleavages that decades of violence had wrought in her and her students' identities, even while she *seemed* to be following white reformers' curricular guidelines to "improve" Native Americans by teaching them marketable and moral industry.

By 1911, things were falling apart at Carlisle.[58] The school's superintendent was under congressional investigation for financial mismanagement. The Native arts program ended in 1914, although De Cora continued to teach. Teaching at Carlisle often seemed a struggle for her; she mentions her desire to leave a few times over years of correspondence with Folsom. Perhaps she was disheartened by administrative changes, perhaps by the difficulties faced by her students, perhaps by the general lack of freedom at a boarding school, even for faculty. When Dietz took a position in Washington state, he and De Cora separated; she kept an apartment at Carlisle and then taught art at Camp Oahe, a summer camp for girls run by Charles and Elaine Eastman in Granite Lake, New Hampshire. By 1918, Carlisle had already closed, and Dietz and De Cora divorced on November 30, 1918. De Cora died from complications of influenza on February 6, 1919.

Just nine years after her death, the 1928 Meriam Report critiqued both allotment and government policies on Native American education. It recommended changes in education along the lines that De Cora had long practiced and advocated for her students—those of *choice* and *self-determination.* The report proposed that teachers be free to provide learning experiences based on the "life of the Indians about her," and thus reinforced De Cora's advocacy of adapting individually specific designs.[59] The autonomy De Cora created for herself and her students, even within the curriculum prescribed by Reel and other Native arts education reformers, helped retain not only her own cultural connection to home, but the connections of her students. De Cora Indigenized the curriculum at a time when white culture presumed total supremacy.

CONCLUSION
A SORT OF HOMECOMING

Objects are mnemonics for stories and mediators between self and place. People tell stories to find themselves in relation to family, community, and landscape: to define their lives and identities. Angel De Cora and Karen Thronson defined their lives and identities by maintaining connection to their home landscapes and to their traditions.

Karen Thronson and her family came to the United States encouraged by advertisements from corporations and letters from fellow countrymen and women. They came hoping to benefit from the promise of property ownership, and they mostly embraced U.S. industrial values. Evidenced by her dress, ornament, and other material culture and social institutions, Thronson followed suggestions like those appearing in magazines such as *Kvinden og Hjemmet* for finding ways to signal new world status; her daughters even more so as they rose into the ranks of middle-class America and embraced its norms. Importantly, they retained connection to family and ethnicity through church and small-town life. In fact, these social networks of mutual support facilitated their acculturation into dominant society. In church groups or within the neighborly reciprocity of a small town, Karen could sustain aspects of Norwegian being, such as embroidery, straw weaving, and lefse. Even while the products shifted to purses and pillows, design patterns remained similar, and a sense of relation within the ethnic community, particularly among the women, was engrained in the Thronsons' immigrant experience. Indeed, the support of family and an ethnic network helps explain why Karen Thronson chose to return to the Story City area of Iowa after her time homesteading in

Kansas. Thronson was able to retain connections to her family and place that allowed her to define her sense of self. In turn, that security facilitated social mobility for her family.

In contrast, De Cora's familial ties were restricted, and her physical relation to her home landscape was blunted. Fundamentally, white society sought to eradicate whatever connections Native Americans had to their families, clans, and places through policies of removal, industrial education, and allotment. They sought to replace Native values with capitalist values. Angel De Cora's family had been forcibly removed from their land a generation prior to hers. She was taken from her family to attend boarding school, and after that she lived far from both her family and the midwestern plains. Making a meager living as an artist-teacher, she survived in a country that had made every effort to repress and exterminate her people and their culture. Although forcibly separated from her community, De Cora never seemed to care much for money or property or for advancing herself, thus retaining some of the "communistic" beliefs of her heritage. She freely shared her knowledge with her students and gave away many of her art works to her friends, suggesting attempts to connect to place and people. De Cora used traditional, specific design patterns on the consumer products she made. In these ways, De Cora resisted the eradication of her group and their individual identities and defined herself.

Despite reformers' rhetoric of "uplifting" Native Americans, the so-called "American" dream of upward mobility was, and continues to be, reserved for those who benefit from the hierarchical structure of an economy that privileges wealth, material assets, and labor geared toward market production. Although De Cora took her allotment on the reservation, she sold it when her patent became unencumbered in 1909, and she never owned a home in the East. Property ownership was not fundamental to her ideas of liberty or identity. Furthermore, De Cora married late in life, her marriage failed, and she remained childless. The consequent independence allowed her to create art, but at a personal cost; even through her art she could not fully create a home for herself.

De Cora's "choices" within the system were mostly false choices. Natalie Curtis suggested in her obituary of De Cora that "the Indian is indeed a foreigner on his own soil when it comes to recognition as a human being."[1] De Cora illustrated the ambivalence she felt as a "foreigner" on her own land because of her personal and tribal displacement. She used the tools at her disposal—illustration and design—to address the demand for Indian art then in vogue and to present truthful representations of distinct Native American homelands, dress, and symbolism. Such representations no doubt helped appease the nostalgia she felt for her homeland.

The modes of colonizing the American lands included first removal and then forcing the colonizer's "civilizing" institutions on the Indigenous people. Government and charitable resources were garnered to support boarding schools, missions, and agricultural development on reservations, ostensibly to "help" Native Americans assimilate to "American" values. Native Americans became immigrants, forced to new homes in this domineering cultural landscape. Many of De Cora's personal letters indicate her tendency to slip into melancholy, even depression, when she was alone working in the eastern cities of New York and Boston, where the contrast between her homeland and traditions and Yankee white cultural spaces was obvious. Like many migrants, she found solace thinking of her home, even while she professed gratitude that she had not succumbed to the effects of reservation life. The psychological trauma she felt as a child and into her adulthood as a result of her boarding-school experience was complicated by her close relationship to her teachers at Hampton and to her friends, white people who wanted to believe their assimilation policies were working. De Cora was strategic in maintaining her autonomy from white culture and her relations to her home via her art, an art that she used to raise her status among whites. Her work resonated with various audiences because its visual language operated on multiple levels.

Although De Cora was recognized as an artist by whites, she was seen as such only within a larger narrative about Native American "success." Whites never let her forget her Indianness—nor did she want to—but she wanted to define it and herself. Lomawaima and McCarty regard choice and self-determination as fundamental human rights that have not only been denied to Native Americans but also to children, especially minoritized children. De Cora asserted herself and her students—all Native Americans—as artists. Artists were creative and free, and this included women artists and designers. In De Cora's model, artists naturally had more space to claim an identity and culture.

To be sure, De Cora made art for a market, as she was asked to do. Commodity capitalism may have emptied her students' work of meaning—at least, for those consumers without cultural connection or a relationship to the objects or motifs. De Cora used the rhetoric of Pan-Indianism and an essentialist view of Native Americans' capacity for design to separate her motivation for production from the market. She cultivated this "essential" aspect of Native identity among her students to help them connect to self, community, and home. Through the generalization of Pan-Indianism, De Cora's and her students' work was commodified, made "safe" for consumers. As demonstrated by their work, she provided her students with choices and the potential to connect, both opportunities they had been denied. Indeed, De Cora employed culturally sustaining pedagogy before the term existed; she Indigenized the curriculum by providing multiple entry points for her students to relate to their pasts and to find autonomy, even self-expression. She helped them to see themselves as Native Americans, even while the United States consistently tried to eradicate that identity through education and displacement.

Karen Thronson maintained tradition by passing down Norwegian symbols and techniques to her daughters and granddaughters. Self-definition and freedom for them was easier in some ways because her community validated her sense of Norwegian female identity. She, her mother, Carrie, her daughter Rachel, and her niece Henrietta relocated from Mankato, Kansas, to a small farm near Ellsworth, Iowa, taking in boarders and likely selling cream and butter for income. To add to the household income, Rachel and Henrietta worked as domestic servants.

Similarly placed immigrant women found support in ladies' aid societies and in the community provided by womens' magazines. The small handcrafted objects women made provided physical connection to both their old-world home and the new homes in the United States they sought to create. For many women immigrants, these goods also provided a mechanism for some economic control in a society that often muted women's voices. As white Protestants, however, people like Karen and her family benefited from the support of community and from the basic ways that community structures correlated with those of the dominant Anglo society.[2]

The stories of women have often been overlooked. The stories of immigrant and Native American women share some aspects, but the distinction between settler immigration and forced migration and the ramifications on community support systems and individual and collective sovereignty loom large. The structural embedding of settler colonial narratives has affected the kind of stories told. Many follow familiar narrative paths: perseverance, labor, and charity, supported by values such as hard work, family, and faith. Values undergird cultural and individual ideologies and ethics — including patriotism, perhaps, or community commitment to a worldview incorporating care for others. Where immigrant stories might be triumphant, Indigenous stories involve perseverance ("survivance") of a different kind. De Cora's visual creations helped her to cope by connecting her to her love of the Nebraska landscape, thereby retaining ties to her home place. De Cora had "her own way" and owned her art. Ostensibly fitting into the capitalist model, at the same time she resisted white supremacy by incorporating styles, materials, and a Native perspective that was not simplistic or exoticized.

SIGNIFICANT FOR my enterprise here, connection to place is facilitated by images and objects and by how their creation helps to keep each of us mindful of our relationships with history, the natural world, and other humans. How objects are used or commodified — or not — matters. How community and solidarity is created or fractured matters. Angel De Cora understood the potential for inculcating students' sense of self and community through making, even if the result was white "industrial" Native arts, and she asserted her own ideas by modifying the Carlisle curriculum. Karen Thronson and Norwegian immigrant women, on the other hand, had ready access to cultural heritage and community.

Situatedness — knowing one's roots and connection to a place and community, both physical and relational — is key to defining self. As art educator Sally Gradle notes,

> The lack of a sense of place — of belonging or attachment — is often a serious by-product of transnational migration, of increased economic and social mobility, and of the pervasive characteristics of a homogenous consumer-scape. If we are to understand an increasingly turbulent and mobile society in which many experience a loss of identity, boundary conflicts that are both long lasting and complex, and symbolic attachments to places both remembered and imagined, a discussion of place is essential.[3]

As the great-granddaughter of Karen Thronson, I have benefited from the structures of settler colonialism. Her daughters became teachers and lawyers;

I am a university professor. The thread that binds Thronson, De Cora, and me goes beyond gender, race, and the legacy of settler colonialism. In the face of white male supremacy, we each find power in situating ourselves through the act making meaning using the phenomena around us and by forming community. If De Cora's motto was to have "her own way," Thronson's was to "stay close to kin." De Cora had to distinguish herself as a Native American woman artist to find community; Thronson already fit into one as a Norwegian woman. Freedom lies in creating—in telling one's own story, one's own past, to define oneself. By telling our interwoven stories, we are all a little more connected and therefore a little more empowered.

NOTES

CHAPTER ONE

1. Readers interested in additional details of De Cora's life should consult Linda M. Waggoner, *Fire Light* (Norman: University of Oklahoma Press, 2008).

2. The pervasiveness of the American "frontier myth" is articulated Richard Slotkin, *Gunfighter Nation: The Myth of the Frontier in Twentieth-Century America* (New York: Atheneum, 1992), 1–26, especially.

3. Between 1866 and 1870, yearly numbers of passengers from Norway disembarking from sailing vessels in Québec averaged 10,413. Québec was the port of choice because, after 1847, duties there were lower than those in New York. Between 1850 and 1865, only two years saw yearly arrivals range as low 6,000: 1857 and 1861. In 1866 alone, 13,506 Norwegians arrived, and in 1867, 11,620. See Odd Lovoll, *Across the Deep Blue Sea: The Saga of Early Norwegian Immigrants* (St. Paul: Minnesota Historical Society, 2015), 45, 105.

4. This was the "first wave" of Norwegian immigration to the United States, in the years 1866 to 1872. L. DeAne Lagerquist, *In America the Men Milk the Cows: Factors of Gender, Ethnicity, and Religion in the Americanization of Norwegian-American Women* (Brooklyn: Carlson, 1991), 42; see also Elliott Robert Barkan, *From All Points: America's Immigrant West, 1870s–1952* (Bloomington: Indiana University Press, 2007).

5. See especially Lovoll, *Across the Deep Blue Sea,* and *Norwegians on the Prairie: Ethnicity and the Development of the Country Town* (St. Paul: Minnesota Historical Society, 2006).

6. The *Helvetia* was built in 1852 at Bremerhafen in Germany. The bark was 451 tons gross and could carry around 250 passengers. Under the captaincy of R. Larsen, Karen and her family sailed six weeks, from May 2 until June 17, 1867, arriving in Québec. Library and Archives Canada preserves the passenger list; see National Archives Canada, C-4522, list 45, RG-76, item 281. The manifest was dated June 18, 1867.

7. In addition to Karen (13), Ole (9), and Sever (Sjur, 8), the manifest includes a Cecelia Sletten (11) and a Marthinus Sletten (6), not mentioned in E. Roy's memoir. Jacob was born in Wisconsin and died in 1942 in Los Angeles; it appears that Cecelia and Marthinus may not have lived past childhood.

8. Population booms in Norway's limited agricultural regions and a tradition of landownership based on primogeniture precipitated migration of families into northern Norway and across the Atlantic to the United States. See Lovoll, *Across the Deep Blue Sea,* 67–72. Lovoll describes port cities like Bergen and Oslo as inundated with *bønde* (landowning) Norwegians waiting for passage on sailing barks bound for North America. *Across the Deep Blue Sea,* 88–89.

9. Lagerquist, *In America the Men Milk the Cows,* 14.

10. Quoted in Theodore C. Blegen, *Norwegian Migration to America 1825–1860,* vol. 1 (Northfield, MN: Norwegian-American Historical Association, 1931), 368.

11. For more on coverture and women, citizenship, and the expansion of suffrage in the Midwest, see Sara Egge, *Woman Suffrage and Citizenship in the Midwest, 1870–1920* (Iowa City: University of Iowa Press, 2018), 12–13.

12. Evelyn Nakano Glenn, *Unequal Freedom: How Race and Gender Shaped American Citizenship and Labor* (Cambridge, MA: Harvard University Press, 2002), 41–43.

13. See especially William Unrau, *The Kansa Indians: A History of the Wind People, 1673–1873* (Norman and London: University of Oklahoma Press, 1986), xix, 148.

14. Concerning the railroads through Kansas Indian territories, see Craig Miner and William Unrau, *The End of Indian Kansas: A Study of Cultural Revolution, 1854–1871* (Lawrence: University Press of Kansas, 1990), 27.

15. From "Committee Report," October 29, 1871. In April 1872, Barclay White reports: "[A]pplications are now pending for the right-of-way for RailRoads across three Reservations, and it is probable one or more RailRoads will soon pass over the lands held by the Santee Sioux." Friends Historical Library, Swarthmore College (FHLSC). "Convention of Delegates from the Seven Yearly Meetings (Hicksite) on Indian Affairs," Central Executive Committee Records, Box 1 (ser. 1), 26–27, 33.

16. Quoted in D. S. Otis, *The Dawes Act and the Allotment of Indian Lands* (Norman: University of Oklahoma Press, 1973), 14.

17. Miner and Unrau, *The End of Indian Kansas,* 3–5.

18. See Waggoner, *Fire Light,* 7–10, 17–23.

19. Significantly, land in Iowa is automatically passed along to the next of kin. Therefore, documenting the marriage at the county seat legalized any potential future land transfer from husband to wife or to their (future) children, upon Mons's or Helge's death. In Kansas and Iowa, joint tenancy on the deed or a transfer on death deed is needed to transfer land. The joint tenancy of Mons and Karen is indicated on the quitclaim deeds for the school and church, where both Mons and Karen are listed, and the mortgages that Mons and Karen took out against the land include "Mons Thronson & W," that is, "and wife." After Mons's death, Karen is listed as "guardian" in the mortgage listed in deed records from 1888.

20. Mons asserted his intention on October 19, 1868, in Dane County, as indicated in the Final Naturalization Paper from the District Court of the Fifteenth Judicial

District of the State of Kansas, included in NARA RG49 Records of BLM Land Entry Files, Kansas, Concordia, 1871–89. Certificate no. 10392, Homestead Application no. 12052.

21. According to family history, the Seversons and Thronsons had seeded wheat and made it through the winter in Iowa, but the families were forced out by what E. Roy described as "a gang of Irish claim-jumpers" armed with revolvers and other weapons. He describes the Seversons and Thronsons as being so scared that they left in wagons as soon as they could, shipping the rest of their goods by rail.

22. Center Township List of Residents, 1872, Jewell County Recorder's Office.

23. Olsen arrived, via Chicago, in 1869 and was originally from Kongsvinger (east of Oslo, in Glåmdalen district). See the entry on "Cloud and Jewell Counties, Kansas" in Martin Ulvestad, *Norwegians in America, Their History and Record*, vol. 1, trans. Olaf Tronsen Kringhaug and Odd-Steinar Dybvad Raneng (Waukon, IA: Astri My Astri, 2010), 188.

24. Ulvestad, *Norwegians in America,* vol. 1, 188.

25. Ole Rynning, "A Truthful Account of America for the Instruction and Help of the Peasant and Commoner Written by a Norwegian Who Came There in the Month of June, 1837," trans. Theodore C. Blegen, *Minnesota History* (1917): 260.

26. Johan Reinert Reiersen, *Pathfinder for Norwegian Emigrants,* trans. Frank G. Nelson (Northfield, MN: Norwegian American Historical Association, 1981), 68, 160, 183. See also Betty Bergland, "Norwegian Immigrants and *Indianerne* in the Landtaking 1838–1862," *Norwegian-American Studies* 35 (2000): 331.

27. Willa Cather elegantly describes the trials of the early years of Swedish immigrants on the Nebraska plains in language suggesting whites' struggle to overcome primitive conditions, but she never addresses the debates over the "reforms" of her day. See, for example, Willa Cather, *O Pioneers!,* ed. Sharon O'Brien, Norton Critical Edition (New York: Norton, 2008), 16.

28. According to the Kanza / Kaw Nation's tribal history, "The treaty of 1825 reduced the tribe's 20 million-acre domain to a 30-mile wide 2 million-acre reservation beginning just west of future Topeka. Promised annuities were seldom delivered or were obligated to unscrupulous traders, while disease decimated the tribal population. When railroad, town and land speculators coveted the 1825 treaty lands, the Treaty of 1846 further reduced Kaw territory to 256,000 acres at present-day Council Grove. The subsequent Treaty of 1859 removed the town of Council Grove from Kaw lands and gave the tribe only 80,000 of the poorest acres, subdivided into 40-acre plots for each family. Finally, on May 27, 1872, over the strong protests of Chief Allegawaho and his people, a federal act moved the Kanza to a 100,137-acre site in northern Kay County, Oklahoma." Accessed April 2, 2018, http://kawnation.com/?page_id=72.

29. Railroad pamphlets and maps served as enticements and guides for white

Yankee Americans and more recent immigrants from Europe. Agents, often working for transport companies, published narratives in Danish and Norwegian to entice possible emigrants. Railroad and transport companies ran advertisements and passed out fliers on church lawns; pastors and agents wrote newspaper articles. Railroads did everything they could to support homesteaders. They helped build grain elevators, ice houses, and stock yards; displayed modern farming equipment; provided free pamphlets on how to increase crop yield and improve livestock; and even provided free stud livestock. Some railroad companies also provided boarding for emigrants searching for homesteads and inexpensive "houseseeker" tickets and special emigrant-rate one-way tickets. For more on the role of emigrant agents, see Lovoll, *Across the Deep Blue Sea,* 90–95.

30. See Waggoner, *Fire Light,* especially 7–12 and 17–23.

31. In 1975, the Winnebago tribe was awarded $4.6 million by the Indian Claims Commission for the land it had lost in the 1837 land cession treaty.

32. Waggoner, *Fire Light,* 20–21.

33. Linda M. Waggoner, "Sibley's Winnebago Prisoners: Deconstructing Race and Recovering Kinship in the Dakota War of 1862," *Great Plains Quarterly* 33, no. 1 (2013): 25–48.

34. Waggoner notes that Ho-Chunk overlapped across the arbitrary boundaries of state lines. "There was an original Wisconsin core group, but all in all the Wisconsin Ho-Chunk were pretty mixed up. There was also a core group who remained in Minnesota and became citizens—but many of their children and grandchildren migrated back and forth to live in Nebraska and Wisconsin." Personal correspondence.

35. Angel De Cora, "An Autobiography," *Red Man,* March 1911, 279.

36. Francis Paul Prucha, "Introduction," *Americanizing the American Indians*, ed. Francis Paul Prucha (Cambridge, MA: Harvard University Press, 1973), 4.

37. Marinella Lentis, *Colonized Through Art: American Indian Schools and Art Education, 1889–1915* (Lincoln: University of Nebraska Press, 2017), 32.

38. Quoted in Otis, *The Dawes Act and the Allotment of Indian Lands,* 9.

39. "We have, to begin with, the absolute need of awakening in the savage Indian broader desires and ampler wants. To bring him out of savagery into citizenship we must make the Indian more intelligently selfish before we can make him unselfishly intelligent. We need to *awaken in him wants. . . .* The Indian must learn that he has no right to give until he has earned, and that has no right to eat until he has worked for his bread. Our teachers on the reservations know that frequently lessons in home-building, and providence for the future of the family which they are laboriously teaching, are effaced and counteracted by the old communal instincts and customs which bring half a tribe of kins-people to settle down at the door of the home." Merrill E. Gates, "Addresses at the Lake Mohonk Conferences," in

Americanizing the American Indian (Cambridge, MA: Harvard University Press, 1973), 332, 334–35.

40. Prucha, "Introduction," 8.

41. The archives of this short relationship between 1869 and 1884 are held in the Friends Historical Library on the campus of Swarthmore College, Pennsylvania (FHLSC).

42. Egge, *Woman Suffrage and Citizenship,* 11.

43. Andrew Jones, *Memory and Material Culture* (Cambridge: Cambridge University Press, 2007), 27.

44. Mihaly Csikszentmihalyi and Eugene Rochberg-Halton, *The Meaning of Things: Domestic Symbols and the Self* (Cambridge: Cambridge University Press, 1981), 16.

45. Some anthropologists and philosophers have moved toward investigating object-oriented ontology. Such an approach may be useful and relevant within some situations (where "things might be treated *sui generis* as meanings") but I choose not to pursue this radical essentialism with my examples. See for example, *Thinking through Things: Theorising Artefacts Ethnographically*, eds. Amiria Henare, Martin Hobraad, and Sari Wastell (London and New York: Routledge, 2007), and Jane Bennett, *Vibrant Matter: A Political Ecology of Things* (Durham: Duke University Press, 2010).

46. Simon Bronner notes that "folk art" as an aesthetic term was publicized and popularized by Holger Cahill of the Newark Museum. He organized the show *American Folk Art: The Art of the Common Man in America, 1750–1900* at the Museum of Modern Art in 1932. Cahill defined folk art as the "expression of the common people, made by them and intended for their use and enjoyment. It is not the expression of professional artists made for a small cultured class, and it has little to do with the fashionable art of its period." He further explained, "It is the work of people with little book learning in art techniques, and no academic training." Quoted in Simon J. Bronner, *Grasping Things: Folk Material Culture and Mass Society in America* (Lexington: University Press of Kentucky, 1986), 192–93. It is worth noting that the alienation many audiences (including many of my undergraduate students) feel from some contemporary art is because they have difficulty accepting any work when they learn that an artist did not manipulate materials.

47. Texts including Alfred Haddon's *The Evolution of Art* (1895) and Thomas Wilson's *Primitive Industry* (1894) confirmed that handmade things were primitive and not modern. See Bronner, *Grasping Things,* 145.

48. Roszika Parker initially noted redefining embroidery from craft to "art" reified hierarchies and thus is problematic. Rozsika Parker, *The Subversive Stitch: Embroidery and the Making of the Feminine* (London: Women's Press, 1984), 5–6.

49. See Bronner, *Grasping Things,* 119.

50. Nancy Osterud writes: "Over time, through a long process of change . . . the ability of women to produce their families' living declined, largely because of capitalist penetration of consumption and capitalist control and reorganization of the farm operations, such as poultry, that were formerly conducted independently by women." Nancy Grey Osterud, "Gender and the Transition to Capitalism in Rural America," *Agricultural History* 67, no. 2 (1993): 27.

51. Waggoner, *Fire Light,* xvii–xviii.

52. See Evelyn Nakano Glenn, *Forced to Care* (Cambridge, MA: Harvard University Press, 2010), 42–45. On white women training Native American women to make lace, see Kate C. Duncan, "American Indian Lace Making," *American Indian Art Magazine* 5, no. 3 (1980): 28–35, 80.

53. Anthea Callen, *Women Artists of the Arts and Crafts Movement, 1870–1914* (New York: Pantheon, 1979), 214–15.

54. Folsom wrote: "Too Indian to consider money values and too modest to push her own work, she made more gifts than sales." Cora Folsom, "Angel Decora Dietz," *Southern Workman* 48, no. 3 (March 1919): 105.

55. See Osterud, "Gender and the Transition to Capitalism in Rural America," 26–7, and Barbara Handy-Marchello, *Women of the Northern Plains: Gender and Settlement on the Homestead Frontier, 1870–1930* (St. Paul: Minnesota Historical Society, 2005), 61, 76–77, 84.

56. Barbara Handy-Marchello, *Women of the Northern Plains,* 84.

57. Appropriation, juxtaposition, metaphor, and trivialization are each methods of coding that can be used in various art forms (literature, poetry, song, visual art). Coding can be complicit, explicit, or implicit. Implicit coding may not be deliberate or even conscious, but it can still convey significant information. With implicit coding, demonstrating evidence of coding in material culture is, then, necessarily part of the feminist enterprise. Joan N. Radner and Susan S. Lanser, "Strategies of Coding in Women's Cultures," in *Feminist Messages: Coding in Women's Folk Culture,* ed. Joan N. Radner (Urbana and Chicago: University of Illinois Press, 1993), 10–17.

58. For coded messages in quilts, see especially Daryl M. Hafter, "Toward a Social History of Needlework Artists," in *Woman's Art Journal* 2, no. 2 (1981–82): 25–29; in crochet and lace, see Rachel Maines, "Fancywork: The Archaeology of Lives," *Feminist Art Journal* 3, no. 4 (1974–75): 1–3.

59. Many periodicals were published by women within the male-dominated Arts and Crafts movement, for example, including the *Craftsman.* See Catherine Zipf, *Professional Pursuits: Women and the American Arts and Crafts Movement* (Knoxville: University of Tennessee Press, 2007), 12.

60. Anne Ruggles Gere, "An Art of Survivance," *American Indian Quarterly* 28, no. 3–4 (2004): 649–84; Gerald Vizenor, *Manifest Manners: Narratives on Postindian Survivance* (Lincoln: University of Nebraska Press, 1999), vii.

61. See especially, Lorenzo Veracino, *The Settler Colonial Present* (London: Palgrave-Macmillan, 2015).

62. Slotkin, *Gunfighter Nation,* 10–14.

CHAPTER TWO

1. Mary B. Kelly, *Embroidering the Goddesses of Old Norway* (Hilton Head, SC: Studiobooks, 2008).

2. Many Norwegian immigrant women on the plains, such as Karen Ødegaard Solem and Martha Lima, initially lamented the lack of trees. Solum wrote to her mother in Nannestad, Norway, from South Dakota in 1886: "I think so often about the dear old mountain ash trees around the cottage at home; there are no trees here." Similarly, Lima wrote to her parents-in-law in Stavanger from North Dakota in 1894: "We have a very wide—to my taste, a much too wide—view from our house. Greatly do I miss water, river, mountain, and woods . . . ." Solum described the flat land of Dakota as "beautiful" when it was covered in wheat and oats. She wrote: "Dakota is a flat land with some hills along the river. The land mostly all over is nice black loam or soil and will yeald [*sic*] good crops once it is broke [*sic*] up. . . . I have never seen such beautiful wheat since I have come here as this year, but we do not have so much planted this year. We have mostly flax; we also have 50 acres of oats that is so beautiful that it is enjoyable to see it." Letter from Karen Solem to "My Dear Amalie," July 21, 1895. Quoted in Lori Ann Lahlum, "'There Are No Trees Here': Norwegian Women Encounter the Northern Prairies and Plains" (PhD diss., University of Idaho, 2003), 92–93.

3. Peggy Lowe, "The Lasting Heritage of the Homestead Act," *Harvest Public Media,* July 8, 2012, accessed October 21, 2018. https://info.umkc.edu/harvestpublicmediaarchive/2012/07/08/the-lasting-heritage-of-the-homestead-act/.

4. In Iowa in 1870 and 1880, only 17 percent of residents were foreign born. See U.S. Census Reports 1870, and Egge, *Woman Suffrage,* 19.

5. Egge, *Woman Suffrage,* 52.

6. NARA RG49 Records of BLM Land Entry Files, Kansas, Concordia, 1871–89, Certificate no. 10392, Homestead Application no. 12052.

7. Jewell County Recorder's Office, Assessment Rolls Value of Taxable Personal Property, Center Township, 1877.

8. This was equivalent to $31.21 in 2017. In 1870, wheat was $1.04/bushel, or $18.91 in 2017 dollars; in 1880, $0.95/bushel ($22.10); in 1890, $0.84/bushel ($22.11); in 1900, $0.62/bushel ($17.71); and in 1910, $0.91/bushel ($22.75). Wheat prices accessed April 5, 2017; see http://www.kansasagland.com/agblogs/how-low-are-wheat-prices-take-a-look-back-at/article_c3a60410-0fbb-581e-a4c5-cbf9d5d0a171.html.

9. Tables 1 and 2 in Wilfred H. Pine, "100 Years of Farmland Value in Kansas,"

Kansas State Agricultural Experiment Station Bulletin 611 (Manhattan: Kansas State University, 1977), 3.

10. Craig Miner, *West of Wichita: Settling the High Plains of Kansas, 1865–1890* (Lawrence, KS: University Press of Kansas, 1986), 56.

11. Perhaps Helge may have taken out mortgages to assist his daughter in these times of need. Helge's sons, Karen's brothers Ole and Sever, were old enough to help farm; Jacob, the youngest, was fifteen, also of age to help.

12. Jewell County Recorder's Office, Land Transfer Index.

13. See also Lagerquist, *In America the Men Milk the Cows,* 59.

14. These traditions are paralleled in the census records of the Thronsons and Seversons. They further explain Carrie and Helge's relatively advanced ages compared to their children: they perfectly fit the Norwegian social norm of having children in one's thirties. Lagerquist, *In America the Men Milk the Cows,* 16–17.

15. Kathleen Stokker, *Keeping Christmas: Yuletide Traditions in Norway and the New Land* (Saint Paul: Minnesota Historical Society, 2000), 66.

16. Kathleen Stokker, "*Julebukk:* Christmas Masquerading in Norwegian America," in *Norwegian American Essays*, ed. Knut Djupedal, 28–39 (Oslo: NAHA, 1993), 32.

17. Stokker, "*Julebukk,*" 29, 36.

18. Laurann Gilbertson, "To Ward Off Evil: Metal on Norwegian Folk Dress," in *Folk Dress in Europe and Anatolia*, ed. Linda Welters (Oxford and New York: Berg, 1999), 199–210; and Kelly, *Embroidering the Goddesses of Old Norway,* 7–9.

19. Kelly, *Embroidering the Goddesses of Old Norway*, 7–9.

20. Frigg is the only one other than Odin permitted to sit on his high seat, Hlidskjalf, and look out over the universe. Galina Krasskova, *Exploring the Northern Tradition* (Newburyport: New Page, 2005), 45. For earthly high seat textiles woven with goddess motifs, see Kelly, *Embroidering the Goddesses of Old Norway*, and *Goddess Embroideries of the Northlands* (Hilton Head, SC: Studiobooks, 2007).

21. Marion Nelson, "Folk Art of Norway," in *Norwegian Folk Art: The Migration of a Tradition*, ed. Marion Nelson, 37–88 (New York and London: Abbeville Press, 1995), 43–44.

22. Gottfried Keller, *Der Grune Heinrich* (1854), quoted in Kelly, *Embroidering the Goddesses of Old Norway,* 9.

23. Hamilton County Recorder's Office Land Transfer Index (accessed April 10, 2017).

24. Joan M. Jensen, *Promise to the Land: Essays on Rural Women* (Albuquerque: University of New Mexico Press, 1991), 189, 202.

25. Women in cities and rural communities pressed flowers, colored and arranged sand, and glued objects together, and with each process transforming "this exciting but dangerous 'outside' into an acceptable component of the 'inside' . . . [t]he craftswoman improved on nature by preserving, cleansing, arranging and

fixing the materials that nature had left in chaos." Talia Schaffer, "Women's Work: The History of the Victorian Domestic Handicraft," in *Crafting the Professional in the Long Nineteenth Century*, ed. Kyriaki Hadjiafxendi and Patricia Zakreski (Farnham and Burlington: Ashgate, 2013), 26–27.

CHAPTER THREE

1. De Cora, "An Autobiography," 281.

2. *Fire Light* (c. 1901), shows a teepee, arbor, and two figures with horses in the foreground. Like this image, the illustrations for "Gray Wolf's Daughter" correspond to the drawings De Cora created at Fort Berthold Reservation in North Dakota during the summer of 1897. Waggoner, *Fire Light,* xiii.

3. Waggoner, *Fire Light,* xxvi, 3–13. De Cora's parents were David De Cora and Elizabeth LaMere. David was the fourth son of Ho-Chunk chief Little De Cora. Elizabeth LaMere was the first child born to a French-Canadian fur trader at Lake Koshkonong, Wisconsin, and a Ho-Chunk métis, Catherine Amelle, making her one-quarter Ho-Chunk.

4. K. Tsianina Lomawaima and Teresa L. McCarty define a safety zone as "an area where dangerously different cultural expressions might be safely domesticated and thus neutralized." *"To Remain an Indian": Lessons in Democracy from a Century of Native American Education* (New York: Teacher's College Press, 2006), xxii.

5. De Cora elucidates for Folsom her recollections of the "kidnapping" in a letter dated January 29, 1912. She wanted to assuage her dear friend of any guilt. She reiterates that neither her mother nor her uncle, Frank LaMere, had any idea she was leaving and did not sign any consent forms. But she also says she is glad for her training. HUA Angel De Cora Boxes 8–9.

6. See for example, Erik Trump, "'The Idea of Help': White Women Reformers and the Commercialization of Native American Women's Arts," in *Selling the Indian: Commercializing and Appropriating American Indian Cultures*, ed. Carter Jones Meyer and Diana Royer (Tucson: University of Arizona Press, 2001), 159–89.

7. See records of the Society of Friends meetings; for example, "An Inventory of the Records of the Executive Central Committee of the Convention of Delegates from the Seven Yearly Meetings (Hicksite) on Indian Affairs, 1869–1884," RG 4/017 Box 1, FHLSC. For discussion of the creation of this stereotype, see Katherine M. Weist, "Beasts of Burden and Menial Slaves: Nineteenth-Century Observations of Northern Plains Indian Women," 29–52, and Mary Jane Schneider, "Women's Work: An Examination of Women's Roles in Plains Indian Arts and Crafts," 101–21, both in *The Hidden Half: Studies of Plains Indian Women*, ed. Patricia Albers and Beatrice Medicine (Washington, D.C.: University Press of America, 1983).

8. Superintendent of Indian Affairs Barclay White concluded in April 1872 that

"The Indians of Nebraska are improving in their condition and gradually advancing in civilization, and if present just and humane policy is continued toward them, I am firm in the opinion that the youth of the present generation may be made useful citizens of the State." From "An Inventory of the Records of the Executive Central Committee of the Convention of Delegates from the Seven Yearly Meetings (Hicksite) on Indian Affairs, 1869–1884," RG 4/017 Box 1, Ser. 1, 32, FHLSC.

9. Waggoner, *Fire Light,* 12.

10. De Cora, "An Autobiography," 281.

11. Cora Folsom, "Angel Decora Dietz," *Southern Workman* 48, no. 3 (March 1919): 104.

12. HUA, De Cora, Box 11. De Cora, "An Autobiography," 285.

13. Report from Lake Mohonk Conference, 1895. Michael Coleman notes that many Native Americans who attended boarding schools in their youth had highly mixed responses to the experience. "At least one hundred other Indian men and women, who attended missionary and government school from 1850 through 1930, remembered that as children they too responded in diverse and ambivalent ways." Michael C. Coleman, *American Indian Children at School, 1850–1930* (Jackson: University Press of Mississippi, 1993), x.

14. More than 1,388 Native American children went to Hampton between 1877 and 1923. Donal F. Lindsey, *Indians at Hampton Institute, 1877–1923* (Urbana and Chicago: University of Illinois Press, 1995), i.

15. Quoted in Waggoner, *Fire Light,* 61.

16. Quoted in Waggoner, *Fire Light,* 77–78.

17. The image is itself based on photographs probably taken at Fort Berthold, extant in the Hampton archives. The photograph of a teepee with trees and horse corresponds directly to the left half of the watercolor, while a photograph of a couple in a wagon may also have provided a source for the wagon on the right half of the watercolor. HUA Angel De Cora Box 11.

18. Waggoner has described the story and its connection to De Cora's "broken home" in *Fire Light,* 44–47. She also notes that the handwritten version of De Cora's other short story for *Harper's,* "The Sick Child," is much more reflective and personal, rather than conforming to the trope of a stoic Indian that appears in the version published by *Harper's.* It also differs from a typescript version of the story that follows reformist ideals. Waggoner, *Fire Light,* 85–86.

19. Robin Kimmerer, *Braiding Sweetgrass: Indigenous Wisdom, Scientific Knowledge and the Teachings of Plants* (Minneapolis: Milkweed Press, 2013).

20. Natalie Curtis describes the eagle at the top and bottom of the title page, and the eagle symbol connecting the symbols of the eagle's song as the border. See Curtis's description of "Drawings" in the prefatory pages of *The Indians' Book* (New York and London: Harper, 1907).

21. Gere, "An Art of Survivance," 661.

22. Jane Simonsen, *Making Home Work: Domesticity and Native American Assimilation in the American West, 1860–1919* (Chapel Hill: University of North Carolina Press, 2006), 198.

23. Radner and Lanser, "Strategies of Coding in Women's Cultures," 23.

24. See also Waggoner, *Fire Light,* 91–95.

25. Letter to Folsom dated October 14, 1902, HUA Angel De Cora Box 8–9. Emphasis in original.

26. See also Waggoner, *Fire Light,* 112, 115, 119–25.

27. As "great summarizers of culture, world's fairs molded the world into an 'ideologically coherent symbolic universe, confirming and extending the authority of the [host] country's leadership.'" Sarah J. Moore, "Mapping Empire in Omaha and Buffalo: World's Fairs and the Spanish-American War," *Bilingual Review* 25 (2000): 111–12. See also Robert Rydell, *All the World's a Fair: Visions of Empire at American International Expositions, 1876–1916* (Chicago and London: University of Chicago Press, 1984), and Nancy J. Parezo and Don D. Fowler, *Anthropology Goes to the Fair: The 1904 Louisiana Purchase Exposition* (Lincoln: University of Nebraska Press, 2007).

28. Margaret Creighton, *The Electrifying Fall of Rainbow City: Spectacle and Assassination at the 1901 World's Fair* (New York: W.W. Norton & Co., 2016), 10; Parezo and Fowler, *Anthropology Goes to the Fair,* 2; Michelle Ryan Bewley, "The New World in Unity: Pan-America Visualized at Buffalo in 1901," *New York History* 84, no. 2 (2003): 200; Rydell, *All the World's a Fair,* 129–30, 157.

29. Rydell, *All the World's a Fair,* 113–14.

30. Rydell, *All the World's a Fair,* 156–57.

31. Quoted in Nancy J. Parezo and John W. Troutman, "The 'Shy' Cocopa Go to the Fair," in *Selling the Indian: Commercializing and Appropriating American Indian Cultures,* ed. Carter Jones Meyer and Diana Royer (Tucson: University of Arizona Press, 2001), 10. Parezo and Fowler's comprehensive study of the Louisiana Purchase Exposition and Creighton's recent work on the Pan-American Exposition illuminate the realities of organizing such large live ethnographic displays, their implications, and the various modes of resistance used by the people in these displays.

32. Parezo and Troutman, "The 'Shy' Cocopa Go to the Fair," 30.

33. *Trans-Mississippi International Exposition, Omaha, June to November 1898: Art, Manufacturing, Mechanics, Commerce, Science, Music: Illustrating the Progress of the West* (n.p.: n.p., 1898), accessed June 29, 2017, http://trans-mississippi.unl.edu/texts/view/transmiss.book.tmie.1898.html.

34. *Official Catalogue and Guide Book to the Pan-American Exposition* (Buffalo: C. Ahrhart, 1901), 26.

35. United States, Office of Indian Affairs, *Annual Report of the Commissioner*, 49.

36. See for example: Arthur Goodrich, "Short Stories of Interesting Exhibits," *World's Work* 2, no. 4 (1901): 1054–96, and Nicholas Murray Butler, "The Educational Influence of the Exposition," *Cosmopolitan* 31, no. 5 (1901): 538–40. The entire September issue (volume 31) of the *Cosmopolitan* is dedicated to the Pan-American Exposition.

37. See Mary Bronson Hart, "How to See the Pan-American Exposition," *Everybody's Magazine* 25, no. 5 (October 1901): 489, and Edward Hale Brush, "Pan-American's Midway: Some of the Amusement Features for the Big Buffalo Exposition," *North Adams Transcript*, June 17, 1901.

38. Brush, "Pan-American's Midway."

39. *The Rand-McNally Hand-Book to the Pan-American Exposition, Buffalo and Niagara Falls* (Chicago and New York: Rand McNally, 1901).

40. *Art Hand-Book, Official Handbook of Architecture and Sculpture and Art Catalogue to the Pan-American Exposition,* ed. David Gray (Buffalo, NY, 1901). For the mention of Tarbell and Tryon, see Hart, "How to See the Pan-American Exposition," 490.

41. United States, Office of Indian Affairs, *Annual Report of the Commissioner*, 47–49.

42. The fair's organizers hoped to highlight the West; many of the exhibitions were put on by western states, including Iowa, Kansas, Nebraska, Colorado, and Montana. De Cora's paintings were shown in the "Indians and Indian-School Life" section of the Government Building exhibit. This exhibit, like the 1901 exhibit, was organized by Alice Fletcher. De Cora contributed three oil paintings she had completed while at Fort Berthold in 1897: *The Medicine Lodge* and two untitled head studies of Native Americans. See Waggoner, *Fire Light,* 83–84.

43. United States, Office of Indian Affairs, *Annual Report of the Commissioner*, 48.

44. Natalie Curtis reprinted images in her article "The Perpetuating of Indian Art," in 1913 (*Outlook,* issue 105, 1913: 630–31). While there are a few photographs by F. A. Rinehart of the 1898 exposition, none suggest De Cora's work specifically; accessed June 29, 2017, http://trans-mississippi.unl.edu/photographs.html. See also F. A. Rinehart, *Photogravures of the Trans-Mississippi and International Exposition, Held at Omaha, Nebraska, June 1st to November 1st, 1898* (Omaha, 1898), accessed June 29, 2017, https://archive.org/stream/photogravuresoftootran#page/n21/mode/2up. Lentis reproduced NARA photos of the Indian schools' display at the Pan-American Exposition in her book, but De Cora's specific contributions are not visible. Lentis, *Colonized through Art*, 238.

45. For more on De Cora and Dietz's contributions to the St. Louis Fair, see Waggoner, *Fire Light,* 123–25.

46. Max Carocci, *Warriors of the Plains: The Arts of Plains Indian Warfare* (Montreal and Ithaca: McGill-Queen's University Press, 2012), 48–49.

47. Ruth B. Phillips, "Dreams and Designs: Iconographic Problems in Great Lakes Twined Bags," in *Great Lakes Indian Art*, ed. David W. Penney (Detroit: Wayne State University Press/ Detroit Institute of Art, 1989), 61.

CHAPTER FOUR

1. Karen Hansen compellingly argues the fluidity of the public and private as gendered spheres in her discussion of *social* spheres among working-class people in antebellum New England. See *A Very Social Time: Crafting Community in Antebellum New England* (Berkeley: University of California Press, 1996).

2. "[W]omen's unpaid caring was simultaneously priceless and worthless" in a political system where earning and property were the primary bases for the entitlements for citizenship. Evelyn Nakano Glenn, *Forced to Care* (Cambridge, MA: Harvard University Press, 2010), 35–36.

3. See especially Glenn, *Forced to Care,* 43–87.

4. Philip Martin, *Rosemaling in the Upper Midwest: A Story of Region and Revival* (Mt. Horeb: Wisconsin Folk Museum, 1989).

5. Marco Santana, "Ladies' Home Journal to Cease Monthly Publication," *Des Moines Register,* April 24, 2014.

6. Laurann Gilbertson and Karen Olsen, "Piecing Together a New Home: Needlework in *Kvinden og Hjemmet* Magazine" (paper presentation, Textile Society of America Ninth Biennial Symposium, Oakland, California, October 7–9, 2004), 15; http://digitalcommons.unl.edu/tsaconf/429. See also the October 1904 issue of *Kvinden og Hjemmet,* which states its circulation as 82,560. Early issues often included copyright and circulation information on the front page.

7. Glenda Riley, *The Female Frontier: A Comparative View of Women on the Prairie and the Plains* (Lawrence: University Press of Kansas, 1988), 56–57, 88. On making the flat landscape "homelike" by making it familiar, see also Julie Roy Jeffrey, "'There Is Some Splendid Scenery': Women's Responses to the Great Plains Landscape," *Great Plains Quarterly* 8, no. 2 (1988): 69–78.

8. Hardanger was the most common form of embroidery worked by immigrants in Utah. See Rachel Gianni Abbott, "The Scandinavian Immigrant Experience in Utah, 1850–1920: Using Material Culture to Interpret Cultural Adaptation" (PhD diss., University of Alaska-Fairbanks, 2013), 332. Also Åse Elin Langeland, "Adjusting to America: A Study in *Kvinden og Hjemmet:* A Monthly Journal for the Scandinavian Women in America, 1888–1947" (master's thesis, University of Bergen, 2001), and Gilbertson and Olsen, "Piecing Together a New Home."

9. Luther College professor Harley Refsal's grandmother, Wilhelmine Tønnesen Brekke, and her family did not have much money when they emigrated to Minnesota. To contribute to the family economy, Wilhelmine made different types of lace work and collected samples of what she could make in a book to show potential

customers. See photograph in Matunda Bigirimana and Karen Sveen, "Det Norske Flyttelasset," *NRK,* January 12, 2018, accessed February 21, 2018. https://www.nrk.no/kultur/xl/det-norske-flyttelasset-til-amerika-1.13861298.

10. *Kvinden og Hjemmet,* June 1908, 228, translated in Langeland, "Adjusting to America," 31.

11. Adaptation by combination also occurred in the language of haandarbeide feature: English terms like *centerpiece* and *pillow sham* and even *tatting* are often used in the same sentence as the Norwegian words for the items being made. Gilbertson and Olsen also surveyed *Ladies' Home Journal* and the textile-specific magazine, *Modern Priscilla,* for the same thirty-year period to compare how these English-language publications included Hardanger needlework and quilting information. Gilbertson and Olsen document that "[d]uring the peak years, 1900 to 1915, 23% of the *Kvinden og Hjemmet* issues examined and 18% of *Modern Priscilla* issues contained patterns and/or advertisements for hardanger embroidery or supplies. From 1915 to 1930, 7% of *Kvinden og Hjemmet*s and 6% of *Modern Priscilla*s contained hardanger embroidery patterns or ads." Gilbertson and Olsen, "Piecing Together a New Home," 17.

12. Gilbertson and Olsen, "Piecing Together a New Home," 17.

13. American thread manufacturers had published patterns for Hardanger as early as 1895. Gilbertson and Olsen, "Piecing Together a New Home," 16.

14. It is interesting to note that the few advertisements for "Indian Art" in *Ladies' Home Journal* were printed in issues from 1900 and 1901. An article, "Charm of the Indian Basket," by George Wharton James, appeared in September 1902 (p. 19), with an advertisement alongside it on the same page. Otherwise, the magazine provides little evidence of interest in Native American Art between 1900 and 1908.

15. "New Designs in Swedish Needlework," *Ladies' Home Journal,* July 1908, 32.

16. Special threads had to be ordered; Norwegian American women could order supplies for embroidery by mail, initially from *Kvinden og Hjemmet* and later from the Norwegian Shop, a Chicago business that frequently advertised in the magazine in both English and Norwegian. My second cousin told me that my grandmother and great-aunt both knew Hardanger.

17. Carol Colburn, "'Well, I Wondered When I Saw You, What All These New Clothes Meant': Interpreting the Dress of Norwegian-American Immigrants," in *Material Culture and People's Art among the Norwegians in America,* ed. Marion Nelson (Northfield: Norwegian American Historical Association, 1994), 118–39.

18. Marion Nelson, "Norwegian Folk Art in America," in *Norwegian Folk Art,* ed. Marion Nelson, 90.

19. Abbott, "The Scandinavian Immigrant Experience in Utah," 287.

20. Henry Glassie, "Structure and Function, Folklore and Artifact," *Semiotica* 7 (1973): 344.

21. Gilbertson and Olsen, "Piecing Together a New Home,"15.

22. Langeland, "Adjusting to America" 38, 45–46.

23. From *Kvinden og Hjemmet,* February 1905, 109; translated and quoted in Langeland, "Adjusting to America," 46.

24. From *Kvinden og Hjemmet,* May 1917, 109; quoted and translated in Langeland, "Adjusting to America," 46.

25. Riley, *The Female Frontier,* 56–57, 100.

26. "Newest Designs in Tatting," *Ladies' Home Journal,* July 1908, 44.

27. Alford established the Royal School of Art Needlework for gentlewomen in reduced circumstances in 1872. In her book *Needlework as Art* (London, 1886), she wrote that "if the unity of nature is an accepted fact, then the acceptance of the unity of art must follow. Art must be considered as the selection of natural phenomena by individual minds capable of assimilating and reproducing them in certain forms and with certain materials adapted to the national taste, needs, and power of appreciation. . . . [I]f man cannot create original materials, he can invent combinations . . . this is Art." Quoted in Kyriaki Hadjiafxendi and Patricia Zakreski, eds., *What Is a Woman to Do? A Reader on Women, Work, and Art c. 1830–1890* (Oxford: Peter Lang, 2011), 262.

28. For a comparison of different ethnic denominations' activities, see Egge, *Woman Suffrage,* 55–64.

29. Osterud, "Gender and the Transition to Capitalism in Rural America," 28.

30. Osterud, "Gender and the Transition to Capitalism," 28.

31. Sandra L. Myres, *Westering Women and the Frontier Experience, 1800–1915* (Albuquerque: University of New Mexico Press, 1982), 204–7.

32. https://www.census.gov/prod/www/decennial.html.

33. Lovoll, *Norwegians on the Prairie,* 4.

34. *The History of Hamilton County* (Dallas: Curtis Media Corporation, 1986), C34.

35. Immanuel was initially Hauge Synod. The United Church, Hauge Synod, and Norwegian Synod all came together in 1917 to form the Norwegian Evangelical Lutheran Church of America. Immanuel's frame church was dedicated September 10, 1899, in a location just east of the present Story City Clinic parking lot. After some short-term pastoral help, the congregation voted in 1900 to extend a call to Pastor Thor T. Heimarck, who served the congregation until his retirement in 1945. See http://www.immanuelstorycity.org/#/about-us/our-history.

36. Immanuel Lutheran Church Annual Meeting Records, vol. 1, beginning 1898, p. 45. The minutes read:

> Immanuel Congregation held their annual meeting on January 6, 1902. The meeting started with song, Bible reading and prayer. Reverend Heimarck was elected chairman of the meeting. Minutes from last meeting read and approved. L. H. Sævereide was elected secretary of the meeting. The following persons had applied for congregation membership:

Andres Matre
Hokan Frette with his family
Sivert Nordskog with his family
Sam Egemo with his family
Mrs Thronson with her daughter
Miss Larson
Elisabeth Gundersen
Ole Gundersen
Edvart Gundersen
Decision: All applicants approved members of Immanuel Congregation.

I am grateful to Harald Dyrkorn for the transcription and translation from Norwegian to English.

37. Lagerquist, *In America the Men Milk the Cows,* 107, 133–36.

38. Immanuel Lutheran Church Annual Meeting Records, vol. 1, beginning 1898, Immanuel Lutheran Budget Records, 1904–1918, 67, 74.

39. The 1905 Iowa census indicates Karen was the head of the household; the 1910 census indicates Carrie was with her, along with a boarder, Elias Rasmussen, and a servant, Christina Larson. The 1910 census also clearly shows just how many more Norwegians and Norwegian-speaking neighbors Carrie and Karen had in Ellsworth than they had had in Mankato, Kansas: Ellsworth was dominated by Norwegians.

40. Ole Rynning, "A Truthful Account of America," 121–22; Lagerquist, *In America the Men Milk the Cows*, 37.

41. "[T]hey are foreigners, they don't even speak English!" is what my mother says the Parretts lamented about Rachel. On the Thronson side, Rachel's choice to marry outside of the Norwegian Lutheran immigrant community may initially have been equally problematic. Young women in Norway often worked on their parents' farm or hired out to other farms until they married, usually late in their twenties. On the relatively late age for marriages in Norway, see Lagerquist, *In America the Men Milk the Cows,* 15–16.

42. Egge, *Woman Suffrage,* 182.

CHAPTER FIVE

1. For more on De Cora's involvement with the Society of American Indians, see Waggoner, *Fire Light,* 189–95, 198–200.

2. See also Waggoner, *Fire Light,* 166–69.

3. Angel De Cora, "An Effort to Encourage Indian Art," in *Congrès International des americanistes XVe Session* (Québec: Dessault and Proulx, 1907), 208.

4. See also Waggoner, *Fire Light,* 173.

5. "Indian Art as Valuable Asset," *Philadelphia Inquirer*, February 2, 1913.

6. Lentis, *Colonized Through Art,* 48.

7. Lindsey, *Indians at Hampton Institute,* 180. See also Waggoner, *Fire Light,* 31–37.

8. "Extracts from the Report of the Commissioner of Indian Affairs: Improvement, Not Transformation," *Arrow* 2, no. 20 (1906): n.p.

9. Elizabeth Hutchinson, *The Indian Craze: Primitivism, Modernism, and Transculturation in American Art, 1890–1915* (Durham and London: Duke University Press, 2009); see also Lentis, *Colonized Through Art,* 76.

10. Simonsen, *Making Home Work,* 184–85.

11. Lentis, *Colonized Through Art,* 35–37.

12. See especially the extract from Morgan in Prucha, *Americanizing the American Indians,* 221–38.

13. United States, Office of Indian Affairs, *Annual Report of the Commissioner*, 69. Quoted in Lentis, *Colonized Through Art,* 37.

14. Lentis, *Colonized Through Art,* 41–44. For a brief history of art education at Carlisle, see especially Linda F. Witmer, *Changing Images: The Art and Artists of the Carlisle Indian Industrial School* (Carlisle: Cumberland County Historical Society, 2008).

15. Lentis, *Colonized Through Art,* 44–45.

16. Lentis, *Colonized Through Art,* 72.

17. Quoted in Lentis, *Colonized Through Art,* 73, from *Report of the Superintendent of Indian Schools,* 1898, 6.

18. An article in the 1906 *Arrow,* "Indian Qualities That Should Be Preserved," concluded that the Indian "is not silly," he is "dignified," "self-possessed," "generous," and devout. Curtis reiterated in her obituary of De Cora that Native Americans are "a people who are natural potters, weavers, designers, workers in metal and in textiles" ("An American Indian Artist," 66). For more information on and an analysis of Carlisle's publications, see especially Jessica Ruggieri Matthews, "Killing a Culture to Save a Race: Writing and Resisting the Discourse of the Carlisle Indian School" (PhD diss., George Washington University, 2005).

19. Dietz and De Cora met at the St. Louis exposition in 1904 and were married in 1907. Dietz's Native American heritage has been widely disputed. Waggoner, *Fire Light,* 186–88, and Waggoner, "On Trial: The Washington R*dskins' Wily Mascot, Coach William 'Lone Star' Dietz," *Montana: The Magazine of Western History* 63, no. 1 (2013): 24–47.

20. The photograph appears on a postcard sent to Carrie Andrews from Angel De Cora, December 24, 1912. HUA Box 11.

21. Lentis, *Colonized Through Art,* 88–89.

22. De Cora, "An Effort to Encourage Indian Art," 206.

23. De Cora, "An Effort to Encourage Indian Art," 207.

24. De Cora, "An Effort to Encourage Indian Art," 205.

25. See Waggoner, *Fire Light,* 157–58.

26. Hutchinson, *The Indian Craze*, 204; Simonsen, *Making Home Work*, 205–6.

27. De Cora, "Native Indian Art," in *Report of the Twenty-Sixth Annual Meeting of the Lake Mohonk Conference of Friends of the Indian and Other Dependent Peoples*, edited by Lilian D. Powers (Lake Mohonk Conference of Friends of the Indian and Other Dependent Peoples, 1908), 17.

28. De Cora, "Native Indian Art," 18.

29. De Cora, "Native Indian Art," in the Report of the Executive Council on the Proceedings of First Annual Conference of the Society of American Indians (Columbus, Ohio, 1911, 1912), 85.

30. De Cora, "Native Indian Art" (1911, 1912), 85.

31. Quoted in Gere, "An Art of Survivance," 665.

32. Cumberland County Historical Society, PI 4-13-5, PI 4-13-8, PI 4-13-10.

33. CCHS PI-7-9, PI-7-11. *Study in Color Harmony* (n.d.) was made by Lillian Rice, and a stencil of the same butterfly design was made by Eunice Bartlette.

34. Lentis, *Colonized Through Art,* 53–54.

35. Bartlette is mentioned as Chippewa in the *Arrow,* 1910, 34.

36. Suzanne Alene Shope, "American Indian Artist Angel Decora: Aesthetics, Power, and Transcultural Pedagogy in the Progressive Era," (PhD diss., University of Montana, 2009), 201.

37. Shope, "American Indian Artist Angel Decora," 203.

38. Shope, "American Indian Artist Angel Decora," 203.

39. Shope, "American Indian Artist Angel Decora," 209–11.

40. Quote from Meskwaki artist Brenda Ackerman, available at Iowa State Textiles and Clothing Museum information page, accessed July 14, 2017, https://textilesclothingmuseum.wordpress.com/tag/meskwaki/.

41. Adapted from University of Iowa Museum of Art information page, accessed July 14, 2017, http://thestudio.uiowa.edu/ocm/artiowa/wp/?page_id=543.

42. Shope, "American Indian Artist Angel Decora," 204.

43. De Cora, "An Effort to Encourage Indian Art," 207.

44. "Winnebago Camp," *Arrow,* June 7, 1907.

45. The *Arrow* reports De Cora's hiking trip as "sport" away from "civilization" where she led "three Indian maidens" to hike and camp, gathering roots and fruit to have an "Indian feast" and sing "Indian Songs." "Winnebago Camp," *Arrow,* June 7, 1907. See also Waggoner, *Fire Light,* 143–44.

46. De Cora, "Native Indian Art," *Arrow* 3, no. 49 (1907), 1; De Cora, "Native Indian Art" (1907), 16–18; De Cora, "Native Indian Art" (1911, 1912), 82–93. These articles, while sharing titles and themes, have slightly different texts. Reports on her talks, cited in Waggoner, 223–25, appeared in the *Wisconsin State Journal,* "The Indian

Girl Must Have Public Education," October 9, 1914, and the *Madison Democrat,* "Women's Club Holds Session in Honor of Feminine Delegates to Indian Conference," October 11, 1914.

47. De Cora, "An Effort to Encourage Indian Art," 208.

48. The Carlisle press printed catalogues with lists and photographs of the art and crafts made by Native American students that were for sale. These catalogues were certainly for a white consumer audience, while the *Arrow* and the illustrated magazines generally seem to have been published for student and staff readership. The title of *Indian Craftsman* was changed to *Red Man* after complaints concerning Gustav Stickley's similarly named journal, *Craftsman.*

49. Quoted in Waggoner, 132, from *Saratogian,* "Miss Natalie Curtis's Talk in Saratoga," May 15, 1912.

50. Natalie Curtis, "An American Indian Artist," *Outlook,* January 14, 1920, 65.

51. De Cora, "Native Indian Art," (1911, 1912), 84. See also Waggoner, *Fire Light,* 189–95.

52. "[W]hite people, who have mixed the different characteristics of the different tribes, so that you cannot tell an Arapahoe from a Sioux now, and cannot tell a Cheyenne from a Crow. I hope that in this gathering we will come to some realization of these things in the proper sense; that we may take a backward step, if you please, in art, not in the sense of lowering our standard, but returning to the old ideas that are really uplifting, and are a purer basis for character building, and that we may conserve and preserve some of these beautiful principles which were the very inspiration of the North American Indian." Response to De Cora, "Native Indian Art," (1911, 1912), 88.

53. Horton G. Elm, response to De Cora, "Native Indian Art" (1911, 1912), 90–91.

54. Rev. Sherman Coolidge, response to De Cora, "Native Indian Art" (1911, 1912), 91.

55. De Cora, "Effort to Encourage Indian Art," 207. Emphasis in original.

56. Shope, "American Indian Artist Angel Decora," 227.

57. De Cora, "An Effort to Encourage Indian Art," 205.

58. Waggoner details the issues at Carlisle; see *Fire Light,* 210–37.

59. See Gere, "An Art of Survivance," 675, and Lomawaima and McCarty, "*'To Remain an Indian,'*" 65.

CONCLUSION

1. Natalie Curtis, "An American Indian Artist," *Outlook,* January 14, 1920, 66.

2. My grandmother, Rachel's daughter Esther, had been a working mother too, teaching first in a one-room school house and then in a school in Fairfield, to provide supplemental income. In addition to these incomes, the women followed

the tradition of their immigrant relatives and continued to make and sell butter and cream to the local co-op, even after my grandmother had moved "in town" to Fairfield with her husband, Leland "Jack," in 1942. Esther did not speak or write Norwegian, but she did know the designs for stars, how to make lefse, and how to make and sell cream; and although she did not use the word *lutefisk,* she described eating salted dried cod. Although Karen and Rachel knew Hardanger, my grandmother Esther may never have learned the technique specifically, or how to tat, but she crocheted, embroidered, and quilted. She was part of the Fairfield First Presbyterian Church Circle, notably attending evening meetings; other Circle meetings took place in the morning and afternoon.

3. Sally Gradle, "Ecology of Place: Art Education in a Relational World," *Studies in Art Education* 48, no. 4 (2007): 392.

BIBLIOGRAPHY

Abbott, Rachel Gianni. "The Scandinavian Immigrant Experience in Utah, 1850–1920: Using Material Culture to Interpret Cultural Adaptation." PhD diss., University of Alaska-Fairbanks, 2013.

Alaimo, Stacy. *Undomesticated Ground: Recasting Nature as Feminist Space.* Ithaca: Cornell University Press, 2000.

Albers, Patricia, and Beatrice Medicine, eds. *The Hidden Half: Studies of Plains Indian Women.* Washington, D.C.: University Press of America, 1983.

Anderson, Laura, and Karen Gold. "Creative Connections: The Healing Power of Women's Art and Craft Work." *Women and Therapy* 21, no. 4 (1998): 15–36.

Appel, Livia, and Theodore C. Blegen. "Official Encouragement of Immigration to Minnesota During the Territorial Period." *Minnesota History Bulletin* 5, no. 3 (1923): 167–203.

Augé, Marc. *Non-Places: An Introduction to an Anthropology of Supermodernity.* Translated by John Howe. London and New York: Verso, 1997.

Barkan, Elliott Robert. *From All Points: America's Immigrant West, 1870s–1952.* Bloomington: Indiana University Press, 2007.

Bergland, Betty A. "Norwegian Immigrants and *Indianerne* in the Landtaking, 1838–1862." *Norwegian-American Studies* 35 (2000): 319–50.

Bergland, Betty A., and Lori Ann Lahlum, eds. *Norwegian American Women: Migration, Communities, and Identities.* St. Paul: Minnesota Historical Society, 2011.

Bewley, Michelle Ryan. "The New World in Unity: Pan-America Visualized at Buffalo in 1901." *New York History* 84, no. 2 (2003): 179–203.

Bigirimana, Matunda, and Karen Brodshaug Sveen. "Det Norske Flyttelasset" [Baggage from Norway]. NRK [Norwegian Broadcasting Company], January 12, 2018.

Bjorkhaug, Hilde, and Arild Blekesaune. "Masculinisation or Professionalisation of Norwegian Farm Work: A Gender Neutral Division of Work on Norwegian Family Farms?" *Journal of Comparative Family Studies* 38, no. 3 (2007): 423–34.

Bjørkvik, Halvard. "The Social and Economic Background of Folk Art in Norway." In *Norwegian Folk Art: The Migration of a Tradition*, edited by Marion Nelson, 119–24. New York: Abbeville Press, 1995.

Blegen, Theodore C. *Norwegian Migration to America 1825–1860*. Vol. 1. Northfield, MN: Norwegian-American Historical Association, 1931.

———. *Norwegian Migration to America: The American Transition*. Northfield, MN: Norwegian-American Historical Association, 1940.

Bogue, Allan G. "The Iowa Claim Clubs: Symbol and Substance." In *The Public Lands: Studies in the History of the Public Domain*, edited by Vernon Carstensen, 47–70. Madison: University of Wisconsin Press, 1962.

Boivan, Nicole. *Material Cultures, Material Minds: The Impact of Things on Human Thought, Society, and Evolution*. Cambridge: Cambridge University Press, 2008.

Brody, J. J. *Indian Painters and White Patrons*. Albuquerque: University of New Mexico Press, 1971.

Bronner, Simon J. *Grasping Things: Folk Material Culture and Mass Society in America*. Lexington: University Press of Kentucky, 1986.

Broude, Norma, and Mary D. Garrard, eds. *The Expanding Discourse: Feminism and Art History*. New York: Icon/Harper and Row, 1992.

———, eds. *Feminism and Art History: Questioning the Litany*. New York: Harper and Row, 1982.

Broughton, Trev. "Auto/Biography and the Actual Course of Things." *Feminism and Autobiography*, edited by Cosslett, Lury, and Summerfield, 241–46.

Brush, Edward Hale. "Pan-American's Midway: Some of the Amusement Features for the Big Buffalo Exposition." *North Adams Transcript*, June 17, 1901.

Buchanan, William. *The Pan-American Exposition*. Buffalo: Baker, Jones, 1901.

Butler, Nicholas Murray. "The Educational Influence of the Exposition." *Cosmopolitan* 31, no. 5 (1901): 538–40.

Cajete, Gregory. *Look to the Mountain: An Ecology of Indigenous Education*. Durango, CO: Kivaki, 1994.

Callen, Anthea. *Women Artists of the Arts and Crafts Movement, 1870–1914*. New York: Pantheon, 1979.

Carocci, Max. *Warriors of the Plains: The Arts of Plains Indian Warfare*. Montreal and Ithaca: McGill-Queen's University Press, 2012.

Casey, Edward. "How to Get from Space to Place in a Fairly Short Stretch of Time: Phenomenological Prolegomena." In *Senses of Place*, edited by Steven Feld and Keith Basso, 13–52. Sante Fe, NM: School of Advanced Research Press, 1996.

Cather, Willa. *O Pioneers*! Edited by Sharon O'Brien, Norton Critical Edition. New York: Norton, 2008.

Cherry, Deborah. *Beyond the Frame: Feminism and Visual Culture, Britain 1850–1900*. London: Routledge, 2000.

Cobb, Amanda J. *Listening to Our Grandmother's Stories: The Bloomfield Academy for Chickasaw Females, 1852–1949*. Lincoln: University of Nebraska Press, 2000.

Colburn, Carol. "'Well, I Wondered When I Saw You, What All These New Clothes

Meant': Interpreting the Dress of Norwegian-American Immigrants." In *Material Culture and People's Art among the Norwegians in America*, edited by Marion Nelson, 118–55. Northfield: Norwegian American Historical Association, 1994.

Coleman, Michael C. *American Indian Children at School, 1850–1930*. Jackson: University Press of Mississippi, 1993.

Conzen, Kathleen Neils. "Historical Approaches to the Study of Rural Ethnic Communities." In *Ethnicity on the Great Plains*, edited by Frederick C. Luebke, 1–18. Lincoln: University of Nebraska Press, 1980.

Cosslett, Tess. "Matrilineal Narratives Revisited." In Cosslett, Lury, and Summerfield, *Feminism and Autobiography*, 141–53.

Cosslett, Tess, Celia Lury, and Penny Summerfield, eds. *Feminism and Autobiography: Texts, Theories, Methods*. London and New York: Routledge, 2000.

Creighton, Margaret. *The Electrifying Fall of Rainbow City: Spectacle and Assassination at the 1901 World's Fair.* New York: W. W. Norton, 2016.

Csikszentmihalyi, Mihaly, and Eugene Rochberg-Halton. *The Meaning of Things: Domestic Symbols and the Self.* Cambridge: Cambridge University Press, 1981.

Curtis, Natalie. "An American Indian Artist." *Outlook,* January 14, 1920, 64–66.

———. *The Indians' Book.* New York and London: Harper and Brothers, 1907.

———. "The Perpetuating of Indian Art." *Outlook,* November 22, 1913, 623–31.

De Cora, Angel. "An Effort to Encourage Indian Art." Paper presented at the Congrès International des americanistes, Québec, 1906. In *Congrès International des americanistes XVe Session.* Québec: Dessault and Proulx, 1907.

———. "Native Indian Art." *Arrow* 3, no. 49 (1907): 1.

———. "Native Indian Art." In *Report of the Executive Council on the Proceedings of the First Annual Conference of the Society of American Indians,* 82–93. Columbus, OH: Washington, D.C., Society of American Indians, 1911, 1912.

———. "Native Indian Art." In *Report of the Twenty-Sixth Annual Meeting of the Lake Mohonk Conference of the Friends of the Indian and Other Dependent Peoples*, edited by Lilian D. Powers, 16–18. N.p.: Lake Mohonk Conference of Friends of the Indian and Other Dependent Peoples, 1908.

———. *See also* Henook-Makhewe-Kelenaka.

Dodge, Richard Irving. *Plains of the Great West and Their Inhabitants, Being a Description of the Plains, Game, and Indians of the Great American Desert.* New York: Putnam and Sons, 1876.

Donovan, Josephine, and Carol J. Adams, eds. *The Feminist Care Tradition in Animal Ethics.* New York: Columbia University Press, 2007.

Duncan, Kate C. "American Indian Lace Making." *American Indian Art Magazine* 5, no. 3 (1980): 28–35, 80.

Eastman (Ohiyesa), Charles. "'My People:' The Indians' Contribution to the Art of America." *Craftsman* 27, no. 2 (1914): 179–86.

Edwards, Richard. “Changing Perceptions of Homesteading as a Policy of Public Domain Disposal.” *Great Plains Quarterly* 29, no. 3 (2009): 179–202.

Effland, Anne B., Denise M. Rogers, and Valerie Grim. “Women as Agricultural Landowners: What Do We Know About Them?” *Agricultural History* 67, no. 2 (1993): 235–61.

Egge, Sara. *Woman Suffrage and Citizenship in the Midwest, 1870–1920.* Iowa City: University of Iowa Press, 2018.

Eldridge, Laurie A. “Ruthe Blalock Jones: Native American Artist and Educator.” *Visual Arts Research* 35, no. 2 (2009): 72–85.

Ellingsgard, Nils. *Norwegian Rose Painting in America: What the Immigrants Brought.* Translated by James Skurdal. Decorah: Vesterheim Museum, 1993.

———. *Rosemaling I Hallingdal.* Oslo: Dreyers Forlag, 1978.

Ellsworth [Iowa] Historical Society. *The Centennial Story of Ellsworth 1880–1980.* New Providence, IA: Providence Printing, 1980.

Emmerich, Lisa E. “‘Right in the Midst of My Own People’: Native American Women and the Field Matron Program.” *American Indian Quarterly* 15, no. 2 (1991): 201–16.

Evernden, Neil. “Beauty and Nothingness: Prairie as Failed Resource.” *Landscape* 27, no. 3 (1983): 1–8.

“Extracts from the Report of the Commissioner of Indian Affairs: Improvement, Not Transformation.” *Arrow* 2, no. 20 (1906).

Fischer, Mike. “Pastoralism and Its Discontents: Willa Cather and the Burden of Imperialism.” In Cather, *O Pioneers!*, edited by Sharon O’Brien, 346–54.

Flom, George T. “The Coming of the Norwegians to Iowa.” *Iowa Journal of History and Politics* 3, no. 3 (1905): 347–83.

Folsom, Cora. “Angel Decora Dietz.” *Southern Workman* 48, no. 3 (1919): 104–5.

Foster, Lance. *The Indians of Iowa.* Iowa City: University of Iowa Press, 2010.

Frykman, Jonas, and Nils Gilje. “Being There.” In *Being There: New Perspectives on Phenomenology and the Analysis of Culture*, edited by Jonas Frykman and Nils Gilje, 6–20. Lund: Nordic Academic Press, 2010.

Gates, Merrill E. “Addresses at the Lake Mohonk Conferences.” In *Americanizing the American Indian*, edited by Francis Paul Prucha, 331–44. Cambridge, MA: Harvard University Press, 1973.

Gates, Paul Wallace. *Fifty Million Acres: Conflicts over Kansas Land Policy, 1854–1890.* Ithaca: Cornell University Press, 1954.

Genetin-Pilawa, C. Joseph. *Crooked Paths to Allotment: The Fight over Federal Indian Policy after the Civil War.* Chapel Hill: University of North Carolina Press, 2012.

Gere, Anne Ruggles. “An Art of Survivance.” *American Indian Quarterly* 28, no. 3–4 (2004): 649–84.

Gerson, Kathleen, C. Ann Stueve, and Claude S. Fischer. “Attachment to a Place.”

In *Networks and Places: Social Relations in the Urban Setting*, edited by Claude S. Fischer, 139–61. New York: Free Press, 1977.

Gesme, Ann Urness. *Between Rocks and Hard Places*. Cedar Rapids: Gesme Enterprises, 1993.

Gilbert, James. *Whose Fair? Experience, Memory, and the History of the Great St. Louis Exposition*. Chicago: University of Chicago Press, 2009.

Gilbertson, Donald E. *A Treasury of Norwegian Folk Art in America*. Osseo, WI: Tin Chicken Antiques, 1975.

Gilbertson, Laurann. "To Ward Off Evil: Metal on Norwegian Folk Dress." In *Folk Dress in Europe and Anatolia*, edited by Linda Welters, 199–210. Oxford and New York: Berg, 1999.

Gilbertson, Laurann, and Karen Olsen. "Piecing Together a New Home: Needlework in *Kvinden og Hjemmet* Magazine." Paper presented at the Textile Society of America Ninth Biennial Symposium, Oakland, California, October 2004.

Gjerde, Jon. "The Immigrant's Luggage: Observations Based on Written Sources." In *Norwegian Folk Art: The Migration of a Tradition*, edited by Marion Nelson, 185–88. New York: Abbeville Press, 1995.

Glassberg, David. *Sense of History: The Place of the Past in American Life*. Amherst: University of Massachusetts Press, 2001.

Glenn, Evelyn Nakano. *Forced to Care*. Cambridge, MA: Harvard University Press, 2010.

———. "Settler Colonialism as Structure: A Framework for Comparative Studies of Race and Gender Formation." *Sociology of Race and Ethnicity* 1, no. 1 (2015): 54–74.

———. *Unequal Freedom: How Race and Gender Shaped American Citizenship and Labor*. Cambridge, MA: Harvard University Press, 2002.

Glimpses of the Rainbow City, Pan-American Exposition, at Buffalo. Chicago: Laird & Lee, 1901.

Gluck, Sherna Berger, and Daphne Patai, eds. *Women's Words: The Feminist Practice of Oral History*. New York and London: Routledge, 1991.

Goodrich, Arthur. "Short Stories of Interesting Exhibits." *World's Work* 2, no. 4 (1901): 1054–96.

Gradle, Sally. "Ecology of Place: Art Education in a Relational World." *Studies in Art Education* 48, no. 4 (2007): 392–411.

Graham, Mark A. "Art, Ecology and Art Education: Locating Art Education in a Critical Place-Based Pedagogy." *Studies in Art Education* 48, no. 4 (2007): 375–91.

Gray, David, ed. *Art Hand-Book, Official Handbook of Architecture and Sculpture and Art Catalogue to the Pan-American Exposition*. Buffalo, NY, 1901.

Green, Richard. "Sioux Performers at the 1901 Pan-American Exposition." *Whispering Wind* 43, no. 1 (2014): 22–25.

Griswold, Robert. "Anglo Women and Domestic Ideology in the American West in the Nineteenth and Early Twentieth Centuries." In *Western Women: Their Land, Their Lives*, edited by Lillian Schlissel, Vicki L. Ruiz, and Janice Monk, 15–34. Albuquerque: University of New Mexico Press, 1988.

Groot, Marjan. "Inscribing Women and Gender into Histories and Reception of Design, Crafts, and Decorative Arts of Small-Scale Non-European Cultures." *Journal of Art Historiography*, no. 12 (2015): 1–32.

Gruenewald, David. "Foundations of Place: A Multidisciplinary Framework for Place-Conscious Education." *American Educational Research* Journal 40, no. 3 (2003): 619–53.

Hadjiafxendi, Kyriaki, and Patricia Zakreski, eds. *What Is a Woman to Do? A Reader on Women, Work, and Art c. 1830–1890*. Oxford: Peter Lang, 2011.

Hafter, Daryl M., ed. *European Women and Preindustrial Craft*. Bloomington: Indiana University Press, 1995.

———. "Toward a Social History of Needlework Artists." *Woman's Art Journal* 2, no. 2 (1981–82): 25–29.

Hale, Frederick, ed. *Their Own Saga: Letters from the Norwegian Global Migration*. Minneapolis: Minnesota Press, 1986.

Handy-Marchello, Barbara. *Women of the Northern Plains: Gender and Settlement on the Homestead Frontier, 1870–1930*. St. Paul: Minnesota Historical Society, 2005.

Hansen, Karen V. *Encounter on the Plains: Scandinavian Settlers and the Dispossession of Dakota Indians, 1890–1930*. New York: Oxford University Press, 2013.

———. "Land Taking at Spirit Lake: The Competing and Converging Logics of Norwegian and Dakota Women, 1900–1930." In *Norwegian American Women*, edited by Betty A. Bergland and Lori Ann Lahlum, 211–45.

———. *A Very Social Time: Crafting Community in Antebellum New England*. Berkeley: University of California Press, 1996.

Hansen, Marcus Lee. "Official Encouragement of Immigration to Iowa." *Iowa Journal of History and Politics* 19, no. 2 (1921): 159–95.

Hart, Mary Bronson. "How to See the Pan-American Exposition." *Everybody's Magazine* 25, no. 5 (1901): 488–91.

Hemmings, Clare. *Why Stories Matter: The Political Grammar of Feminist Theory*. Durham and London: Duke University Press, 2011.

Henare, Amiria, Martin Hobraad, and Sari Wastell. "Introduction." In *Thinking through Things: Theorising Artefacts Ethnographically*, edited by Amiria Henare, Martin Hobraad, and Sari Wastell, 1–31. London and New York: Routledge, 2007.

Henook-Makhewe-Kelenaka. "An Autobiography." *Red Man*, March 1911, 279–85.

———. "Gray Wolf's Daughter." *Harper's New Monthly Magazine* 99 (1899): 860–62.

———. "The Sick Child." *Harper's New Monthly Magazine* 98 (1899): 446–48.

———. *See also* De Cora, Angel.

Henricksen, Vera. *Christmas in Norway*. Oslo: Tanum-Norli, 1981.

Herring, Joseph B. *The Enduring Indians of Kansas: A Century and a Half of Acculturation*. Lawrence: University Press of Kansas, 1990.

Hertzberg, Hazel W. *The Search for an American Indian Identity: Modern Pan-Indian Movements*. Syracuse: Syracuse University Press, 1971.

Hexom, Charles Philip. *Indian History of Winnishiek County*. Decorah, IA: A. K. Bailey, 1913.

Hibbard, Benjamin Horace. *A History of the Public Land Policies*. Madison: University of Wisconsin Press, 1965.

The History of Hamilton County. Dallas: Curtis Media Corporation, 1986.

Holand, Hjalmar Rued. *History of the Norwegian Settlements*. Translated by Malcolm Rosholt and Helmer M. Blegen. Waukon, Iowa: Astri My Astri, 2006.

Hutchinson, Elizabeth. "Handicraft, Native American Art, and Modern Indian Identity." In *Seeing High and Low: Representing Social Conflict in American Visual Culture*, edited by Patricia Johnston, 194–207. Berkeley and Los Angeles: University of California Press, 2006.

———. *The Indian Craze: Primitivism, Modernism, and Transculturation in American Art, 1890–1915*. Durham and London: Duke University Press, 2009.

———. "Modern Native American Art: Angel Decora's Transcultural Aesthetics." *Art Bulletin* 83, no. 4 (2001): 740–56.

Huyssen, Andreas. "High/Low in an Expanded Field." *Modernism/Modernity* 9, no. 3 (2002): 363–74.

"Indian Art as Valuable Asset." *Philadelphia Inquirer*, February 2, 1913.

"The Indian Girl Must Have Public School Education." *Wisconsin State Journal*, October 9, 1914.

James, Edwin. *An Account of an Exploration from Pittsburgh to the Rocky Mountains, Performed in the Years 1819 and '20*. 3 vols. London: Longman, Hurst, Pees, Orre and Brown, 1823.

Jeffrey, Julie Roy. "'There Is Some Splendid Scenery': Women's Responses to the Great Plains Landscape." *Great Plains Quarterly* 8, no. 2 (1988): 69–78.

Jensen, Joan M. *Promise to the Land: Essays on Rural Women*. Albuquerque: University of New Mexico Press, 1991.

Johnston, Patricia. "Introduction." In *Seeing High and Low: Representing Social Conflict in American Visual Culture*, edited by Patricia Johnston, 1–24. Berkeley and Los Angeles: University of California Press, 2006.

Jones, Andrew. *Memory and Material Culture*. Cambridge: Cambridge University Press, 2007.

Kahn, Eve. "Echoes of an Exposition, and an Assassination." *New York Times*, November 4, 2016.

Kelly, Mary B. *Embroidering the Goddesses of Old Norway*. Hilton Head, SC: Studiobooks, 2008.

———. *Goddess Embroideries of the Northlands*. Hilton Head, SC: Studiobooks, 2007.

Kimmerer, Robin Wall. *Braiding Sweetgrass: Indigenous Wisdom, Scientific Knowledge and the Teachings of Plants*. Minneapolis: Milkweed, 2013.

Kinsey, Joni L. *Plain Pictures: Images of the American Prairie.* Washington, D.C.: Smithsonian Institution, 1996.

———. *Thomas Moran's West: Chromolithography, High Art, and Popular Taste.* Lawrence: University Press of Kansas, 2006.

Kinzie, Juliette. *Wau-Bun, the Early Day in the Northwest*. Philadelphia: J. B. Lippincott, 1873.

Kolodny, Annette. *The Land before Her: Fantasy and Experience of the American Frontiers 1630–1860*. Chapel Hill and London: University of North Carolina Press, 1984.

Krasskova, Galina. *Exploring the Northern Tradition*. Wayne, NJ: Career, 2005.

Lagerquist, L. DeAne. *In America the Men Milk the Cows: Factors of Gender, Ethnicity, and Religion in the Americanization of Norwegian-American Women*. Brooklyn, NY: Carlson, 1991.

Lahlum, Lori Ann. "'There Are No Trees Here': Norwegian Women Encounter the Northern Prairies and Plains." PhD diss., University of Idaho, 2003.

———. "Women, Work, and Community in Rural Norwegian America, 1840–1920." In *Norwegian American Women,* edited by Betty A. Bergland and Lori Ann Lahlum, 79–117.

Langeland, Åse Elin. "Adjusting to America: A Study in *Kvinden og Hjemmet*: A Monthly Journal for the Scandinavian Women in America, 1888–1947." Master's thesis, University of Bergen, 2001.

Legreid, Ann M. "Home, Health, and Christian Respectability: Norwegian Immigrant Women in Family and Community Health." In *Norwegian American Women,* edited by Betty A. Bergland and Lori Ann Lahlum, 181–209.

Leland, Charles Godfrey. *The Union Pacific Railway, Eastern Division: Or, Three Thousand Miles in a Railway Car.* Philadelphia: Ringwalt and Brown, 1867.

Lentis, Marinella. "Art Education in American Indian Boarding Schools: Tool of Assimilation, Tool of Resistance." PhD diss., University of Arizona, 2012.

———. "Art for Assimilation's Sake: Indian School Drawings in the Estelle Reel Papers." *American Indian Art Magazine*, Winter (2013): 44–51.

———. *Colonized through Art: American Indian Schools and Art Education, 1889–1915*. Lincoln: University of Nebraska Press, 2017.

Lindsey, Donal F. *Indians at Hampton Institute, 1877–1923*. Urbana and Chicago: University of Illinois Press, 1995.

Lippard, Lucy R. "Independent Identities." In *Native American Art in the Twentieth Century*, edited by W. Jackson Rushing III, 134–48. New York: Routledge, 1999.

Lokken, Roscoe L. *Iowa Public Land Disposal*. Iowa City: State Historical Society of Iowa, 1942.

Lomawaima, K. Tsianina. "Estelle Reel, Superintendent of Indian Schools, 1898–1910: Politics, Curriculum, and Land." *Journal of American Indian Education* 35 (1996): 5–31.

Lomawaima, K. Tsianina, and Teresa L. McCarty. *"To Remain an Indian": Lessons in Democracy from a Century of Native American Education*. New York: Teacher's College Press, 2006.

Lovoll, Odd. *Across the Deep Blue Sea: The Saga of Early Norwegian Immigrants*. St. Paul: Minnesota Historical Society, 2015.

———. "Emigration and Settlement Patterns as They Relate to the Migration of Norwegian Folk Art." In *Norwegian Folk Art: The Migration of a Tradition*, edited by Marion Nelson, 133–48. New York: Abbeville Press, 1995.

———. *Norwegian Newspapers in America: Connecting Norway and the New Land*. St. Paul: Minnesota Historical Society, 2010.

———. *Norwegians on the Prairie: Ethnicity and the Development of the Country Town*. St. Paul: Minnesota Historical Society, 2006.

———. *The Promise of America*. Minneapolis: University of Minnesota Press, 1999.

Lowe, Peggy. "The Lasting Heritage of the Homestead Act." *Harvest Public Media*, July 12, 2012.

Luckman, Susan. *Craft and the Creative Economy*. London: Palgrave Macmillan, 2015.

Luebke, Frederick C., ed. *Ethnicity on the Great Plains*. Lincoln: University of Nebraska Press, 1980.

Lurie, Nancy Ostereich. "Mountain Wolf Woman, Sister of Crashing Thunder: An Autobiography of a Winnebago Indian." In *Native Women's History in Eastern North America before 1900: A Guide to Research and Writing*, edited by Rebecca Kugel and Lucy Eldersveld Murphy, 417–32. Lincoln: University of Nebraska Press, 2007.

Maines, Rachel. "Fancywork: The Archaeology of Lives." *Feminist Art Journal* 3, no. 4 (1974–75): 1–3.

Mann, Bonnie. *Women's Liberation and the Sublime: Feminism, Postmodernism, Environment*. Oxford, New York: Oxford University Press, 2006.

Martin, Philip. *Rosemaling in the Upper Midwest: A Story of Region and Revival*. Mt. Horeb: Wisconsin Folk Museum, 1989.

Matthews, Jessica Ruggieri. "Killing a Culture to Save a Race: Writing and Resisting the Discourse of the Carlisle Indian School." PhD diss., George Washington University, 2005.

McAnulty, Sarah. "Angel Decora: American Indian Artist and Educator." *Nebraska History* 57 (1976): 142–99.

Miner, Craig H. *The Corporation and the Indian: Tribal Sovereignty and Industrial Civilization in Indian Territory, 1865 1907*. Columbia: University of Missouri Press, 1976.

———. *West of Wichita: Settling the High Plains of Kansas, 1865–1890*. Lawrence: University Press of Kansas, 1986.

Miner, Craig, and William E. Unrau. *The End of Indian Kansas: A Study of Cultural Revolution, 1854–1871*. Lawrence: University Press of Kansas, 1990.

Moore, Sarah J. "Mapping Empire in Omaha and Buffalo: World's Fairs and the Spanish-American War." *Bilingual Review* 25, no. 111–27 (2000).

Myres, Sandra L. *Westering Women and the Frontier Experience, 1800–1915*. Albuquerque: University of New Mexico Press, 1982.

Nattestad, Ole Knudsen, and Rasmus B. Anderson. "Description of a Journey to North America." *Wisconsin Magazine of History*, 1917/18, 149–86.

Nelson, Marion. "Folk and Decorative Arts before 1970." In *Norway in America*, 7–24. Decorah, IA: Vesterheim Norwegian-American Museum, 1989. Exhibition catalogue.

———. "Folk Art and Faith among Norwegian Americans." In *Crossings: Norwegian-American Lutheranism as a Transatlantic Tradition*, edited by Todd W. Nichol, 73–92. Northfield, MN: Norwegian-American Historical Association, 2003.

———. "Folk Art in Minnesota and the Case of the Norwegian American." In *Circles of Tradition: Folk Arts in Minnesota*, edited by Willard Moore, 24–44. St. Paul: Minnesota Historical Society, 1989.

———. "Folk Art of Norway." In *Norwegian Folk Art*, edited by Marion Nelson, 37–88.

———, ed. *Material Culture and People's Art among the Norwegians in America*. Northfield: Norwegian American Historical Association, 1994.

———. "Norwegian Folk Art in America." In *Norwegian Folk Art*, edited by Marion Nelson, 89–118.

———, ed. *Norwegian Folk Art: The Migration of a Tradition*. New York: Abbeville Press, 1995.

Nevergold, Barbara Seals. "'Doing the Pan': The African-American Experience at the Pan-American Exposition, 1901." *Afro-Americans in New York Life and History* 28, no. 1 (2004): 23–41.

Noddings, Nel. *Caring: A Relational Approach to Ethics and Moral Education*. Berkeley, CA: University of California Press, 2013.

Norwood, Vera. "Women's Place: Continuity and Change in Response to Western Landscapes." In *Western Women: Their Land, Their Lives*, edited by Lillian Schlissel, Vicki L. Ruiz, and Janice Monk, 155–82. Albuquerque: University of New Mexico Press, 1988.

Noss, Aagot. "Rural Norwegian Dress and Its Symbolic Functions." In *Norwegian Folk Art*, edited by Marion Nelson, 149–55.

Nostrand, Richard L., and Lawrence E. Estaville. "Introduction: Free Land, Dry Land, Homeland." In *Homelands: A Geography of Culture and Place across America*, edited by Richard L. Nostrand and Lawrence E. Estaville, xiii–xxiii. Baltimore: Johns Hopkins University Press, 2001.

O'Brien, Sharon. "Gender and Creativity in *O Pioneers!*" In Cather, *O Pioneers!*, edited by Sharon O'Brien, 379–95.

Official Catalogue and Guide Book to the Pan-American Exposition. Buffalo: C. Ahrhart, 1901.

Orwig, Darrek D. *Story City*. Charleston: Arcadia, 2012.

Osterud, Nancy Grey. "Gender and the Transition to Capitalism in Rural America." *Agricultural History* 67, no. 2 (1993): 14–29.

Otis, D. S. *The Dawes Act and the Allotment of Indian Lands*. Norman: University of Oklahoma Press, 1973.

Parezo, Nancy J., and Don D. Fowler. *Anthropology Goes to the Fair: The 1904 Louisiana Purchase Exposition*. Lincoln: University of Nebraska Press, 2007.

Parezo, Nancy J., and John W. Troutman. "The 'Shy' Cocopa Go to the Fair." In *Selling the Indian: Commercializing and Appropriating American Indian Cultures*, edited by Carter Jones Meyer and Diana Royer, 3–43. Tucson: University of Arizona Press, 2001.

Parezo, Nancy J., Kelley A. Hays, and Barbara F. Slivac. "The Mind's Road: Southwestern Indian Women's Art." In *The Desert Is No Lady*, edited by Vera Norwood and Janice Monk, 146–73. New Haven: Yale University Press, 1987.

Parker, Rozsika. *The Subversive Stitch: Embroidery and the Making of the Feminine*. London: Women's Press, 1984.

Parker, Rozsika, and Griselda Pollock, eds. *Framing Feminism: Art and the Women's Movement* 1970–1985. London and New York: Pandora, 1987.

———. *Old Mistresses: Women, Art, Ideology*. New York: Pantheon, 1981.

Petrowski, William R. *The Kansas Pacific: A Study in Railroad Promotion*. New York: Arno, 1981.

Phillips, Ruth B. "Dreams and Designs: Iconographic Problems in Great Lakes Twined Bags." In *Great Lakes Indian Art*, edited by David W. Penney, 52–68. Detroit: Wayne State University Press / Detroit Institute of Art, 1989.

———. "Like a Star I Shine: Northern Woodlands Artistic Traditions." In *The Spirit Sings: Artistic Traditions of Canada's First Peoples*, 51–92. Toronto: McLelland and Stewart, 1987. Exhibition catalogue.

Pine, Wilfred H. "100 Years of Farmland Value in Kansas." *Kansas State Agricultural Experiment Station Bulletin* 611. Manhattan: Kansas State University Agricultural Experiment Station, 1977.

Pratt, Stephanie. "Restating Indigenous Presence in Eastern Dakota and Ho Chunk (Winnebago) Portraits of the 1830s–1860s." In *Indigenous Bodies Reviewing, Relocating, Reclaiming*, edited by Jacqueline Rebecca Tillett Fear-Segal, 17–30. Albany: State University of New York Press, 2013.

Prucha, Francis Paul, ed. *Americanizing the American Indians: Writings by the "Friends of the Indian" 1880–1900*. Cambridge, MA: Harvard University Press, 1973.

———. "Introduction." In *Americanizing the American Indians*, edited by Francis Paul Prucha, 1–10. Cambridge, MA: Harvard University Press, 1973.

Raaen, Aagot. *Grass of the Earth: Immigrant Life in the Dakota Country*. St. Paul: Minnesota Historical Society, 1994.

Radin, Paul. "The Clan Organization of the Winnebago: A Preliminary Paper." *American Anthropologist* 12, no. 2 (1910): 209–19.

———. *The Winnebago Tribe*. Lincoln: University of Nebraska Press, 1970.

Radner, Joan N., and Susan S. Lanser. "Strategies of Coding in Women's Cultures." In *Feminist Messages: Coding in Women's Folk Culture*, edited by Joan N. Radner, 1–29. Urbana and Chicago: University of Illinois Press, 1993.

The Rand-McNally Hand-Book to the Pan-American Exposition, Buffalo and Niagara Falls. Chicago and New York: Rand McNally, 1901.

Reel, Estelle. *Course of Study for the Indian Schools of the United States: Industrial and Literary*. Washington, D.C.: Government Printing Office, 1901.

Reiersen, Johan Reinert. *Pathfinder for Norwegian Emigrants*. Translated by Frank G. Nelson. Northfield: Norwegian American Historical Association, 1981.

Relph, E. *Place and Placelessness*. London: Pion, 1976.

Riley, Glenda. *The Female Frontier: A Comparative View of Women on the Prairie and the Plains*. Lawrence: University Press of Kansas, 1988.

Rinehart, F.A. *Photogravures of the Trans-Mississippi and International Exposition, Held at Omaha, Nebraska, June 1st to November 1st, 1898*. Omaha, 1898.

Romnes, Harriet. *Rosemaling: An Inspired Norwegian Folk Art*. Madison, WI: Norse Chalet, 1970.

Rosaldo, Renato. "Imperialist Nostalgia." *Representations* 26 (1989): 107–22.

Royce, Charles C. *Indian Land Cessions in the United States, 1784–1894*. Vol. 2. *Eighteenth Annual Report of the Bureau of American Ethnology to the Secretary of the Smithsonian Institution, 1896–1897*. H.R. Doc. No. 736, 56th Cong., 1st Sess. (1899).

Russell, Charles H. *Undaunted: A Norwegian Woman in Frontier Texas*. College Station: Texas A & M University Press, 2006.

Rydell, Robert. *All the World's a Fair: Visions of Empire at American International Expositions, 1876–1916*. Chicago and London: University of Chicago Press, 1984.

Rynning, Ole, and Theodore C. Blegen, trans. "A Truthful Account of America for the Instruction and Help of the Peasant and Commoner Written by a Norwegian Who Came There in the Month of June, 1837." *Minnesota History* (1917): 220–69.

Schaffer, Talia. "Women's Work: The History of the Victorian Domestic Handicraft." In *Crafting the Professional in the Long Nineteenth Century*, edited by Kyriaki Hadjiafxendi and Patricia Zakreski, 25–42. Farnham and Burlington: Ashgate, 2013.

Schiffer, Michael Brian. *The Material Life of Human Beings*. London: Routledge, 1999.

Schlissel, Lillian, Vicki L. Ruiz, and Janice Monk, eds. *Western Women: Their Land, Their Lives.* Albuquerque: University of New Mexico Press, 1988.

Schneider, Mary Jane. "Women's Work: An Examination of Women's Roles in Plains Indian Arts and Crafts." In *The Hidden Half: Studies of Plains Indian Women*, edited by Patricia Albers and Beatrice Medicine, 101–21. Washington, D.C.: University Press of America, 1983.

Schnell, Steven M. "The Kiowa Homeland in Oklahoma." In *Homelands: A Geography of Culture and Place across America*, edited by Richard L. Nostrand and Lawrence E. Estaville, 139–54. Baltimore: Johns Hopkins University Press, 2001.

Schrader, Robert Fay. *The Indian Arts and Crafts Board: An Aspect of New Deal Indian Policy*. Albuquerque: University of New Mexico Press, 1983.

Scott, Astrid Karlsen. *Norway's Fest Days*. Olympia, WA: Nordic Adventures, 1993.

Sennett, Richard. *The Craftsman*. New Haven: Yale University Press, 2009.

Setterdahl, Lilly. "*Kvinnan Och Hemmet*: A Women's Journal Written in Swedish, Edited by a Norwegian, Published by a Dane." In *Scandinavians in America: Literary Life,* edited by J. R. Christianson, 92–103. Decorah, IA: Symra Literary Society, 1985.

Sheldrake, Philip. *Spaces for the Sacred: Place, Memory, and Identity*. Baltimore: Johns Hopkins University Press, 2001.

Shope, Suzanne Alene. "American Indian Artist Angel Decora: Aesthetics, Power, and Transcultural Pedagogy in the Progressive Era." PhD diss., University of Montana, 2009.

Simonsen, Jane. *Making Home Work: Domesticity and Native American Assimilation in the American West, 1860–1919*. Chapel Hill: University of North Carolina Press, 2006.

Slotkin, Richard. *Gunfighter Nation: The Myth of the Frontier in Twentieth-Century America*. New York: Atheneum, 1992.

Stankiewicz, Mary Ann. "Drawing Book Wars." *Visual Arts Research* 12, no. 2 (1986): 59–72.

Starr, Jeanette. *Fun with Straw*. Minneapolis: Prompt Printing, 1979.

Stegner, Wallace. "Remnants." In *American Places*, edited by John Macrae III, 189–211. New York: E. P. Dutton, 1981.

Stewart, Janice S. *The Folk Arts of Norway*. Madison: University of Wisconsin Press, 1953.

Stokker, Kathleen. "*Julebukk:* Christmas Masquerading in Norwegian America." In *Norwegian American Essays*, edited by Knut Djupedal, et al., 28–39. Oslo: NAHA, 1993.

———. *Keeping Christmas: Yuletide Traditions in Norway and the New Land*. Saint Paul: Minnesota Historical Society, 2000.

Stratton, Joanna L. *Pioneer Women: Voices from the Kansas Frontier*. New York: Simon and Schuster, 1982.

Sundberg, Sara Brooks. "Picturing the Past: Farm Women on the Grasslands Frontier, 1850–1900." *Great Plains Quarterly* 30, no. 3 (2010): 203–19.

Trans-Mississippi International Exposition. *Trans-Mississippi International Exposition, Omaha, June to November 1898: Art, Manufacturing, Mechanics, Commerce, Science, Music: Illustrating the Progress of the West.* N.p.: n.p., 1898. Accessed June 29, 2017. http://trans-mississippi.unl.edu/texts/view/transmiss.book.tmie.1898.html.

Trump, Erik. "'The Idea of Help': White Women Reformers and the Commercialization of Native American Women's Arts." In *Selling the Indian: Commercializing and Appropriating American Indian Cultures*, edited by Carter Jones Meyer and Diana Royer, 159–89. Tucson: University of Arizona Press, 2001.

Ulvestad, Martin. *Norwegians in America, Their History and Record*. Vol. 1. Translated by Olaf Tronsen Kringhaug and Odd-Steinar Dybvad Raneng. Waukon, IA: Astri My Astri, 2010.

United States, Office of Indian Affairs. *Annual Report of the Commissioner of Indian Affairs to the Secretary of the Interior for the Fiscal Year 1901*. Washington, D.C.: Government Printing Office, 1902.

Unrau, William E. *The Kansa Indians: A History of the Wind People, 1673–1873*. Norman and London: University of Oklahoma Press, 1986.

Veracino, Lorenzo. *The Settler Colonial Present*. London: Palgrave Macmillan, 2015.

Vizenor, Gerald. *Manifest Manners: Narratives on Postindian Survivance.* Lincoln: University of Nebraska Press, 1999.

———. *Native Liberty: Natural Reason and Cultural Survivance*. Lincoln: University of Nebraska Press, 2009.

Waggoner, Linda M. *Fire Light: The Life of Angel De Cora, Winnebago Artist*. Norman: University of Oklahoma Press, 2008.

———. "On Trial: The Washington R*dskins' Wily Mascot, Coach William 'Lone Star' Dietz." *Montana: The Magazine of Western History* 63, no. 1 (2013): 24–47.

———. "Sibley's Winnebago Prisoners: Deconstructing Race and Recovering Kinship in the Dakota War of 1862." *Great Plains Quarterly* 33, no. 1 (2013): 25–48.

Wangsness, Sigrid Brevik. "*Kvinden og Hjemmet*: A Magazine for Scandinavian Immigrant Women, 1901–1910." In *Norse Heritage Yearbook*, edited by Hans Storhaug, 105–16. Stavanger: Norwegian Immigration Center, 1986.

Weist, Katherine M. "Beasts of Burden and Menial Slaves: Nineteenth-Century Observations of Northern Plains Indian Women." In *The Hidden Half: Studies of Plains Indian Women*, edited by Patricia Albers and Beatrice Medicine, 29–52. Washington, D.C.: University Press of America, 1983.

West, Elliott. *The Way to the West*. Albuquerque: University of New Mexico Press, 1995.

White, Richard. *Railroaded: The Transcontinentals and the Making of Modern America*. New York: W. W. Norton, 2011.

Witmer, Linda F. *Changing Images: The Art and Artists of the Carlisle Indian Industrial School.* Carlisle: Cumberland County Historical Society, 2008.

Young, Carrie. *Nothing to Do but Stay: My Pioneer Mother.* Iowa City: University of Iowa Press, 1991.

Zakreski, Patricia. *Representing Female Artistic Labour, 1848–1890*. Aldershot: Ashgate, 2006.

Zipf, Catherine W. *Professional Pursuits: Women and the American Arts and Crafts Movement*. Knoxville: University of Tennessee Press, 2007.

INDEX

IOWA AND THE MIDWEST EXPERIENCE

Angel De Cora, Karen Thronson, and the Art of Place: How Two Midwestern Women Used Art to Negotiate Migration and Dispossession
By Elizabeth Sutton

The Archaeological Guide to Iowa
By William E. Whittaker, Lynn M. Alex, and Mary De La Garza

Carnival in the Countryside: The History of the Iowa State Fair
By Chris Rasmussen

Dakota in Exile: The Untold Stories of Captives in the Aftermath of the U.S.-Dakota War
By Linda M. Clemmons

The Drake Relays: America's Athletic Classic
By David Peterson

Dubuque's Forgotten Cemetery: Excavating a Nineteenth-Century Burial Ground in a Twenty-First Century City
By Robin M. Lillie and Jennifer E. Mack

Duffy's Iowa Caucus Cartoons: Watch 'Em Run
By Brian Duffy

Equal Before the Law: How Iowa Led Americans to Marriage Equality
By Tom Witozky and Marc Hansen

From Warm Center to Ragged Edge: The Erosion of Midwestern Literary and Historical Regionalism, 1920–1965
By Jon K. Lauck

Harvest of Hazards: Family Farming, Accidents, and Expertise in the Corn Belt, 1940–1975
By Derek S. Oden

Iowa Past to Present: The People and the Prairie, Revised Third Edition
By Dorothy Schwieder, Thomas Morain, and Lynn Nielsen

The Iowa State Fair
By Kurt Ullrich

The Jefferson Highway: Blazing the Way from Winnipeg to New Orleans
By Lyell D. Henry, Jr.

The Lost Region: Toward a Revival of Midwestern History
By Jon K. Lauck

Main Street Public Library: Community Places and Reading Spaces in the Rural Heartland, 1876–1956
By Wayne A. Wiegand

Necessary Courage: Iowa's Underground Railroad in the Struggle against Slavery
By Lowell Soike

On Behalf of the Family Farm: Iowa Farm Women's Activism since 1945
By Jenny Barker Devine

The Sacred Cause of Union: Iowa in the Civil War
By Thomas R. Baker

The Small-Town Midwest: Resilience and Hope in the Twenty-First Century
By Julianne Couch

A Store Almost in Sight: The Economic Transformation of Missouri from the Louisiana Purchase to the Civil War
By Jeff Bremer

Transcendental Meditation in America: How a New Age Movement Remade a Small Town in Iowa
By Joseph Weber

What Happens Next? Essays on Matters of Life and Death
By Douglas Bauer

Woman Suffrage and Citizenship in the Midwest, 1870–1920
By Sara Egge